DEFIANCE

DEFIANCE

*Racial Injustice, Police Brutality,
A Sister's Fight for the Truth*

JANET ALDER

with Dan Glazebrook

dialogue
books

DIALOGUE BOOKS

First published in Great Britain in 2024 by Dialogue Books

1 3 5 7 9 10 8 6 4 2

Copyright © Janet Alder and Dan Glazebrook 2024

The moral rights of the authors have been asserted.

All rights reserved.
No part of this publication may be reproduced, stored in a retrieval system, or transmitted, in any form or by any means, without the prior permission in writing of the publisher, nor be otherwise circulated in any form of binding or cover other than that in which it is published and without a similar condition including this condition being imposed on the subsequent purchaser.

A CIP catalogue record for this book
is available from the British Library.

Hardback ISBN 978-0-349-70285-8

Typeset in Caslon by M Rules
Printed and bound in Great Britain by
Clays Ltd, Elcograf S.p.A

Papers used by Dialogue Books are from well-managed forests and other responsible sources.

MIX
Paper | Supporting
responsible forestry
FSC
www.fsc.org FSC® C104740

Dialogue Books
An imprint of Dialogue
Carmelite House
50 Victoria Embankment
London EC4Y 0DZ

www.dialoguebooks.co.uk

Dialogue, part of Little, Brown Book Group Limited,
an Hachette UK company.

To my children and grandchild, Caroline, Nathan and Justice, who have battled on and endured the ups and downs in the fight for justice with me over the years; to all my family; and to all families who have lost loved ones at the hands of the British state. I feel you. The battle is long and arduous but it is essential. Keep fighting and surviving.

Some names have been changed to protect the privacy of some individuals from the author's past.

Contents

Christopher Alder, the Man	xi
Introduction	1
The Custody Suite	5
Christopher	9
The Nightclub	17
Finding Out	21
Hull	26
Making Enquiries	30
Last Days in Hull	34
Back to Burnley	41
Campaigning	48
Piecing it Together	82
Disclosed Documents	90
Making the Documentary	97
Viewing the Video	103
After the Video	110

An Uphill Battle	114
The Crane Report	116
The Inquest	119
The Funeral	148
Mr O'Doherty	154
Battling the CPS	169
Before the Trial	174
The Trial of the Officers	181
The Trial Takes Its Toll	201
Christine and Herbert	211
After the Trial	216
Going into Care	219
Injustice	221
The Goodhands	224
Police Disciplinary	228
Care	233
Ben Almond	237
Taken but Unwanted	240
The CPS	246
Life in the House	252
Death on Camera	260
School	267
Elections	273
Holidays	280
The IPCC Report	289

Weekends	293
Life with Ben	299
Weekends 2	306
Preparing the Civil Case	309
After the Goodhands	323
Civil Case Against the CPS	328
Leaving Hull	343
The CPS in the Dock	350
Life Before Christopher's Death	358
Body Swap	365
Christine Omoregie	371
Another Sham Investigation	379
Spying	390
The Horror Never Stops	413
The Struggle Continues	421
Acknowledgements	431
Notes	433

Christopher Alder, the Man

'My brother Christopher was a fun-loving child. He was always open to new experiences as well as a bit of a joker and really good at impressions. He could go into his shell and be a bit quiet around people he didn't know. But he was very caring and protective and thought nothing of putting himself forward for the weak. I felt proud when he was around.'

JANET ALDER

'I, along with many other people, would describe my brother Christopher as a gentleman. He was a quiet and calm man who would, in my experience, avoid trouble rather than start it.'

RICHARD ALDER

'I would describe Chris as a very popular guy who knew a lot of people. He would chat to anyone and everyone, "colour" was not a problem with him. He was a very calm person.

'Physically he was very fit, he had a gymnasium rigged up in one of his bedrooms and used it regularly. He certainly gave the appearance of being able to "handle" himself.'

RICHARD, Christopher's friend

'I have seen people try to goad him but Chris has just ignored them saying he didn't want to get involved in trouble. In all the time I have known him I have never known him lose his temper or fight with anyone.'

CHRISTOPHER, Christopher's friend

'Chris was a very nice man whom I was lucky to know for the last six months. We both attended a computer course and Chris was a very humorous man and a very generous friend, and was thought of warmly by all that knew him. I wrote a few cards for him which he was going to send to girls because he didn't feel as confident as I because I wrote poetry. He never spoke very much, he was usually quiet, even when out for the night. He was always good fun to be with.'

JOHN, Christopher's friend

'Chris? He was the best bloke I ever met. It's hard to describe Chris. He was a mate, he was great. And tough. You could have broke a stick over that guy's back and he wouldn't have moved.'

PHIL, Christopher's friend

Introduction

This book has been a long time coming. I wrote the core of it back in 2010, after what I thought would be the final UK legal proceedings arising from Christopher's death, my civil case against the Crown Prosecution Service for failing to prosecute anyone for his death.[1] I had represented myself in this case, having been dropped by my lawyer shortly before it began, and had been preparing for it at night while working as a cleaner and on the run from an abusive partner. Having been immersed in all the documents of the case for months, I wanted to write it all down while it was fresh in my mind, and to give myself, I hoped, some kind of closure. But these hopes were dashed. Little did I know, the worst was yet to come.

I have met many other families like mine who have been devastated by the loss of a loved one at the hands of the police or in the 'care' of the state. Such families are growing in Britain at the rate of more than one per week;[2] one of the tragedies of becoming involved in groups like the United Families and Friends Campaign – which brings together people from all over the country whose loved ones have died in state custody – was meeting more and more newly traumatised families at the annual demonstration that has been held each year since 1999.

New Christopher Alders are emerging all the time – people like Chris Kaba, shot dead by the Metropolitan Police through the windscreen of his car in September 2022, or Oladeji Omishore, who fell to his death from Chelsea Bridge after being repeatedly tasered by the police three months earlier. Neither men posed any threat when they were subjected to these violent attacks, and yet no police officer has been prosecuted for them; in Omishore's case, no one was even suspended. By the time this book goes to print, there will have been dozens more cases like these. The British state likes to pride itself on its rule of law, but after meeting the many other families it became clear to me that this is rarely upheld when it comes to the state itself. Instead of those responsible being held to account, our families are badly let down, left with unresolved feelings of grief, and all too often made out to be criminals ourselves, while those who have killed or failed to prevent the deaths of our loved ones are exonerated. Victims are slandered, grieving relatives spied on and evidence is destroyed – all, it seems, as a matter of course.

Part of the purpose of this book is to provide some guidance to those families who will go through this experience – to let them know what to expect, and what they are up against. You will need to ask a lot of questions, because you are not necessarily going to be told the truth – and you will need to be prepared for all your taken-for-granted assumptions about how things work to be drastically changed. Holding these institutions to account is not an easy task. The situation can be very isolating, and the state you encounter when you need answers and justice is completely different from the one we have been taught to see on the surface. Just because people are in certain positions or jobs does not necessarily mean they are going to do the right thing for you; in fact, their jobs are often more important to them – and to the state – than you or the case or justice. People will put themselves first, and things like institutional reputation, good relations with colleagues and not ruffling feathers are powerful motivators.

But for these very reasons, standing up for justice is a worthwhile task, as the state will never deliver it when left to its own devices. You are defending your rights as a human being and demanding better treatment of your fellow humans. Though it will be hard, it is important not to give up when you have a feeling that something is radically wrong. A situation like this will knock you completely off kilter and plunge you into a state of extreme vulnerability – and when you are vulnerable it is hard to trust your instincts. But it is important that you do so. This is one of the major lessons I have had to learn – that my instincts were usually spot on, yet I questioned myself and ignored them too often.

This is a story – among many others – of justice denied. Fighting this battle over the past quarter of a century has been a lesson in collusion, cover-up, and all the sophisticated – as well as the crude – methods employed by different parts of the British state to maintain the status quo, protect itself and those in its employ, and evade justice. The state's own official processes have repeatedly failed to investigate who was responsible for Christopher's death or the institutions who should have looked after him. This book is my attempt to bring some kind of accountability, simply by telling the truth.

The Custody Suite

1998

At 3.46 on the morning of 1 April 1998, PC Neil Blakey and PC Nigel Dawson dragged the unconscious Christopher Alder into the custody suite of Queen's Gardens police station in Hull, leaving a smear of blood along the walls of the corridor as they did so. Bleeding from a head wound, with his trousers round his ankles, he was dumped face down on the floor, his hands cuffed behind his back. Concerned, the custody sergeant, John Dunn, requested they take him to hospital. 'This is acting now,' Dawson told the others. 'Oh, he's right as rain,' added Blakey, 'this is a show, this.' Dawson and Blakey seemed to be doing all they could to convince their colleagues not to take him back to the hospital. Were they worried about the staff there seeing what had happened to him?

Earlier in the evening, Christopher had been treated as the victim of a possible assault, and taken to hospital with a head injury, but the staff had been unable to treat him due to his erratic behaviour – a typical consequence of injuries of this type. The two officers, who had been at the hospital to interview him about the assault, dragged him out of the hospital, with clear instructions from the medical staff to bring him back for treatment once he had calmed down. Outside the building, Christopher continued to object to the police's treatment of him. That was the officers' cue to make the arrest. Christopher had not committed any crime; he had been arrested, the two constables explained to their colleagues, to 'prevent a breach of the peace'. They handcuffed him and he stepped unassisted into the van. By the time he arrived in the police station, however, he was unconscious and had seemingly lost another tooth and his belt, and had incurred further injuries to his head, lower lip and eye. Exactly what went on between the hospital and the police station has never been properly investigated.

In the custody suite, Blakey and Dawson continued to reassure their colleagues about the bleeding man lying on the floor, motionless. 'This is an acting thing,' Dawson said again. 'He kept doing dying swan acts, falling off the trolley,' chimed in Blakey. 'He's shit himself,' noted Matthew Barr, the jailor. No one responded. 'He's shit himself, I reckon,' he repeated. Still, no one reacted to Barr's observation; the conversation moved on to what Christopher had been arrested for.

Christopher was still motionless, struggling to breathe. 'Can we get him on his side?' Barr asked shortly afterwards. 'He's going to be restricted with them cuffs on.' Blakey went to take them off, struggling because, he later explained, the 'keyhole ... was on the wrong side'. 'Are you winning, love?' Dawson asked him. Eventually, around forty minutes after they'd been put on, Blakey managed to get the cuffs off. He was suddenly overcome by several sneezes as he leaned over Christopher.

At Christopher's inquest, the Force Medical Examiner Patrick Naughton-Doe explained that if there is any doubt as to whether a potentially ill patient was 'faking it', the correct procedure is to call for medical advice. Meanwhile, the airways should be checked, and the patient left either in the recovery position, or on their back if their breathing was severely compromised. When asked whether he would leave a patient face down in the prone position, his reply was: 'Obviously not.' All of this is basic first aid procedure, as taught on the most elementary first aid courses, and certainly on the courses undertaken by all the officers attending to Christopher. None of it was followed.[1]

Instead, after his cuffs were removed, Christopher was left face down, his arm remaining bent backwards across his back. 'They don't show you this on the joining video, do they?' asked Dawson, as the station matron entered the room. 'Just hang on, Bridget,' said Dunn. 'A man's down here with no trousers on.' Nothing was done to preserve Christophers dignity as the officers busied themselves discussing how to find Christopher's details on their system.

At 3.51, after five minutes face down on the police station floor, Christopher started making what were later described by investigators as 'deep gurgling' sounds signifying 'that someone is having difficulty'. Dunn immediately stood up and peered over his desk at Christopher. But no one attempted to move him into the recovery position, or even went over for a closer look. The police continued to discuss what to do with him. 'The trouble is,' said Blakey, 'he was not like this at his time of arrest.' Indeed, when arrested, Christopher was fully conscious, had an additional tooth, appeared to be wearing his trousers with a belt, and his head wound was not bleeding. 'Outside ... well, he's fronted us up. Just fronted us up,' Blakey explained. 'He basically said he can have us any time if he fancied. We had to escort him off the premises and then in the street we give him—' but Dawson interrupted him: 'several options to go.' How Blakey had been intending to finish his sentence we will never know.

Instead, the officers made a plan to charge him with a public order offence.

The gurgling noises continued. Blakey would later claim he thought they were 'snoring noises'. They were actually Christopher's death rattle.

At 3.57, Barr noticed that 'he's not making any of them noises anymore, lads. There's fucking blood coming out of his mouth as well.'

'Well, there's blood been coming out of his mouth since he's been in hospital,' replied Dawson, still attempting to persuade his colleagues that there was no cause for alarm. Blakey continued to try to argue the case that Christopher could not be taken back to hospital: 'We can't follow him around like minders, can we? This is the trouble.'

'He's not fucking breathing, lads,' continued Barr.

It was then that the officers finally attempted to put him in the recovery position, *for the first time since they'd dragged him in unconscious eleven minutes earlier*. Barr then took his pulse. 'We've lost him, sarge,' he concluded, 'we've fucking lost him.'

Christopher

1960–98

Christopher Ibikunle Alder was born on 25 June 1960, a year before me, making him the third in line of our family of five children.

I was so proud of him when we were growing up. He was a bit of a comedian – I think you can see that in his face, in the photographs. When we were little, we used to play a game where he would bury my head in the pillow until I admitted that I was in love with Engelbert Humperdinck! I would laugh my head off.

He was also a fantastic dancer. When we used to have school discos everybody would crowd round him as he did the snake on the floor. His speed and agility was something else; I was in awe of him.

He was a brilliant runner, and fantastic at sports – a real athlete. Watching him do so well on the track inspired me to take up running and gymnastics, which became a major part of my life.

Later in life, he took up photography. I hadn't realised how talented he was until I got his paperwork, which included piles of beautiful photos. He evidently had a fascination with nature: there were lots of pictures of swans, ravens and bees, as well as two photographs of a tree taken from the same angle in two different seasons. It was easy to see that through his photography he was in tune with nature. Some people walk about, day in, day out, and don't even look at a bird or a tree. They've forgotten they even exist. But he still had a zest for life in that way, and all life – humans, animals and plants – clearly meant a lot to him.

Our childhood wasn't easy, growing up in state authority care in Hull. At school he was quite protective of me. I've learned that there are always some who fear anything or anyone different from what they perceive as the norm. So being the only Black family at school we suffered quite an extraordinary amount of racism. We were attacked on a daily basis either verbally by those with intentions to demean and degrade, or in testosterone-fuelled brawls. As a minority we were seen as either an exotic curiosity or something to be feared; race discrimination in those days was blatant yet barely ever mentioned: the only time teachers got involved was to punish us when we reacted to it. Everyone seemed to accept that we were a target and it tended to be the older boys that would give me grief. By the time I reached senior school my eldest two brothers had left and Christopher was my only brother left at the school. So, whenever I had a problem – if someone had upset me by calling me 'nigger' or 'rubber lips' – I'd go to Christopher and he'd sort it out. He protected me an awful lot – and he had to protect himself a lot too. He was doubly taunted at school, both for his race and his psoriasis, which covered him from top to toe. It was sore all the time, and he would often scratch it until it bled. The other kids at school called him 'map of the world'.

Yet he never seemed to allow the taunting he was subjected to to bother him that much; he took everything in his stride at school – not like me. I got upset and lashed out at times. This was how I looked after myself in school, where I felt so isolated. It was only at night that the stress of our situation really came out. He would constantly bang his head on the headboard, like children I've seen on TV in Romanian orphanages. You'd hear the headboard going off of the wall all the time, and the house parents, who ran our care home, would go mad at him.

As an adult, he was a quiet and sensitive type of guy, but very sociable; he had many friends. Before his death, he was living in a little flat on the quayside of Hull just minutes away from the Waterfront nightclub, sharing his home with a mate who was trying to sort out his own accommodation. That's how he was: he would help out anyone if he could. After Christopher's death, I got several letters from his friends and neighbours offering their condolences, saying how kind he had been to them. One older couple got in touch to pay their respects and told me how he would help move furniture or go to the shops for them. At the funeral, a girl came up to me in tears, telling me that everyone had been picking on her in a nightclub but Christopher had stood up for her and protected her. She said she would never forget it. No one had anything but good to say about him. But I didn't know him very well as an adult myself. After leaving the care home, we all went our separate ways – I was looking after my daughter as a single parent and ended up in Scotland, fleeing an abusive relationship, and I feared going back, so I didn't see much of my brothers after that. I think we were all dealing with the demons of growing up in care.

In 1976, British unemployment approached 6 per cent, the highest it had been since the early years of World War II. That was the year Christopher left school. Job prospects were bad, but a career in the army seemed to offer a stable income, travel and an opportunity to develop his athletic abilities and physical fitness. Christopher enlisted that September. He was sixteen.

One of Christopher's army comrades, Phil Waring, got in touch with me after his death, and we met up. He had joined at the same time as Christopher and they were part of the same battalion.

'When I joined up it was jail or the army for a lot of the kids,' Phil explained. 'They came out of care, there was no jobs, so we joined as boy soldiers. I was a springboard diver at junior class and then I went into the army and saw the gymnast class and I thought: get me in! And Chris was the same.'

In the early years, it must have felt like a dream come true for Christopher and Phil. They joined the army's junior gymnastic team and, for a year, they did army recruitment, performing gymnastic displays at 'schools, colleges, fetes, fairs – anywhere we could get booked in'. It was, said Phil, 'the best time ever'. They performed at the Cardiff Military Tattoo, and, in 1977, at the FA Cup final at Wembley Stadium.

After a year, when they were seventeen, they started 'army training for serious', including a gruelling two-week stint in the Brecon Beacons. This involved digging six-foot trenches into what is known, for obvious reasons, as 'concrete hill', and marching for miles up the treacherous Pen y Fan in rain and snow, with full equipment. 'That was mad,' Phil told me. Then there was the running: 'Everywhere in the camp, you didn't walk, you ran. The only time you'd not run was after a meal. And then you do the run on the shale beach and that's murder.' This is more than a metaphor; in 2013, two young men died in the Brecon Beacons during these very exercises.[1]

Then there was 'P Company', which Phil described as 'five days of sheer hell'. P Company is the pre-parachute regiment selection training programme, in which all parachute regiment candidates must complete a series of eight tests which push them to the limit of their physical endurance. Among other things, it involves a ten-mile hike carrying 16 kilos and a rifle; a stretcher race, in which teams of four must carry a stretcher carrying 80 kilos five miles; a log race; and 'milling' – where two recruits wear boxing gloves and pummel each other. 'These days they wear headguards, but we never had them,' Phil remembered. 'It's to figure out how well you can handle the stress. It's only about a minute, but it feels a hell of a lot longer when you're doing it.'

Both Christopher and Phil passed P Company and were accepted as candidates for the parachute regiment. The next stage was actually jumping out of aircraft. Phil could not remember his first jump, but one US soldier told historian Robert Kershaw that 'until I had actually taken that helicopter fall from 1,500 feet to treetop level, I had no idea how exhilarating and terrifying that manoeuvre was … your stomach felt as though it had just been pitched into the roof of your mouth.'[2] Kershaw, in his book *Sky Men: The Real Story of the Paras*, wrote that 'nobody liked parachuting but everybody had to do it.'[3] Yet this does not seem to have been the case for Phil and Christopher, who, once they'd got the hang of it, would take every opportunity to leap, badgering hot air balloonists to take them up whenever they were in the vicinity.

Then came six weeks of parachute training in Canada: 'We did what was called a "brigade jump" with the Canadian airborne, which involved nearly 4,000 people in the air. There were two deaths and multiple broken limbs. And they expected more. On paper, they expected at least ten deaths,' Phil told me. Both men completed their training and were accepted into the third battalion of the parachute regiment, known as 3 Para. This was an elite unit with deep colonial roots and a history of atrocities from Aden to Ireland. Racism was rife.

3 Para's posting between 1976 and 1981 – the exact years of Christopher's time as a serving soldier – was to the deadliest area of the whole of Northern Ireland for the British forces: South Armagh. Nicknamed 'Bandit Country' by Northern Irish secretary Mervyn Rees, South Armagh was the heartland of the armed wing of republican nationalism, the IRA. During the course of Operation Banner, no fewer than 1,255 bomb attacks and 1,158 shooting incidents took place within just one ten-mile radius in the county, with its largest city, Crossmaglen, 'a place of hostility, isolation and the constant threat of death,' according to historian Toby Harnden.[4] This is not mere hyperbole; 123 British soldiers were killed in South Armagh during the conflict, leading Harnden to conclude that 'no other part of the world has been as dangerous for someone wearing the uniform of the British army.'[5] Briefing his men in advance of their deployment to the province, Brigadier Peter Morton 'reminded them that on average only one PIRA terrorist had died for every 50 British soldiers who had lost their lives there.'[6] For several years, roads were deemed too dangerous for use by soldiers, and all supplies and personnel had to be moved by helicopter. Even this became dangerous after 1986, when Libyan leader Muammar Gaddafi began supplying the IRA with shoulder-to-air RPG missile launchers in retaliation for British support for a US bombing raid on his home that killed his baby granddaughter.

By the time Christopher arrived, Britain was already sustaining heavy losses, with soldiers leaving the army in droves. As one marine recalling this period wrote, 'Years ago, when [the Troubles] first started, soldiers viewed the conflict in Northern

Ireland as an opportunity to get some active service in. To many young soldiers who had not served in Aden and Malaya, despite the dangers, Northern Ireland seemed very exciting, it was the real thing, something to boast about back home. However, the novelty wore off. By 1975 when I was discharged, a tour of Northern Ireland was the worst thing that could happen. The number of soldiers deserting or going AWOL would increase, alcoholism and violence was prevalent, and the cost to family relationships was immeasurable.'[7]

Christopher was part of the third 3 Para tour to be deployed in the territory, from December 1980 to April 1981. 'They hated the paras in Northern Ireland,' Phil told me. Harnden writes,

> The very mention of South Armagh can send a shiver down the spine of any one of tens of thousands of soldiers who have served there ... Before going out on patrol, troops are briefed that every gorse bush, stone wall or ditch, every cowshed, milk churn or haybale could hide a bomb; if a sniper decided to strike, the victim would probably never even hear the crack of the bullet being fired.[8]

Sixteen paratroopers were killed in two explosions in the country in the year before Christopher and Phil arrived.[9]

Yet Phil explained that the posting was 'nothing spectacular.' They came into very little contact with locals, and only tended to leave the base for border patrol or guard duty. Phil spent most of his time in the orderly room due to a foot injury. Christopher somehow managed to acquire a dog while he was there, a 'little brown and white thing', according to Phil, probably during a dog-handling course, and likely used for sniffing out the huge 'culvert bombs' that were planted under roads.

After that, said Phil, 'we got posted back to the good place': Tidworth. 'For about five miles square it's all garrison town. Living there is like hell on earth. If the world was an arsehole, Tidworth would be a pile.' Christopher requested to leave the army immediately on his return, the first point at which he would legally have been allowed to do so since joining up.

I don't know exactly what Christopher experienced during his time in Northern Ireland, or in the army more generally. I remember him coming home for a break at one point with razor cuts on his face. It must have been quite a shock to have been recruited, as a child, into what was effectively a gymnastics team, and then suddenly finding yourself as an armed enforcer of British imperialism, while your own comrades treated you as the enemy within.

The Nightclub

1998

Early in the evening of Tuesday 31 March 1998, Christopher was getting ready for a night out with some of his friends. His time in the army had instilled a sense of pride in maintaining a smart appearance, so dressing himself in navy corduroy trousers, a light blue speckled jumper and a pair of smart black slip-on shoes, he set out to meet his friends Benjamin and Neal.

At around 7 p.m., he arrived at Neal's flat, which adjoined his own. The three of them went to a few local bars – the Buzz bar, the White Horse and Circus Circus – having a drink in each one before heading to McDonald's for a bite to eat. Benjamin says Christopher then began 'pestering me to go with him to the Waterfront club', but in the end this was to no avail. Neal and Benjamin decided to return to Neal's flat while Christopher borrowed £5 from them and headed to the Waterfront. At this point, said Benjamin, 'he was perfectly all right: he was sober and seemed his normal cool self'.

Christopher was a regular at the club and had been for around five years, living only a few doors away. The staff at the club knew him well and spoke of him as being friendly and pleasant, always taking the time to speak to them. One of the club's doormen described him as 'an easy-going guy', the other adding that 'we never had any trouble from him'.

Christopher spent most of his time in the club that night in the 'Soul Suite', the Waterfront's chill-out lounge. There he spoke with a number of people, including a local doctor, who described him as 'pleasant and good natured', and a couple of young women who joked that he was too old to be chatting them up. Some of the bar staff, however, thought he looked 'nervous' and 'unhappy', and at around 1.30 a.m., Christopher got into a scuffle with a man called Jason Ramm. What it was about remains unclear, but it was soon broken up and no one appeared to have been hurt. Jason Ramm was ejected from the club soon afterwards, and was allegedly heard by one witness to be shouting at Christopher, 'I'll fucking kill you – you fucking niggers are all the same!'[1] The club closed half an hour later, and Christopher left, telling the DJ, 'Don't worry – we'll all be friends tomorrow'.

Once he got outside, however, Christopher found Jason Ramm waiting for him, agitated and shouting about the incident earlier in the night. Initially Christopher ignored him, and started heading for home. Jason tried to follow him, but another man, David Okwesia, intervened and offered to talk to Christopher himself to try to sort things out. While they were talking, Jason Ramm approached and a fight broke out between him and Christopher. Various attempts were made to break it up, including one by Jason Paul.

Jason Paul and Christopher had had an altercation two weeks previously at the Tower nightclub in Hull, when Christopher had intervened in an argument between Jason and Christopher's niece Laura (the daughter of his brother Richard). Laura had seen Jason kissing a girl in the club, which had surprised her because, as far as she knew, he was seeing her friend. Laura asked this friend, who was also in the club, if she and Jason were still together. She said they were and so Laura told her what she had seen. Later on, Jason got angry at Laura, shouting, 'What did you do that for?' He started pushing her, and poked her in the cheek. Christopher saw this and intervened, demanding to know what Jason thought he was doing. Jason continued shouting and made a fist, as if he was going to hit her. Christopher stood between the two of them and pushed Jason backwards with both hands. Jason walked away, so Christopher sat back down and carried on his conversation with his friend. Later on, Jason again started shouting at Laura, this time grabbing her clothing, and then her chin. She turned away in fright, and went to tell Christopher what had happened. He reassured her that everything would be all right, and then left the club with her and her friend before wishing them good night.

Some witnesses say Jason Paul was intervening in the fight between Christopher and Jason Ramm, and Christopher lashed out at Jason Paul; others say it was Jason Paul who struck Christopher first. It's hard to say from the statements of those who were outside when the brawl occurred, but a blow from Jason Paul knocked Christopher over. He fell straight back, hitting his head on the cobbled road. It appeared to witnesses that he was knocked semi-unconscious. This was a typical fight between lads on a night out, the likes of which happen just about every Saturday night in most towns and cities of Britain.

An ambulance was called, and some of the nightclub staff put Christopher into the recovery position and checked his breathing. According to the doorman Michael Coombs, 'after a minute or so of waiting, the injured man regained consciousness and he tried to get up', although he was persuaded not to do so until the ambulance arrived. Another staff member, Karen Mills, placed a blanket over Christopher, who had taken his jumper off during the fight.

Eleven minutes after being knocked to the ground, the ambulance arrived, and the paramedics ushered a now somewhat disorientated Christopher into the vehicle. 'He walked slowly but normally,' one of them later told the inquest, but he did have a large lump or swelling (known as a haematoma) on the back of his head from where he had hit the ground. He had also lost a tooth.

Paramedic Stephen Krebs travelled in the back of the ambulance with Christopher on the way to the hospital. In his statement to the police, he noted that 'at no point whilst in my company at the scene was the patient abusive, uncooperative or violent towards anyone'.[2] Stephen and Christopher apparently developed a good rapport over the course of the journey, during which they discovered that both had a background in the armed forces. Nevertheless, others at the scene had described Christopher's behaviour as erratic and aggressive following his fall, attempting to kick people while he was on the ground, and insulting those who tried to help him. Dropping him off at the hospital, the paramedic mentioned to the nursing staff 'just to be a little bit aware that Chris was having mood swings, you know, and to just be a little bit extra careful'.

Finding Out

1998

It was Friday 17 April 1998 when I found out.
I had just settled down to watch a bit of TV before bed after a night out with friends at a pub near my home in Burnley. The kids were asleep and I was getting into my nightwear when there was a loud knock on the door. It was one of those very official-sounding knocks – a firm, heavy banging – and it made me jump. Wondering who was visiting at this time of night, I peeped behind the curtain and saw a silhouette looking like a man in uniform. I had an instant feeling of dread; something was very wrong. I opened the door to see a police officer.

'Are you the sister of Christopher Alder?'

'Yes,' I said, 'why, what's happened?'

I could feel my stomach sink, as if someone had just dropped a rock in it, even before I had chance to hear what he had to say. I was pacing up and down the room, hyperventilating; I knew I was about to get the worst news I had ever been approached with. He seemed nervous, and was unable to make eye contact.

'Your brother Christopher has died in police custody.'

I lost my breath.

'Police custody?' I said.

'Yes.'

'What do you mean?'

'I don't know any more than that. It could just mean he was sat next to a copper when he died,' he said.

I couldn't believe what I was hearing. Emotionally, I felt like I'd been hit with a sledgehammer; I was shocked, confused and frightened. Everything I knew as normal collapsed with that knock on the door.

I immediately became quite hysterical. I sent the officer away; in fact, I couldn't get him out of my door quickly enough. My brother had died in police custody and a police officer had come to tell me. I was shaking; I grabbed my mobile phone, going through the numbers trying to find someone who would be awake, or just not out on a Friday night. I just wanted to speak to someone, to anyone.

A lump in my throat appeared and I couldn't dislodge it. I had a sick feeling in the pit of my stomach. I knew I needed to call the police back, but I was scared about what I would find out. Eventually I forced myself to call Burnley police station, only to be told it had nothing to do with them. All they could tell me was that they received the news of Christopher's death in a two-line fax message, and that I should contact Humberside Police. When I did, the officer on the other end of the line spoke in a very abrupt tone, as if I was wasting his time. 'Do you want to know how your brother died?' he asked. I said yes. Sharp and cold in his tone of voice, he was quick to emphasise that Christopher had been in a fight, and that due to his injuries he had died. That's all he could tell me, saying I should call again in the morning as there was no one available to talk to just now. I put the phone down. My mouth was dry. I did not sleep much that night for crying.

I spent the weekend not knowing what to do or how to handle things. Nothing could have prepared me for such traumatic news. I just got drunk, cried, got drunk, cried. On the Saturday, I went to the pub to meet a friend, but she was too distressed about her own financial situation to really listen. I didn't have anyone to turn to, or any clue what to expect, but eventually I made up my mind to go to the police station in Hull where it had happened. I phoned the station that night and spoke to an officer at the advice desk. He put me through to the switch board, but all I heard was a recorded message about a death in custody, which obviously distressed me. I shouted, 'What do you mean, a death in custody?'

It was not until late on the Sunday morning that I finally dropped off to sleep for a few hours. In my sleep, I dreamed of a raven landing on a chimney, its beak touching a TV aerial. But when I looked closer, I saw its feathers were broken and charred, as if it had been struck by lightning. I woke up with a start, sweating and fearful. Immediately the voice of the policeman came back into my head, telling me Christopher was dead. I knew I was going to Hull the next day, to the place where he had died, but had no idea what to expect or whether I was prepared to hear what I was going to be told. I just needed to see if I could find anything to add to the very little I knew so far.

The lump was still in my throat, making it hard to swallow, and my mouth was permanently dry. I grabbed some clothes and packed a bag, telling my daughter I would have to go to Hull for a few days and that she would have to look after herself and her brother.

I got the train to Hull on 20 April. Two of my surviving brothers still lived there, but with a busy working life, bringing up children and dealing with some difficult situations, I hadn't seen them for some time. Emmanuel (then living in Leeds) and Stephen were in full-time psychiatric care; we'd had a difficult childhood and it had taken its toll. On arrival in Hull, I went straight to see my other brother, Richard.

Richard and I sat up most of the night, speaking about our days in the children's home and the horrors of discipline and punishment, finding we were even able to giggle a bit and make light of some of the things we remembered. The five of us had suffered some serious emotional and physical abuse at the hands of our 'guardians'. How we managed to laugh at those nightmare days I do not know; I guess it was just the sheer relief of not being in that situation anymore. It was great being together as brother and sister. We tried to instil a little humour in the empty, uncomfortable, silent atmosphere that kept creeping in as our minds went back to the ordeal of Christopher's death, knowing the news we had just been given, yet almost nothing about what had actually happened.

My older brother had had to identify Christopher's body, something I know I would have found impossible. He left with the vision of Christopher on a cold slab in a mortuary etched in his mind for ever. Richard mentioned Christopher having a cut above his eye when he saw him, which had been stitched up, and said that he couldn't understand where it had come from or who had stitched it. I didn't see the relevance of what he was saying at the time, and didn't think to ask.

No one made us aware that we were entitled to be represented at the original post-mortem. I only learned later, from others who had been through similar experiences, that families are permitted to instruct that their own independent medical representative attend the post-mortem process. This had been denied to us, however, as the first post-mortem had been arranged without our knowledge. Not being able to make much sense of where my brother was coming from as far as Christopher's eye injury was concerned, I just put his comments to the back of my mind – as I did when he mentioned that Christopher had collapsed in the custody suite while being booked in.

My brother raised his gaze from the computer now and then, and we chatted a bit more before I left him with his thoughts, cracking a joke that I was going to wet the bed, as I had done so often in the children's home, and no one could stop me. We giggled, and then I went through to my bedroom. I spent the night tossing and turning, thinking about our discussion and fearful of what the next day would bring.

Hull

1998

The next day I phoned the police again to see if they had now identified the cause of Christopher's death. They transferred me to the coroner's office. 'No,' said the coroner's assistant, 'we have a toxicology test to do yet.' I spent the rest of the day calling anyone I could think of who might be able to help, even Amnesty International.

The following morning I awoke at dawn: too early to call anyone. I sat with a cup of coffee in my hand, nervously glancing at the clock. The minute it turned nine, I left the house for the phone box across the road to call the coroner again. But I got the same reply: the cause of death had still not been established. Starting to get impatient, I asked the coroner's assistant why, more than a fortnight after it had happened, he still couldn't give my family the reason for our brother's death. I told him I wanted to know if I should involve a solicitor and he replied that it wouldn't do any harm. Suspicious, I braced myself to make a visit to Queen's Gardens police station.

This was the first time I had been back to Hull for some years, and little had changed. I passed through the central square, with its statue of Queen Victoria, and saw people feeding the pigeons just as I used to, despite the cold, grey April weather.

Queen's Gardens itself was a special place to sit when I was a child, with a huge pond in the centre surrounded by well-tended beds with some of the brightest flowers I have ever seen. It was always full of birds, bees, ducks, swans, people having picnics and children running around freely.

But this time it was nothing like that. The gloom in the air seemed to reflect my own mood, and all those familiar feelings of insecurity that I'd tried to leave behind twenty years earlier at our Hull care home began to creep back as I walked into the police station.

I was so nervous as I waited to be seen; as a society we are brought up to feel intimidated by police stations. After what seemed like an age, an officer sat at a desk behind glass knocked on his window and in a very aggressive voice told me to 'come here'.

I was instantly angry about the way he was talking to me, and became defensive. I told him not to speak to me like that because I hadn't done anything wrong, and that I was there to understand what had happened to Christopher. The officer walked into a back room.

Sitting in the building where he had died, I wondered if Christopher had suffered in this intimidating environment. He must have been scared, just like I was, I thought. I remembered feeling this way as a child around the bullies and racists at school, and how Christopher would protect me. Now he was dead.

After another long wait, a thin, sandy-haired officer in his late thirties emerged from the back office behind reception. Detective Inspector David Brookes led me into an interview room, where I sat down and felt a little more at ease. I hoped he could tell me something more about what had happened, but like everyone else I had dealt with, he told me very little. He said that Christopher had been in a fight, and that he had collapsed sat next to a policeman while being booked in and subsequently died.

Hands behind his head and chewing gum, Brookes wouldn't have looked out of place on a deckchair on Blackpool beach, with nothing more to do than swat away the odd horsefly – maybe that's all I was to him. In contrast, I felt like a frightened pufferfish: trying not to let my fear show, while also trying to appear bigger than I was. I told him Amnesty International was supporting the family, and as I did so, I felt like my words were coming from somewhere else.

I *had* phoned Amnesty – that part was true – but they had told me that while they sympathised, they could not assist as they dealt with atrocities affecting a multitude of people, not individual cases.

I asked Brookes how many police officers were involved in Christopher's arrest. He picked up the phone and after making an 'uh-huh' sound down the phone, he told me he was asking his colleagues. But I was pretty sure his lips moved only to gnaw on the gum in his mouth – and I told him so. As I realised that our conversation had become pointless, his radio called in a murder. I took this as my cue to leave.

As I passed through the police station foyer, I was gripped by a strange feeling and turned around. Behind me, I could see a crowd of police officers behind the counter, with more heads bobbing around the corner, all competing to get a good look at me. I felt the adrenaline rush of fear coming over me. My heart pumping wildly, I just managed to blurt out a sarcastic 'BYE!'

before stepping out of the building and bursting into tears. The more frightened I was, the more I seemed to open my mouth.

I was none the wiser as to what had happened to Christopher after my conversation with Brookes. Instead, I left feeling even worse: more frightened, and as if I was making trouble for his well-ordered police station.

Making Enquiries

1998

After my distressing visit to Queen's Gardens police station, I realised it was pointless looking to the police for information about what had happened to Christopher; I was going to have to make my own enquiries. Richard said Christopher's death had been reported in the local newspaper, so I began by heading to the office of the *Hull Daily Mail* on Beverley Road.

It was a large 1970s two-storey block, almost resembling a squat pyramid – one of those buildings that must have looked very stylish when they were built, but which had dated very quickly. Inside, they kindly gave me a bundle of newspapers from the past month.

The day after his death, the newspaper had published a photograph of Christopher, and I wondered where they'd got it from. The reports didn't say much about the police's involvement in Christopher's death: just a line at the end of one article noting that Christopher had 'collapsed' while in police custody, after which 'officers and paramedics made desperate attempts to resuscitate him'.[1]

Instead, the focus all seemed to be on a fight outside the Waterfront nightclub that Christopher had apparently been involved in earlier in the night, with one edition of the newspaper containing a big picture of a line of officers in uniform combing the cobbled area outside the club for evidence. Some of the reports included pleas for witnesses to come forward, even printing freeze-frames of some of those they wanted to talk to.

The headline of the second day of coverage was 'Death Probe: Man Charged'.[2] It said that a twenty-seven-year-old man, Jason Paul, who was involved in that fight, had been arrested and charged with GBH in connection with the death. I felt sick and confused. Anyone reading the papers would have been led to believe that Jason Paul was responsible for Christopher's death. Yet during my visit to Humberside Police, no one had mentioned there was a possibility that Christopher had been murdered, nor that they'd arrested a suspect.

As I read through the news reports, this seemed to be the pattern of each newspaper article. I was later to find this was also the pattern of the press releases written by the Police Complaints Authority. All I knew at this point was that Christopher had died in police custody. I noticed the articles also said he had been 'arrested for assaulting a hospital worker'.[3] That stopped me in my tracks; it just didn't fit with the Christopher I knew, who protected me and others.

I asked the desk staff where that claim about the hospital workers had come from. They told me they got it from a press release issued by the police. I was shocked that the police had been feeding this claim to the media before completing any investigation. It seemed that different accounts were being given to the media and our family, and added to this was the possibility Christopher had been murdered. Nothing was clear.

I left the newspaper offices in turmoil and headed back to Richard's flat. After a cup of tea I decided to visit the Hull Royal

Infirmary, where Christopher had supposedly assaulted staff. My niece Laura came with me. We entered the towering 1960s silver building through the doors to A & E and went straight to the desk. I asked if we could talk to someone who knew what had happened while Christopher was there on the night of 31 March. The receptionist told me she would find the specialist who had been working that night, so I took a seat. The area was open and brightly lit and luckily not very busy, and a few minutes later she returned with a tall middle-aged man with blond hair and glasses, wearing a white coat.

He introduced himself, shook my hand and offered his condolences. He took me into a side room, perching on the edge of a trolley with one foot touching the floor while we talked. The first thing he told me was that 'this is now a murder inquiry, and I am bound by law not to say anything'.

My eyes widened. This was the first time I had heard anything about Christopher being murdered. Well, who murdered him, I asked myself? Neither Richard nor I had been told anything about a murder. Did this mean that Jason Paul had killed Christopher? I was stunned that DI Brookes had not mentioned it to me, when even the hospital consultant seemed to know.

I explained that all I wanted to know was what state Christopher had been in when he left the hospital. He replied, 'He had a superficial head injury and a mouth injury.' At no time did he mention anything about Christopher being aggressive or assaulting anyone.

It didn't appear from what the consultant was saying to me that the injuries from the punch were life-threatening. And if they had been, surely they would not have released him from the hospital?

The last time I'd been at this hospital was in 1980, when our father was being treated after a stroke. He was unable to move and the right side of his body was paralysed. I remember looking up at the huge building back then, seeing it reaching up into the sky, trying to work out exactly where our father was, the passing clouds making it look like it was moving. It seemed to reflect my own feelings of instability, of the world shifting under my feet. Now that same feeling was engulfing me again, and far from providing answers, everything I found out just seemed to add to the confusion.

On my way home, I was stopped by a woman who looked around Christopher's age, a couple of years older than me. She asked if I was his sister and told me she knew Christopher very well and couldn't believe he was dead. She had seen him a couple of weeks previously and she told me what a good person he was, how bubbly and kind. It was a relief to hear someone describing the brother I knew and loved after all the hostile comments in the press.

Last Days in Hull

1998

It was late afternoon by the time I got back to Richard's and tried to process what I'd learned. I was angry that the police hadn't told us about the murder charges against Jason Paul. Back in the phone box, they transferred me to a police liaison officer named Beatrice Ogunleye-Smith. Her name and voice instantly told me she was of African origin; she spoke with the same Nigerian accent as our father.

This knocked me for six; Hull was over 96 per cent white, and I had never even seen a Black policeman before. What were the chances of this case being randomly assigned to an officer apparently hailing from Nigeria? I could feel the hairs on my arms standing on end; had the police drafted her in after going through our family background?

Even more astonishing was that she had no knowledge of the case; Ogunleye-Smith knew nothing about the investigation and her role was purely to liaise with the family. But how could she do this if she was unable to answer any of our questions?

It later emerged she had been specially drafted in from Grimsby, and was qualified not in dealing with bereaved families but with victims of sexual abuse. In other words, not only did she know nothing about the investigation she was liaising with us about, she wasn't even qualified for the role she was supposed to be performing. I told her that I needed to know what had happened to my brother, and I found it offensive that we were being contacted by someone who knew nothing about the case. The police seemed to me to be using Beatrice as a lightning rod, putting a Black face at the front of the force to take the pressure off themselves.

I insisted I be allowed to meet with someone who knew about the murder charge and the police made an appointment for me with Superintendent Ken Bates, the officer responsible for investigating the charges against Jason Paul. The day after the call with Beatrice, I met Bates. I was not keen to return to the police station where Christopher had died, especially after my last experience there, but I was not going to turn down any chance to find out exactly what had happened to my brother. Extremely nervous, I walked into Queen's Garden police station once again and as I stood at the reception, officers walked through the foyer smirking at me and sniggering.

It was so obvious that even the other person waiting noticed it; he told me he was willing to be a witness to their behaviour if I needed, and gave me his contact details. I also noticed the camera on the wall and wondered if I was being watched by the officers who found me so amusing.

After about forty minutes, Bates opened the inner police station door, called my name and led me up some steps to an office, where we were joined by Ogunleye-Smith. Bates offered me a tea, but I declined; I just wanted to get on with it. Although very nervous, I told him I needed to know what had happened to my brother. I explained that I was confused by the misleading press releases issued by his police force, and by the contradictory information we had been getting from them, the press and the hospital.

As he talked, I started to make notes that I could relay to Richard when I got home. Apparently rattled, Bates aggressively wheeled towards me on his chair and told me in a bullish tone that he did not deal with outside organisations, only with family. I presumed he was referring to the conversation I had had two days earlier with Brookes. Trembling, I responded, 'I *am* family, I'm the sister of Christopher Alder and I didn't come here for an argument.' I told him all communication in the future would be through a solicitor, and then, my nerves shredded, I walked out of the door. He followed closely behind. 'We don't deal with solicitors,' he snarled, 'who is your solicitor?' I could feel him towering above me as I walked out.

It appeared that whereas I had been seen by his colleague Brookes as a nuisance, Bates saw me as a threat. He certainly didn't treat me like a distressed sister, nor take any heed of the shock I was in following my brother's death. His explosive reaction caught me by surprise and I left feeling totally drained of energy. And still, at no point during our meeting had he mentioned the ongoing murder inquiry into Christopher's death which had run through the whole of April; neither did he tell me that Christopher had met his death on the custody suite floor and that the whole thing had been captured on CCTV.

I've always found that in times of stress, I tend to have vivid dreams; I believe this is my brain trying to make sense of what has gone on during the day: a way of sorting out the confusion of daily life. After I found out about Christopher's death, my dreams, if I managed to sleep at all, were vivid and scary. As I walked away from the menacing confinement of the police station in a haze, detached from everything around me, an image of the raven from the dream I'd had at the weekend I found out about Christopher's death flashed suddenly into my head. I'm not usually one for superstition; but for some reason I clung on to this dream, believing it to be significant and important in some way; all the more so when I later discovered that Christopher had had something of an obsession with ravens himself.

My eyes began welling up and as I walked towards the town centre I burst into tears, releasing the shock and fear I felt following the meeting with Bates. Most people see me as a confident, loud and gobby woman, but those visits to the police station made any insecurities and feelings of worthlessness I might have unconsciously been hiding come flooding over me like a tsunami. I was petrified.

Wanting to go somewhere that would calm me down, I headed to a Waterstones bookshop in town. I had decided to get a book on dream interpretation to try to make sense of the charred-raven image that had embedded itself in my mind so powerfully since Christopher's death. I chose a couple of books and headed for the checkout. As I did so, I happened to glance towards the door, and noticed a white man in his early fifties standing outside, wearing what appeared to be navy-blue overalls and a navy-blue fleece jacket. I was sure I had seen him earlier, coming into the police station, walking through the foyer and out through the door at the back. Then I saw in his hand a small notebook bearing the silver badge of the police force. I was startled, like a rabbit in the headlights. I pointed to the door, and shouted, 'My brother died in police custody and the police are following me!'

Several staff and customers started walking towards the door and the undercover officer quickly walked to the opposite side of the road. I remained in the shop, my knees shaking, overcome with paranoia. I realised at that moment that I had to get a solicitor. I needed someone to protect me from the police, the very organisation that is supposed to keep us safe. I felt hunted, like a fox being chased by hounds.

Once I had steadied myself, I headed out to search for a solicitor's office. I was jittery and apprehensive, and afraid of sounding crazy. In fact, I probably did sound crazy. In the first office I went to, I strode up to a man putting his coat on and asked, 'Excuse me, are you any good?' He didn't seem best pleased with the manner in which I approached him, and I am not even sure he was necessarily a solicitor.

'What do you mean, am I any good? What is the problem?' he said.

'My brother has died in police custody,' I told him.

'Well, there is nothing I can do about that at this time,' he said.

'Well, you are no good to me then,' I replied, 'goodbye.' I must have seemed supremely arrogant; I didn't mean to offend him, but I was anxious and scared, and looking for someone who could help and reassure me.

The next solicitors I walked into told me they were acting on behalf of Jason Paul. I left immediately, wanting nothing to do with them. In hindsight I wish I had stopped and spoken to them; my feelings towards Jason had started to change after my visit to the police station, and I was starting to think that perhaps he was not responsible for Christopher's death. I had sensed a defensiveness in the police's hostility towards me that made me increasingly suspicious that they had something to hide.

As I left Jason's solicitors, I saw another man I recognised from the police station; like the officer outside the bookshop, he too was just standing there, apparently waiting for me to leave. Had they sent a whole team to follow me?

Panicking, I ran up a flight of steps into the offices of Stamp Jackson & Procter. 'It's like the fucking Gestapo out there,' I screamed as I entered, 'get them told!' I was shaking and out of breath. One of the receptionists came out from behind her desk and calmed me down. I explained what had happened, showed her the newspapers, and told her about my suspicions that the police were withholding information. It was the first time that day that I felt someone believed me and was on my side.

She booked me in for an appointment with a solicitor and then led me through the back entrance out onto the street where I got into the first taxi I saw. My heart still beating wildly, I said to the driver, 'I can't believe it, the police are following me!'

'Get out,' he replied. I suppose he thought I must have done something wrong. In the next taxi I said nothing. As we drove, I looked out of the rear window in case a police car was tailing us, but thankfully saw nothing. When I reached Richard's house, I couldn't believe my eyes; there was a patrol car parked right outside. I now felt sure I was being trailed. I wrote down the car's registration number and walked into the house with my head held high, but I had entered a totally different world, one that was scary and distorted, where victims are hounded and nothing is as it should be.

By now, news of Christopher's death had spread nationally. I was contacted by Paul Macey, a journalist from the national Black newspaper *The Voice* who wanted to write a piece on Christopher, and asked if I had a photograph of him they could use. I didn't, but we knew the police had a picture, because they had provided it to the local press. Paul helped me work out they must have taken it from Christopher's flat and used it without the consent of our family. I gritted my teeth and phoned Queen's Gardens. At first Bates requested that the police be allowed to keep the photo. 'No,' I said, 'it is to be returned to the family.' He said I could collect it from Tower Grange police station the next day.

That night I couldn't sleep. I was anxious and my head was pounding with conflicting thoughts. I had originally been angry with Jason Paul because of my conversation with the hospital doctor and the media reports suggesting he had been responsible for Christopher's death. Yet I was becoming sceptical about everything the police had told us. I couldn't understand why they had withheld vital information from me and felt humiliated by their treatment. I really didn't know what to think.

Back to Burnley

1998

The morning after my call with Superintendent Bates, I caught the train home. It was now 24 April and I needed to get back to my kids. Aside from feeling scared by Humberside Police's intimidation and stalking, I realised I knew little more than I had the night the officer first brought me the news.

I was glad when I finally got back and hugged my children.

Hull seemed like a bad dream and I was determined to return to ordinary life. But people treated me differently now that Christopher's death was national news, either not knowing what to say or offering unsolicited advice. It began to unnerve me. Under my tough exterior, I was starting to feel extremely vulnerable and ill at ease. As a child I craved reassurance, tenderness and somebody to tell me things were going to be OK – and now, apart from my kids, I was alone again.

Meanwhile I was beginning to feel that the police were more connected with Christopher's death than they had let on. Jason had been kept in a bail hostel in York, miles from Hull, since April, but it wasn't until June that all the charges against him were dropped. In early May, the national press reported that the five police officers connected to Christopher's death – the two who had arrested him, the one who had driven him to the police station, and two more who were with him in the custody suite – had been suspended from duty.

It was around then that I received a phone call from Jim Elliott of the Police Complaints Authority. I'd never heard of the PCA (the forerunner of today's IOPC), but apparently it was their job to make sure deaths in police custody were properly investigated, and Elliott had been appointed to supervise an investigation into the role of the police in Christopher's death. He asked if he could visit me at home, and we arranged a meeting for the afternoon of 12 May 1998, over a month after Christopher had died. I cleaned the house and carefully arranged the living room with the two settees opposite each other, with enough distance between them so I did not feel intimidated; I did not want a repeat of my meetings with the police. I asked Marie, a close friend from work, to join me so I did not have to face him alone.

As the fresh spring air blew in through the open windows, I sat with Marie, my hands sweating, awaiting a knock on the door. Elliott arrived at midday. He was a man in his late forties, with greying hair and gold-rimmed glasses, wearing the blue shirt and grey tie that seems to be the uniform of officialdom. He took out a notepad, removed his jacket and sat down. After some initial remarks – including curtly explaining that his role did not include consoling the victim's family – he got down to business.

He explained that the PCA had the power to supervise police investigations and make recommendations in relation to police discipline. He gave examples of previous investigations, but made no mention of any prosecutions or even successful disciplinary action arising from any of them, and no examples of any investigations into deaths in custody. He said nothing that reassured me. I got the distinct feeling that these investigations had little to do with holding officers to account for someone's death; they seemed to be more along the lines of an internal audit or a performance review.

In our case, he said, the PCA had appointed West Yorkshire Police to conduct an independent investigation. He told us that the highest level of independence at police level was appointing another police force. But it was still the police investigating themselves – surely that wasn't right?

Then he said something that shocked me: 'Your brother came out of the police van unconscious.'

'What?' I asked. Neither DI Brookes nor Superintendent Bates had told me this when I went to the police station. I felt sick, plunged back into that same state of shock as when I first found out that Christopher was dead. My body immediately became rigid, the tension in my neck making it hard to move. Marie stroked my back, trying to console me.

I couldn't help but notice that Elliott's body language appeared uncomfortable, with wet circles of perspiration starting to cover a large area under his armpits. As a child it had become important for me to watch facial expressions and body language; I had become hyper-sensitive to being let down, finding the words people spoke did not always match the way they acted. Finding myself once again in a world of uncertainty, I fell back on the skills I had learned to survive.

He continued the conversation by telling me not to forget that 'there are five other families involved'. He meant the families of the suspended officers. I was furious.

'But none of them are dead, are they?' I replied. They had not lost their loved ones; yet he seemed to be suggesting I should have more sympathy for the very people I suspected of being responsible for my brother's death.

Elliott seemed to be avoiding eye contact with me, finding it easier to stare out of the window while he spoke or concentrating on his notepad. In one particularly strange moment, he described a case where police officers had been disciplined for stealing boxes of chocolates from a lorry. He explained that a lorry had crashed, tipping all its goods onto the road, and when the police arrived, the driver gave them some chocolates as a goodwill gesture for their assistance. The officers involved later faced disciplinary action for taking the chocolates.

I was stunned. With all the hundreds of deaths in custody, was this the only case that had ever resulted in action being taken against the police? Did the PCA only discipline police officers in cases as trivial as this? Marie also thought it was insulting to compare a few boxes of chocolates to a person's life. But there it was in black and white, in the 1997 PCA Annual Report he later handed to me.

While Elliott went to the bathroom, my friend and I had a swift discussion. She was shocked by his callous manner towards a grieving sister while constantly reinforcing his concern for the five other families. She also felt he wasn't being truthful and told me to rip the pages out of his book.

When he returned, I asked to see his notebook and ripped out the pages where he had been taking notes. They seemed to be a record of what I had been asking, and he looked very sheepish. 'I'm sorry, but I just don't trust you,' I told him.

As he had attended the post-mortem held on the night of Christopher's death, I asked him about the eye injury that Richard had seen when he identified Christopher's body. I thought this injury would have been considered significant in an inquiry into someone's death, and I asked Elliott who had stitched it up. But, staring out of the window, Elliott replied that he didn't recall seeing any eye injury. He told me that the questions I was asking him were properly suited for the inquest and that's where I would get the opportunity to ask them.

After I asked him to leave, I pictured Christopher being pulled unconscious out of a police van. Why had this only come out now? Why had the police been telling everyone that he had collapsed in the police station? Something wasn't right and Jim Elliott's visit had only compounded my suspicions.

I didn't see Elliott face to face again, but I had many conversations over the telephone with him to ask whether they had found the cause of Christopher's death. I got the impression that if it wasn't for his obligation to keep the family informed, he wouldn't have spoken to me at all.

It was during one of those conversations that I discovered that Christopher's death in the custody suite had been captured on CCTV video. A wave of nausea immediately washed over me knowing someday I would have to watch it.

Not long after Elliott's visit I called Superintendent John Holt of West Yorkshire Police and made a desperate plea for Christopher's clothes to be returned to the family. Holt was leading the investigation into the conduct of the police on the night of Christopher's death.

'Your brother's clothes have been destroyed,' he casually replied. I was staggered; they had not even consulted the family. I asked him why.

'For health reasons,' he replied.

It was an insult. I had read of cases in which the clothes of murder victims were kept as evidence for decades – and yet

Christopher's clothes were supposedly too unhygienic to have around even long enough for us to pick them up.

'I've dealt with plenty of Black and Irish deaths in the past,' he continued, in a very cocky tone of voice. Was this supposed to be reassurance or an insult? Why did he feel he needed to tell me this? Were these the type of investigations on which Superintendent Holt prided himself, with his colourful ribbons? It felt like he was trying to say they were all much of a muchness, they happen all the time, it's just what Black and Irish people *do*. I ended the call, enraged.

Already struggling to keep it together, one June morning I found myself going into the shop where I worked only to be falsely accused of stealing watches and selling them in my local pub. What truly hurt was that my so-called friends were the star witnesses: two girls I knew from the estate where I lived who I had recommended for the jobs. I was sacked on the spot. It couldn't have happened at a more vulnerable time, when my defences had been shattered by the news of Christopher's death.

Could things get any worse? I had been the store manager, a position I had got just weeks before finding out the devastating news about Christopher. It paid £200 a week, which had allowed me to feed my children well, dress them in the latest fashions, and take them places on the weekends. Now I was unemployed.

As usual, I put on a brave face, but I felt hurt and betrayed. It upset my daughter, Caroline, even more than me; she was ready to storm over to the house where one of them lived and demand she hand back all the clothes I had lent her over the years. Stopping her took some persuading.

My head was in a mess; all I wanted was to hide and wake up from this nightmare. I made a feeble attempt to clear my name, but with the ongoing fight to find out what had happened to Christopher, I had no energy or commitment for more confrontation. It was too much of a strain having to plead my innocence when I had not done anything wrong. I couldn't fight on all fronts at the same time; I had to pick my battles. And as Christopher Alder's sister, the choice was clear to me.

Campaigning

1998–9

In early May, I met up with my South African friend Noxi, a seasoned campaigner from the days of apartheid. She believed that if I wanted justice for Christopher, I would have to start a campaign. This sounded daunting, and I didn't have a clue how to go about it; I had never even been on a demonstration. So she took me to see her activist friends, Maggie and Andy Makin, at their vegetarian cafe in Burnley. They were immediately sympathetic to Christopher's case, and I warmed to them instantly. Andy had years of campaigning experience and had been present at the anti-racist march where the young teacher Blair Peach had met his death at the hands of the police in 1979. He had contacts all over the country and knew just who to talk to if you wanted a demonstration. Maggie was softly spoken, and principled, with a no-nonsense but caring approach. I can't have been easy to deal with; I was suspicious, panicky and probably at times incoherent. But over time, my confidence in Andy and Maggie grew. They gave me constant support as well as the opportunity to meet many people.

The following month, Andy rallied a group of people together to meet with us in Burnley to show me I had support in my battle to find out the truth. Many of them had come from Hull; they had seen and followed the developments in Christopher's case and as we spoke it became clear that they didn't see this as a one-off. They had heard about many other unresolved deaths in custody, and said that a disproportionate number of victims were Black. None of them seemed surprised I was having difficulty getting answers, and everyone said they would lend support in any way they could. The Hull campaigners, although too many to name individually, were phenomenal. They helped design T-shirts, leaflets and badges, laid wreaths every year outside Queens Gardens Police station and began collecting funds to build our campaign. They also approached Hull MPs and councillors, although we didn't find much support on that front. That was how the 'Justice for Christopher Alder' campaign was born.

One of the first things we did was make ourselves known to local journalists, so that the press could put our side of the story across, challenging the narratives fed to them by the police. The Hull campaigners also leafletted the city centre on several occasions, and found a lot of support when they did so. It seemed that many ordinary people in Hull had taken Christopher's death as personal to them; this was their police force, paid for with their taxes, and they would need them in times of emergency. They didn't like the idea that they too could end up being left to die on the floor of the police station.

For me, the campaign was a lifeline. When you are thrown into a situation like this, many people find it hard to believe or relate, and might even treat you as if you are crazy. It can be scary and isolating, almost like living in another dimension at times. So it was incredibly important for me to have contact with other family campaigns and to meet people who had been through similar experiences, who were able to provide the solidarity and understanding that was so absent in my dealings with the authorities. Even just being listened to and believed was an invaluable source of support, and it is no exaggeration to say it probably saved my sanity.

The campaign has also been important for Christopher's memory. The police tried to smear Christopher and treated both his life and his death as totally insignificant. But he is now a well-known name and what has happened to him has become public knowledge, with the police's narrative shot to pieces. Campaigning has forced the system to act, and even though it has never brought formal justice, it has kept the heat on everyone involved; the police, the officers who were there the night he died and the institutions protecting them. And it has triggered a widespread questioning of the police, contributing to a different understanding of their role and how they operate. It has woken up the public and shaken up the state.

And the campaign has also been important for other families. Over the years, so many people have been in touch with me following state killings of their own friends and relatives. Our campaign has inspired them to stand up for their loved ones too, to not let them be forgotten and written off, their memories besmirched, but to hold the authorities accountable and keep up the pressure. We may not get state-sanctioned justice, but we make sure there are consequences for state killings. We don't let them forget what they have done. For me, the campaign has ensured that Christopher's death would not be brushed under the carpet.

Around the time I was taking my first tentative steps campaigning, the police made what seemed like a blatant attempt to intimidate my brother Richard. On 16 August, two officers pulled up beside him in their car after claiming he had sworn at them, and placed him under arrest. He stood his ground and demanded to know what he was being arrested for, and struggled as they attempted to grip him. According to Richard, once they had got him into the van, they said they were going to take him to where his brother died, and that Christopher 'deserved what he got'. Richard was charged and ultimately convicted of 'using threatening, abusive, or insulting words or behaviour', and ended up doing community service. To me, it just felt totally vindictive, like the police were mocking what had happened to Christopher. And I also wondered whether they were trying to punish us for my moves to expose them. They couldn't get to me as I wasn't in Hull – so they went for Richard instead. It felt like they were trying to send us a message, telling us to keep quiet.

Conversations with people in Andy's circle who had campaigned following the death of Blair Peach, meanwhile, led me to believe the chances of justice were bleak; despite a major public outcry, the police who killed him had never been held accountable. In fact, despite hundreds of similar cases to Christopher's, no police officer had been held responsible for a death in custody since 1969.[1] Even in the handful of cases that have resulted in prosecutions, juries have been reluctant to convict police officers. The state seems to assume that the police are just not capable of brutality and therefore if someone dies in police custody, it must have been either their own fault or a tragic accident. It was becoming painfully clear that getting justice for Christopher wasn't going to be easy.[2]

It became clearer still a few days later when I received a letter from Stamp Jackson & Procter solicitors in Hull, explaining that they were not prepared to represent me. They said they would still represent my brother Richard, but I felt they couldn't or wouldn't deal with me opening my mouth the way I had been. I was upset and took the knock-back quite personally, especially coming from the one institution that had, until then, shown me sympathy and support. I can see now it was an early sign of how even those tasked with supporting families can end up sowing divisions within them, however inadvertently, over how to respond to deaths in custody if everyone isn't on the same page and is getting different advice. I was left feeling despondent and abandoned.

I went to the cafe and showed the letter to Andy. His words were, 'we'll find another solicitor', as if he wasn't in the least surprised. Asking around soon led us to Ruth Bundey, a reputable solicitor with vast experience dealing with deaths in police and prison custody. Ruth had dealt with cases like that of Helen Smith, a nurse who died in Saudi Arabia, whose father Roy challenged the Home Office claim that the death was an accident. That case established for the first time the duty of a coroner to hold an inquest following the death of British citizens abroad. She had also successfully represented several of the 'Bradford Twelve', who were prosecuted, and eventually acquitted, for their attempts to defend their community against a planned fascist attack.

We met in her office in Chapeltown in Leeds, and I liked her straight away. She had a warm smile, a firm handshake and expressive eyes; you could tell immediately that she had a gutsy character as well as a deep commitment to justice. Having dealt with family campaigns before, she did not see my campaigning work as a threat, and I trusted her immediately. She agreed to act on my behalf almost as soon as I'd walked through the door, and after that, we were in contact almost daily. She always listened without judgement and promptly followed up on what I told her with a letter to the appropriate people. At last, I felt I had a real ally.

One of the first things Ruth did was to get hold of the official medical report into Christopher's death. His post-mortem had been conducted in Sheffield on the night after Christopher's death by a Home Office-appointed pathologist called Dr John Chalmers Clark. I braced myself to read it, desperate to find out exactly how and why Christopher died, yet knowing that the details would be disturbing.

The report was unequivocal that the injuries Christopher sustained from the fight outside the club 'did not cause, or even directly contribute to, his death'. The head injury, it said, was 'relatively minor'. The pathologist had made this finding on 1 April, and the full report was completed five days later. Yet the police had arrested Jason Paul on a murder charge (later reduced to GBH), denied him bail, and not dropped charges against him until July. I found it hard to believe that they would actually try to frame a man for a death that they knew he had nothing to do with. Yet that seemed to be exactly what had happened. And there was worse to come.

At some point on the journey in the police van, the report said, Christopher had vomited and inhaled this vomit into his lungs, making it harder for him to breathe. Yet when he was brought into the police station, 'he was placed face down on the floor' with his arms handcuffed behind his back. I felt the rage inside me start to swell: Christopher was unconscious, choking on his own vomit, and yet not only was he not taken back to the hospital, he was not even put into the recovery position. Instead, he was dumped face down on the floor, hands behind his back, and left to choke to death. It is an image that haunts me to this day.

The report concluded that Christopher died 'from a combination of factors, of which inhalation of vomit, acute alcohol intoxication and postural asphyxia were the most important,' although it noted that his blood alcohol level was not high enough for alcohol poisoning to have played a significant role in and of itself. Postural asphyxia, I discovered, was when someone's breathing is restricted due to the position they are in. Being left face down on the floor meant that his choking was 'potentially compounded by him ending up lying face down on the floor of the police station'. I tried to make sense of what I was reading. Did this mean because his chest was pressed against the floor his lungs couldn't adequately inflate? If Christopher choked to death on his own vomit, surely those who facilitated this by dumping him face down rather than in the recovery position were criminally responsible for his death? But the pathologist seemed to then row back from his own conclusions, saying that the ultimate cause of death was 'undetermined'. I couldn't understand it – what did this mean? Everybody dies of *something*, and the pathologist said unequivocally that Christopher had been sick and inhaled his own vomit, and then been left face down and struggling to breathe until he died.

Still it got worse. The report stated that in the police station, Christopher was lying on the floor, 'naked from the thighs up', his trousers and pants pulled down to his knees, and with mud staining on both his thighs. No one had mentioned that before. What could have caused him to lose consciousness, and end up with his trousers round his knees and mud on his thighs? What the hell had happened to Christopher on the way to the police station? As far as I was told, he had stepped into the van fully compos mentis with his trousers up. I started to imagine the worst.

Attached to the report was a 'supplementary statement' claiming that there was no other cause for Christopher's unconsciousness but cardiac arrhythmia or cardiac arrest. That made no sense to me; Christopher had no history of heart trouble, and there was no evidence of any now. Nevertheless, Dr Clark recommended sending Christopher's heart to a specialist for further examination.

My mind kept turning over what could have happened to Christopher after leaving the hospital. Just as in childhood, I would have the most vivid and horrible nightmares the minute I drifted off, and I became afraid to go to sleep. For the police it seemed all too convenient that Christopher's death remained mysteriously unexplained. But for us it was frustrating, infuriating and traumatic, the waiting for answers tortuous. It drained me mentally and physically, making me ill and feel helpless.

I sent the pathologist's report to the press and did some interviews with local TV about it. I wanted to put maximum pressure on the police to force them to explain what had gone on. But I was not comfortable with this new role I felt compelled to take on. I have always had an inner shyness and uncertainty of myself in distressing times, and now I found myself suddenly thrust into the public eye. This was completely unknown territory for me, and it felt at times like my privacy was being invaded. The pressure I was under made me want to hide; I started to wonder whether perhaps I really should just shut up and go away, just as the police and PCA seemed to be suggesting.

Not long after receiving Dr Clark's report, we were sent the results of Christopher's second post-mortem. This had initially been commissioned by Jason Paul's solicitors after his arrest, and was carried out on 10 April by a Dr Gray. It made me start to wonder whether the police had assaulted Christopher on the way to the police station. Clark had recorded small bruises to the strap muscles in his neck, and believed they probably occurred during resuscitation attempts. But Gray said these injuries indicated that 'there may have been gripping or restraint to the neck to some extent during a struggle'. Christopher had not been gripped by the neck outside the nightclub, and so if this 'struggle' had happened, I reasoned, it could only have been when he was with the police.

Like Clark, Gray concluded that the cause of death was undetermined and the result of multiple factors. However, his actual findings seemed to be at odds with this conclusion. Like Clark, Gray noted that Christopher's blood alcohol level was too low to be a direct cause of death, although it might have caused vomiting or contributed to Christopher's 'excited state', identified as another possible contributory factor. Yet such a state, he noted, was usually associated with cocaine use or psychiatric illness, neither of which applied to Christopher. Moreover, even if he were in this state, Gray said that it would only have caused death had it generated a serious cardiac dysrhythmia, of which there was no evidence, and which is anyway 'unusual in fit young men'. He also backed Clark's conclusion that Christopher's injuries were not a direct cause of his death. Yet when it came to choking on his own vomit, he was unequivocal, saying he 'had inhaled significant gastric contents and this must have contributed to the terminal respiratory failure'. Furthermore, 'the final posture' in which he had been left by the police 'did cause postural asphyxia'. To me, it seemed clear – while there were unknowns in what caused Christopher to lose *consciousness*, it was beyond doubt that he *died* as a result of his airways being blocked by vomit and the position in which he was left. In other words, the police's failure to clear his airways and put him in the recovery position is ultimately what killed him. Yet, like Clark, he seemed unwilling to draw the obvious conclusions from his own findings, saying it was 'undeterminable' what had killed Christopher or whether the police could have saved him. I felt these pathologists were terrified of saying anything that might implicate the police, as if they felt obliged to prevaricate and muddy the waters of their own clear-cut medical evidence. And his comments about the police at the end of the report were bizarre, claiming that Christopher's family 'can be reassured that an exhaustive investigation of the events' by the police is underway, and that 'deaths in custody in England are subject to diligent enquiries with full disclosure of events and information, however unwelcome to the authorities'. This had certainly not been the experience of any of the families I had met – besides which, this doctor's remit was to examine the body, and I failed to see how this would have helped him reach conclusions about the quality of the police investigation. His report noted that his father was a retired Humberside police officer, and his brother a serving police officer, and I worried that he was too close to the force to risk saying anything that might cast them in a bad light. Much as I hated the idea of Christopher's body being opened up again, I became convinced that we needed to have our own independent post-mortem carried out.

It was from Gray's report, however, that I learned more about the events of the night Christopher died. After being punched outside the nightclub, Christopher had been taken to hospital to treat his injuries. In the hospital, according to the police account, he became 'abusive and uncooperative' – a result, Gray believed, of his 'post-concussive state' – and, although a few tests were done, the attempt to X-ray his skull was abandoned. But I couldn't help feeling that the police had aggravated the situation. For some reason the police officers Dawson and Blakey felt it was ok to 'physically escort' Christopher to the toilet, threatening him with CS gas in the process. Shortly afterwards, he was 'dragged backwards' out of the hospital by the same officers. It didn't seem like a very compassionate way of dealing with a distressed and injured assault victim, who the hospital felt needed a skull X-ray.

Before leaving, the medical staff advised Christopher 'to return when he was in a calmer state of mind' so they could complete their assessment. Outside the hospital, said the report, he wanted to go back in, but the police refused, again threatened him with CS gas and arrested him. Gray notes he was fully compliant while being cuffed and put into the van, but claims he 'appeared to be asleep' on arrival at the police station a few minutes later.

All this talk of CS spray made me nervous that he had been gassed after leaving the hospital. Could this have explained his sudden difficulty breathing? Gray's report noted that 'CS spray was not detected' in toxicology tests, but added that 'CS can disperse quickly', meaning it would not necessarily have shown up in these tests even if it had been used.

Throughout this time, I was filled with a constant need to know what had happened to Christopher and why. My initial expectation was that if anyone was responsible for Christopher's death, they would be held accountable. But when I started to think it could have been the police themselves who were responsible, I was struck with fear. Because of the reception I was getting asking questions, I was slowly losing trust in all that I had once believed. I was having to mentally disentangle everything I had believed about the British justice system. I was fearful and uncertain. But at the same time I knew myself to be the type of person that stood steadfast on serious matters; I'm just not someone who can walk away and forget it. I would be left with it going over and over in my mind; there was no way I could just forget about it and 'move on'.

In an age when scientists can exhume a body that has been buried for hundreds of years and find out how the person has died, I couldn't accept that someone could die in police custody in full view of five people, and no one know the cause of death.

I began to have visions of Christopher being beaten, handcuffed behind his back while being sprayed with CS gas, attempting to defend himself while the officers stood towering above him, raining blows down on his head, kicking his groin, dragging his legs to restrain him and putting him in a neck hold. Learning that his trousers were down to his knees left excruciating thoughts which are still painful if I stop and consider them. But everything was in the hands of other people – people employed to administer truth and justice and yet who were seemingly doing nothing to alleviate this psychological torture.

As news spread of Christopher's case and our campaign, activists and anti-racist campaigners started contacting Andy, inviting me to speak at meetings. Losing my job had left me with time on my hands, and so I began to travel around the country to speak at their events, letting people know about Christopher's death, what we had been told and what we hadn't. It was through these events, where I met so many others who'd suffered the loss of their loved ones at the hands of the state, that I started to realise the scale on which this was occurring. It seemed to be far more common than I would ever have suspected.

On 19 August 1998 I spoke at a meeting with Ricky Reel's mother, Sukhdev, in Blackburn library, organised by the Justice for Ricky Reel campaign. Ricky was a young Asian man who was chased by a gang of white youths one night in 1997, and ended up dead in the River Thames. Many suspect he was murdered, but no one had ever been held accountable; his family believe the police failed to take it seriously because he was Asian. All I could think about was how easily this could happen to my own children, and I found it incredible that she had found the strength through her grief to speak out and fight for justice.

I also met the family of Michael Menson, a musician and songwriter who had been part of the dance band Double Trouble. Their 1989 hit 'Street Tuff' was a landmark record in the evolution of British Jamaican dance music and had reached number three in the charts in 1989; I had danced to it many times. I was horrified to hear that in January 1997, after getting off a bus in Edmonton, London, Michael had been chased by three boys who stole his personal stereo, poured petrol on him and set him alight. He was still on fire when he was later found staggering down the road and taken to hospital, and he died two weeks later from horrific burns. Michael's last words to his brother were 'Don't let them get away with it'. There were serious failings by the police who had not sealed the area as a crime scene, simply assuming Michael had done this to himself. It took them over two years to admit he had been murdered, while those responsible were still walking the streets. It was only after the investigation had been taken over by the new 'racial and violent crimes taskforce' that any charges were brought, and this was purely due to the family's determination and steadfast stand for justice, as even the police themselves admitted. I became close to Michael's brother Kwesi, who gave me some very wise words of advice: 'Pace yourself: it's a long, hard slog.'

I knew now that, when confronting institutions who just wanted you to give up without telling you anything, it was important to maintain public pressure, and this meant attracting support from family, friends and the wider community, including as many organisations as possible. Without this you would be sidelined, ignored, dismissed, intimidated or worse. But I was also beginning to see just how important Kwesi's words were – because the people we were up against were, it seemed, as deeply committed to evading justice as we were to achieving it.

These were just two of the many justice campaigns I came into contact with, and it began to gnaw at me to see the number of ordinary families torn apart by the injustice of unaccountable killings. The lack of regard the police appeared to have for Black and brown life left me feeling extremely vulnerable; case after case demonstrated how uninterested they seemed to be in investigating ethnic minority deaths, and how frequently they were implicated in those deaths themselves. At the same time, however, meeting other family members in a similar position to me gave me the inspiration and strength to carry on fighting. I certainly needed it.

In late August I received a letter from the Police Complaints Authority telling me they had completed their investigation and their findings had been sent to the Crown Prosecution Service. It would now be for the CPS to decide whether or not any of the officers involved in Christopher's death would be prosecuted. I desperately wanted to have confidence that the criminal justice system did not discriminate, and would act impartially in accordance with the evidence, and I dared to hope that justice would be done.

But I found the waiting and delays excruciating and decided to phone the CPS directly. I was told that Philip Fleming, the lawyer in charge of the case, would call me back. Waiting for that call was nerve-wracking; I paced around the room, feeling sick, until, finally, the phone rang. He had come to a view, he explained, that there was insufficient evidence at this stage to prove the police had caused Christopher's death. My heart sank. Four months after an investigation had been launched into Christopher's death, there were still no plans to prosecute anyone. I was devastated.

Soon afterwards, my lawyer Ruth phoned Fleming to arrange a meeting to discuss his thinking in more detail, but he refused to meet us. I decided to call him again.

I told Fleming that I was amazed he had come to the view that no one should be charged just five days after receiving the file from the PCA. He replied that he had already been aware of the case because it had received press interest and he had also been aware of the police investigation. He said that prior to the case he worked on a secondment to the police complaints division in the CPS headquarters in London and was known by the CPS as one of the few experienced lawyers that dealt with cases of deaths in custody, under what was known as the safeguard procedures, and that he had experience of prosecuting police officers. Clearly this listing of his credentials was supposed to reassure me of the validity of his decision.

One thing that particularly concerned me was why Christopher's clothes had been destroyed. If they had not been needed as evidence, they should have been returned to his family, and yet surely they *had* contained crucial DNA evidence as to whether Christopher had been assaulted by the police? I asked whether they had been tested for CS gas before being destroyed, and he said no. I found this deeply troubling and suspicious; I had thought his clothes would have been forensically tested. So I asked Fleming why they had been destroyed; he simply said he didn't know.

He then explained the reasoning behind not charging the

officers. They could not be prosecuted for neglect, Fleming suggested, as Christopher might have died even if they *had* tried to help him. I couldn't understand it. Christopher choked to death because of the position he was left in. Yet the CPS apparently believed that, even had he not done so, he might still have died *of something else*, some unknown medical condition for which there was no evidence. It was as if they were refusing to prosecute a man who had shot someone dead on the grounds that the victim might have ended up being killed by a bus. There seemed to be no logic in what was being said. And if something had happened in the police van to render Christopher unconscious and put him on the path to death, there was an obvious explanation as to what that was. I plucked up the courage to ask Fleming whether the possibility that the police had assaulted Christopher themselves had been investigated.

'No,' he replied.

I was shocked. The question as to whether these officers could have subjected Christopher to an assault was regarded as irrelevant, written off without even being raised. Instead, the CPS were fixated on the idea that some unknown and unprovoked medical condition or event had caused his death.

Following this call, Ruth wrote to Fleming to ask for a written explanation as to why Christopher's clothes had been destroyed. He replied that the investigating officer had destroyed them three months after Christopher's death because they posed a health hazard, and that it had not been done to conceal anything. This was how we learned that Christopher's clothes had been destroyed before the investigation into the police officers' conduct had been concluded.

In September of that year, for the first time in my life, I went on a march. The Labour Party was having its annual conference in Blackpool, and Andy arranged for me to go there to drum up support among the delegates and demonstrators attending. I had never been anywhere near a politician and wasn't particularly politically minded, but he persuaded me that this was a golden opportunity to speak to a lot of people who would be sympathetic to our campaign.

Our coach pulled up outside the conference centre on a street awash with people and banners: socialist parties, dozens of trade unions, and thousands of people from all regions of Britain. I'd never seen so many people congregated together. Some were fighting to stop university fees, some demanding better pensions, some trying to prevent the privatisation of the NHS. I was mesmerised and a little overwhelmed; this was totally different from the world I was used to, and I would never have imagined people did this type of thing. I'd not really thought about politics before; I just believed that things ran as they should, or at least as they had to. The idea that people could come together to demand change was completely new to me.

As soon as our coach pulled up, Andy and some of the others darted off in the direction of a black saloon car that was parked on the opposite side of the road. I heard Andy say 'Mo Mowlam, we want to know what happened to Christopher Alder', while waving his placard in her face. I thought, my god, what is he doing? Without answering him, this small rather round woman got into the car and was driven swiftly off. And then it dawned on me. These people have power; power over those who are refusing to give us answers. If we can reach them, they can force the police to tell us the truth. It was like a lightbulb switching on in my head, and I realised that if we wanted justice, we'd need to go to the top.

Later on, I addressed a meeting of over a thousand people on the fringes of the conference. I stood on a big platform outside the centre, a sea of people in front of me, terrified, but feeling I owed it to Christopher to speak out. As soon as I started talking, everything came flooding out – all that I had found out over the past few months, what we'd been told and what we still did not know. My fury with the authorities must have been obvious; I had not written a speech and it was all very raw. But people were prepared to listen, and it didn't take a lot to convince them something was wrong.

When I got home, my body started shaking like a dog with fleas. Once again I wanted to hide, to finally awake from this terrible dream. I felt like my body was folding in on itself: I was hunched over, unable to straighten my shoulders or stand upright, and I still had my children to look after, my household chores to do, the shopping and cooking and everyday things to take care of. Holding everything together was becoming more and more of a struggle.

Meanwhile I felt my thought process changing: my outlook was becoming less naive and more sceptical. I was starting to see the relevance and impact of wider society, of politics – things that I had once thought did not affect me. I was watching the news more and taking more notice of things going on in the world. Hearing about atrocities and injustices would hit me hard; I was hurting inside, but the crying stopped. I became more determined, more steely. I knew I had to stop fighting for the simple life that I once had, and accept my life as it was now. I had made the decision on that very first day I went to the police station that I would fight for the truth, whatever the trials and tribulations, yet there was still a fear in me, and a desire for my former life of ignorant bliss, walking around with my eyes closed. But deep down I knew those days were gone.

The next few months were a whirlwind of campaigning. I was

speaking in different parts of the country every other week, and awareness and funds were growing, financing printing costs and making it easier for me to travel to meetings. In December, the campaigners organised a massive leafleting of Hull, which generated some decent press coverage, keeping Christopher's name alive and maintaining pressure on the force to provide answers.

That autumn an inquiry was held into the death of Stephen Lawrence, who had been murdered as a teenager by racists in London in 1993. Stephen and his friend Duwayne Brooks had been waiting at a bus stop when a gang of white thugs started taunting them with racist abuse, before chasing Stephen and stabbing him to death. Those responsible remained at large after the police refused to properly investigate the murder. An inquiry was set up by the then home secretary, Jack Straw, on 31 July 1997, to examine what had gone wrong, with Sir William Macpherson as its chair. I saw many parallels with Christopher's case, most obviously the police's lack of concern for Black life. Those involved in the Lawrence case had ignored key evidence (such as a list of names and addresses of the possible killers, which was provided to them within 24 hours of Stephen's death) and failed to arrest any suspects for two weeks – and yet all of those officers were exonerated of any wrongdoing by the Police Complaints Authority. This did not exactly bolster my confidence in the organisation.

The inquiry was held at the Stakis Hotel in nearby Bradford, so, on 21 October, Andy, Noxi, my friend Sophia, who worked in Andy's cafe, and I attended to hand out leaflets. It was there I met Stephen's father, Neville Lawrence, having seen him and his wife Doreen on television many times. His words of support are still with me now: 'Keep fighting!' They themselves had been fighting for justice for five years by then, and it would be another twelve before the main suspects finally faced a criminal trial: it was not until 2012 that Gary Dobson and David Norris were found guilty of his murder. I felt inspired and encouraged by the Lawrence family's words and example.

Macpherson's report concluded that the Metropolitan Police were institutionally racist and that this problem filtered down to the other organisations within the criminal justice system. This was not news to many Black people, but was nevertheless a staggering admission. Stephen's parents had fought a tenacious campaign and shaken up a racist system. The inspiration they gave to me and many others is immense – they showed us that as Black people we didn't have to sit and endure the disregard for our loved ones' lives – we could challenge it.

The last Saturday in October was chosen as the date for the annual silent march of the United Families and Friends Campaign (UFFC) from Trafalgar Square to Downing Street. It was through the UFFC that I was to meet many other families around the country in a similar position to mine. Since then, I have travelled to London religiously every October to attend. The group and the marches have always been a great source of support and courage; but it has shocked me to see more and more new families attending each year, as people continue to die in state custody in horrific circumstances.

Trafalgar Square became a sea of banners and placards bearing the names and faces of those who the system had cast aside as insignificant collateral damage, calling for the cover-ups to be stopped and for justice to be done. The strain and tears on our faces bore witness to a common loss, but at the same time we were infused with an intense and fiery defiance, energised by the strength we drew from each other. Shouts of 'What do we want? JUSTICE!' and 'NO JUSTICE, NO PEACE!' echoed from our mouths, airing the anger and hurt caused by the contempt we felt from a state which had turned its back on us.

When we arrived at the gates of Downing Street, anyone who wished to was given the opportunity to speak. First was Brenda Weinberg, a powerful and articulate speaker, who told the story of her brother Brian Douglas. Brian was a music promoter in Clapham who died after being struck on the head by the police, with a force equivalent to having fallen on his head from eleven times his height. As is so often the case, the police's initial claims about the incident were contradicted by multiple eyewitnesses.[3]

Brenda explained that the experience of families whose loved ones died in police custody is that investigations are conducted purely for the convenience of the authorities and to limit reputational damage. She said it was a process that left families alienated and she criticised the persistent failure of the CPS and the PCA to press charges against officers responsible for deaths in custody. 'How can the PCA expect the public to believe the police can investigate the police?' she asked, calling for the PCA to be abolished and replaced with an independent body. 'We find ourselves having to fight for basic information,' she said. 'And if we become emotional that is used as evidence of a negative characteristic of Black people.' This struck a deep chord with me; I had felt all along that the police treated my concerns with contempt, and then used my upset at this treatment to justify dismissing me. It was a vicious circle, which led the police to be more and more dismissive towards us while leading us into ever deeper frustration and despair.

The next speaker was Myrna Simpson, a little old Black lady with chubby cheeks and a beaming smile, who had probably campaigned longer than anyone else there. Myrna came to

Britain from Jamaica as a British citizen in the 1960s, and her daughter Joy Gardner joined her in 1987. By that time Thatcher's government had stripped Commonwealth citizens of British citizenship, so Joy entered Britain on a visa. Shortly afterwards, she gave birth to a baby boy. But the authorities refused to extend her visa and in 1993 she was arrested by the immigration department to be deported. In the process, immigration officials wrapped thirteen feet of tape around her mouth, in front of her young son, until she lost consciousness. She suffered brain damage and was put on a life-support machine, but died from cardiac arrest four days later. None of the officers involved were prosecuted, or even given an internal disciplinary. Myrna should really be able to retire and find some peace and relaxation in her old age, but for her this will never be, as justice has not been served.

I would hear new stories like these every year on that march, as more families were torn apart by unaccountable police violence. Year after year.

In early December, Ruth was sent the medical report on Christopher's heart that had been requested following his postmortem. Conducted by a Dr Cary, it noted that Christopher's heart was slightly larger than normal, probably as a result of his fitness – but that quite apart from the lack of evidence of any underlying heart disease, the sequence of events in terms of Christopher's collapse and death would not be typical of a sudden cardiac death. He said that while there were some changes in his heart, they were mild and non-specific and not the sort of changes that would be expected if the heart were responsible for sudden death. He didn't feel it had caused Christopher's death and believed his deterioration and failure to recover would appear to be related at least in part to the lack of attention by the officers.

This report was given to Dr Clark, who then added an amendment to his own report stating that in the light of Dr Cary's findings, the face-down, prone position into which Christopher was placed took on a greater significance, and that he was not now inclined to view that cardiac abnormality caused his death. This gave us renewed hope that any attempt to pass off Christopher's death as the result of some supposed heart condition was not going to fly.

A few days later came the official launch of the Justice for Christopher Alder campaign, at the Campanile Hotel in Hull on 9 December 1998. The event was part of a joint meeting with another family campaign fighting against the attempted stitch up of a local lad by the police. When I arrived there were already around fifty people in the room as well as a camera crew from the BBC programme *Rough Justice*. The whole room was filled with cigarette smoke. I was very nervous, but the atmosphere was friendly and supportive.

From then on, the Hull campaign was very active, regularly organising meetings, writing to MPs and fundraising. The campaign had brought together local socialists with members of the Black community, some of whom had worked with my dad at British Aerospace in Brough, and it was their collective efforts that kept Christopher's name alive in the city.

Press interest continued to grow. Local media in Hull and Lancashire covered the case quite extensively, *The Voice* published a piece on the questions raised by the pathologist's report, and I did a short film interview with the local TV BBC news programme, *Look North*. In mid-December, I received a phone call from a television producer, John McGee, who wanted to make a programme about Christopher's death for Channel 4, and I met him at Andy and Maggie's cafe in February to discuss the idea. I agreed to take part and a date was arranged for them to take me to Hull for a day's filming.

In March 1999, I received another medical report. A pathologist, Dr Cook, had been asked by the PCA to give his opinion on the medical evidence; and while he agreed with Clark and Gray that multiple factors caused Christopher's death, crucially he believed that none of them were irremediable: with the correct treatment, Christopher should have lived. 'In conclusion,' he wrote, 'I consider that Mr Alder most likely died as a result of an obstruction to his airway ... should Mr Alder have received the appropriate first aid care of being placed in the recovery position and clearing his airway when he first arrived at the police station, then transported by ambulance back to the hospital, it is most likely that he would have survived.' I felt vindicated that my common-sense reading of the earlier reports had been correct, and I believed this now meant that manslaughter charges would finally be brought against the officers involved. I believed we were finally on our way to justice.

Yet the report also contained some horrifying revelations. Cook noted that there were several discrepancies between the injuries recorded at the hospital and those recorded at the post-mortem. At the hospital, Christopher was only missing one tooth, but two were recorded missing at the post-mortem. At the hospital, only one lip had injuries, but both were injured by the time of the post-mortem. The wound on Christopher's head had grown significantly and started bleeding again after he left the hospital, and there was a further 1–1.5 cm laceration. This difference, Cook concluded, must have occurred as a result of a further injury sustained to the back of his head after leaving the hospital.

All those images of what could have happened to Christopher on the way to the police station flooded into my mind once again.

There were more revelations too. Cook reported that the doctor at the hospital had given the police firm advice that if Christopher became unwell he should be brought back for treatment. The only reason I could imagine for why they refused to do so was that they didn't want to let the doctors see the additional injuries that were not documented at the hospital on his arrival.

But it seemed the CPS were still determined to avoid a prosecution. On 1 April 1999, exactly a year after Christopher's death, Fleming wrote to Ruth to explain that he was seeking further medical opinion. I was shocked. They already had four medical experts whose findings all pointed towards the culpability of the police, so what more evidence was needed? It seemed to me they were clutching at straws, desperate to find anything that would take blame away from the police and justify a decision not to prosecute.

This suspicion was only confirmed when the opinions of their new 'expert' were revealed. Dr Dearden, a consultant anaesthetist, stated that 'Negroes have larger lips and tongues and lips that significantly increase the risk of airway obstruction'. The implication was that it was not police brutality or negligence that had caused Christopher's death, but rather his Blackness. In my view, this was little more than barefaced racism. I couldn't believe it was being put forward as a serious medical explanation in 1999.

As I spoke out about Christopher's death, I was coming into contact with more and more people fighting similar battles, and it soon became clear that the difficulties I was having with the CPS had been experienced by many other families before me. An official report by Judge Gerald Butler had criticised the CPS for their reluctance to prosecute state officials responsible for deaths in custody. His report dealt with cases such as Brian Douglas, Shiji Lapite, Richard O'Brien, Michael Dempsey, Robert Dixon, Donovan Williams, Wayne Douglas, James Gailey, David Howell, Ian Muskett, Ziya Bitirim, Alton Manning and Dennis Stevens, all of whom died in either police or prison custody, often following restraint or beating at the hands of their captors. Despite many of these deaths being ruled 'unlawful killings' by inquests, in all cases, the CPS initially refused to prosecute, and in no case did they bring a successful prosecution. On 8 March 1999, we held a peaceful vigil outside the CPS office at 50 Ludgate Hill in London, to demand that the police officers I believed to be responsible for Christopher's death be charged with manslaughter. We were joined by several of the other Family Justice Campaigns who had been let down by the CPS, and it was here that I first met Ruggie Johnson. Ruggie was a Sheffield man with a heart of gold and a steely courage and determination when it came to fighting for justice. He was a volunteer with the Monitoring Group who supported families who had experienced racial injustice at the hands of the state, and he would become a pillar of support for me during the inquest.

There was a good turnout and after the speeches and chanting had finished, I was able to mingle and talk to the other families. So many of the cases were similar: delays, lack of communication with family members, and the failure of the CPS to hold officers to account. I was shocked by what I was discovering – that what could be written off as careless and sloppy in our case appeared in fact to be part of a systematic and deliberate approach. More and more I started to feel like there was an unwritten rule at work, one that prevailed over all the other laws of the land, up to and including even murder and manslaughter – that police officers were not to be held responsible for deaths in custody.

A year to the day after Christopher's horrific death, on 1 April 1999, the campaigners organised a meeting of remembrance for family, friends and supporters outside the Queen's Garden police station where he died. Over two hundred people turned out, some from as far as London, but with a large contingent from Hull itself: it was their local police station, and they knew that what had happened to Christopher could just as easily happen to a member of their family too.

I was shocked but also humbled to see so many families of other men that had died at the hands of the police, or in prisons and psychiatric hospitals. I appreciated that they had joined us. There were people there who told me that their own experiences of being roughed up by the police had opened their eyes to the many injustices that were happening around the country. More and more people kept arriving, making their way from buses, coaches and trains, and the atmosphere was electric, the power of all that collective emotion almost overwhelming. Once the crowd was assembled, we marched through the centre of Hull's shopping precinct, across Victoria Square, and then towards Queen's Gardens. The anger and upset welled up inside all of us as we drew closer to the police station, and the crowd swelled as people continued to join us along the way. Walking through the town centre, we had been guided by the police, but at the last minute we took a detour as I led the crowd right to the doors of the police station. We shouted and screamed, demanding that those responsible be brought to account; we wanted justice, we wanted truth, and we wanted an end to the cover-up. Emotions were running high and looking back, the police must have been a little concerned. I was running on pure adrenaline. Angered by the way I had been treated on my previous visits to the police station, and by the constant delays, I didn't hold back: I let it all out. I screamed that we didn't believe a word they had told us in the past or what they were going to tell us in the future. Emboldened by the number of people that had turned out, my intention was to face them and demand answers.

Ruggie had come along with his six-year-old daughter and he stood beside me on the steps, demanding that the line of police officers stood in front of us allow the family to lay wreaths in the police station foyer. 'Move aside,' Ruggie shouted, 'show some respect for the family!' The police sergeant in front of us then began to give me a weak and feeble apology. This was a year down the line and nothing had been done to bring the police officers I considered to be responsible for Christopher's death to any kind of justice, when ordinary civilians would have been dealt with within weeks. I said to him, 'If you meant any word of what you have just said you would have sorted this out a long time ago. You would have made sure those culpable were held to account.' In the past I had always found the blue uniform and the sheer mention of the police intimidating; I had been brought up to believe that the police were there for our safety and are always right, so it felt very empowering to tell them exactly how I felt. Eventually they backed down and allowed us into the foyer to lay our wreaths. Everything seemed surreal. Tears rained down my face; I had lost all control, but the power of all the people together was immense. The police had shown no respect for my brother or the rest of my family, but all these ordinary people came from all over the country to give us respect as a family and to honour Christopher's life. It was very emotional. All two hundred people seemed to be crying and holding each other.

The peaceful protest on the grounds of Queen's Gardens had turned into a heated demand for truth and a challenge to the police and their actions. After my altercation with the police sergeant, Jason Paul turned to lend his support. How must he have felt sitting in the bail hostel, questioning himself as to whether he had caused another man's death? He told me how he had expected to chat to Christopher the next day and make up, and I could see from the look on his face that he wasn't responsible.

On the journey home I fell asleep on the floor of the coach. I was physically and mentally exhausted, probably from the massive adrenaline rise and fall. Sleeping was not a problem that night; it was one of many days when I was totally washed out.

On 6 April 1999, Ruth wrote to Fleming at the CPS to ask when I would be able to view the CCTV footage from the night of Christopher's death. He replied that he did not want me to view it because he feared it could lead me to make a 'comment' about it, presumably to the press. I wondered what was on the video that he was so concerned about, and for a long time that was all I could think about. Fleming seemed not to care about the emotional damage that the waiting and apprehension was causing us. His concern seemed to be simply with what I might say, and how the police would look.

Not long afterwards, I decided to call Fleming myself in relation to the revelations from Cook's medical report. I asked him about the missing tooth and additional injuries that had been identified at the post-mortem that had not been there at the hospital, and about whether the possibility of a CS gas attack had been investigated. He simply said there was no evidence of CS spray being used. This seemed to me to be missing the point, as the prime potential evidence – Christopher's clothing – had been intentionally destroyed. I found this deeply troubling and suspicious, and Ruth and I kept raising the issue with the CPS. The response was frustrating – they basically dismissed our concerns and told us it was too late to do anything about them anyhow.

Then on 26 July 1999, Ruth received another letter from Fleming to tell us that the officers would not be charged with manslaughter. Once again, I was angry and shocked – but, deep down, not surprised. All along, the CPS had shown their desire to brush Christopher's death under the carpet, protect the police and avoid accountability. In this, they were nothing if not consistent.

I read on. Their decision, he explained, was based on the 'medical evidence' – presumably a reference to Dr Dearden's report with its outdated stereotypes, as all the other medical opinion would surely have *supported* a manslaughter charge.[4] Instead, the letter continued, the police officers were to be charged with wilful misconduct in a public office, as they had 'wilfully failed to take reasonable and proper care' of Christopher. This left me even more confused. If the officers had indeed 'wilfully' conducted themselves in a way that led to Christopher's death, I struggled to see how this wasn't manslaughter. Then it clicked. The CPS were going to try to argue that, yes, of course the police officers should have looked after him better, but ultimately it wouldn't have made any difference, and he would have died anyway. The officers' treatment of Christopher was wrong, but not fatal; they did not have anything to do with his death. It was to be, in other words, a parody of justice, rather than the real thing; and it would result in a token wrist slap at best.

It was an insult. Misconduct to me sounded like urinating

in the street or some other minor infraction of the law. It just didn't seem to capture the gravity of what had happened – that a man had been rendered unconscious in police custody and left to choke to death face down on the floor by the police.

Worse still, what I didn't know at that time was that once someone has been charged, they could not be questioned again. This meant that because they would be charged before my concerns about additional injuries and CS spray had been investigated, they could never be questioned about them, and these issues could not then be part of any case against them.

By this time, I believed that Christopher's race had affected the way the police treated him. I knew that a disproportionate number of Black men died in police custody, and this made me wonder whether racism had been a factor in Christopher's death. It had just been established by the Stephen Lawrence Inquiry that the Metropolitan Police, at least, were institutionally racist and that there was an importance in identifying racism that may be unconscious, unwitting or unintentional. The Macpherson report had explicitly stated that should the family or anyone else believe an incident to be a racial one then it must be treated as such.

I decided to call Fleming; but as soon as the issue of race was raised, his tone of voice became very stern. It rattled him; he seemed irritated with me and curtly told me there was no evidence of racism. I said I simply wanted the issue to be considered, but he had clearly made up his mind and did not wish to discuss the matter further.

I didn't think this was good enough. I wanted the CPS to take seriously the possibility of racism and to investigate it. I was experienced enough to know that in this day and age, people are unlikely to express blatant racism in a telephone call, or in a letter, much less in an official document or statement. Racism is generally far more subtle than that, manifest not in explicit comments, but in the way someone views you or treats you, making you feel out of place or unaccepted. It can be a 'slow drip' of rebuffs or failures to engage, or an attitude that is not even conscious. I again asked Fleming if he had considered whether the officers' behaviour could have been influenced by race but again, he was adamant there was no evidence of racism and that was that. I came off the phone feeling despondent, my feelings dismissed. I felt that the authorities were transferring their guilt onto me, making me feel ashamed for even raising the issue. But I was struggling to find any reason why anyone would so callously leave another human being on the floor fighting for their life.

On 23 August 1999, Andy, Maggie, Ruggie, Ruth and I attended something called a pre-inquest review at Hull Coroner's Court. This is where the coroner meets with the different parties involved and their representatives to agree on the format and conduct of the inquest and iron out any issues that might arise. This was the first time I had seen the coroner, Geoffrey Saul.

The personnel enlisted for the defence of the state authorities was formidable. Each of the five police officers had their own QC or barrister, and each barrister had their solicitors or juniors. In addition, there was a QC for the hospital, representation for the ambulance crew and representation for the chief constable of Humberside Police. God knows how much all these representatives were costing the public purse. The coroner insisted that the barristers wore suits rather than wigs and gowns. I don't know why, but this slight symbolic change did little to put me at ease. It felt like we were surrounded by wolves in sheep's clothing.

In court, the coroner acknowledged that although the cause

of death, which remained uncertain, was unlikely to be central to a trial on misconduct in a public office, it would be central to the family. He then pointed out that with a trial pending, the officers would be advised not to answer any questions at the inquest. He also expressed concern that the inquest verdict might influence a future criminal jury. On these bases, he strongly recommended that there be no inquest until after the trial was over. I understood what he meant: holding the inquest first would allow the officers to use the rule of incrimination to avoid answering any questions. Yet Humberside Police had insisted the inquest *should* be held before the trial. I immediately became suspicious. At no point had anyone prepared me for the possibility that the officers – the only people who could tell us what had really happened to Christopher – might simply refuse to answer any questions at the inquest, on the grounds that they had been charged with a crime and were awaiting trial. The decision to charge them before the inquest, along with Humberside's insistence that the trial be held only afterwards, would allow them to get away without answering a single question. I began to suspect that this had been the police's intention all along. I just hoped the coroner's recommendation for holding the trial first prevailed over Humberside. But I wasn't confident; Superintendent Holt had written to him to say that it would be 'nine to twelve months before a trial commences'.

Eventually, on 14 September 1999, the five Humberside Police officers involved in Christopher's death – PCs Nigel Dawson, Neil Blakey, Mark Ellerington, Matthew Barr and Sergeant John Dunn – appeared at Hull Magistrates' Court charged with misconduct in a public office. Ruth, Andy, Ruggie, Suresh Grover (who had been involved in the Ricky Reel and Stephen Lawrence campaigns) and I met with some of our supporters from Hull outside the court with banners and placards, giving leaflets to passers-by. We got a great reception from the Hull residents, with people shouting support from cars and beeping their horns.

Inside the court, I got to see the officers for the first time. What shocked Richard was that he recognised one of the officers who had arrested Christopher. It turned out that Richard and Christopher had known Blakey at school. We were concerned that this may have affected how Christopher was dealt with, and later raised the issue with the CPS, but they told us this was something we would have to question at the inquest.

When I saw the officers, the anger welled up inside me, but looking at them standing in the dock, part of me believed that there was still a chance for some sort of justice, that this was the moment we'd been waiting for for over a year.

As I saw the officers leave the court, my adrenaline surged. They had been surrounded by their colleagues from Queen's Gardens, who swarmed round them like bees protecting their queen. I ran up to them and, catching sight of Dawson and Blakey, called out: 'I hope you see Christopher's face every night when you try to sleep'. They scuttled off around the corner protected by their minders and disappeared out of sight.

The hearing had been over in a matter of minutes, but the judge seemed to understand. I clung on to his words with hope, and convinced myself that we were now on our way to justice.

Piecing it Together

1999–2000

The more I raised issues with the CPS, the more they seemed to regard me as a nuisance, a fly in the ointment as they attempted to quietly bury the case. Fleming was unwilling to discuss anything with me and all the delays and dismissal of my concerns were making me feel very dispirited. I felt they were fighting me with passive aggression. I began to see that no matter how devastated you were as a relative, it made no difference to the authorities; they still treated you like you didn't matter.

In early October, there was another preliminary hearing at Hull Magistrates' court. The officers did not attend, but on the way out I spotted Fleming from the CPS and told him I wasn't happy with the investigation and the discrepancies in the evidence. Three days later, he sent a letter to Ruth requesting to be contacted by her from now on rather than me. Ruth replied, reminding him that the CPS were responsible for direct liaison with victims of crime and were obliged to take our views into account, especially after the publication of the Macpherson report.

Meanwhile, Ruth had a telephone conversation with Dr Cary, the medical specialist who had examined Christopher's heart. He told her he didn't think the fact that Christopher's heart was slightly larger than normal made any difference, and believed Christopher would have survived had he been given medical attention; he was not at all convinced by the cardiac arrhythmia scenario that seemed to have been developed without any evidence.

I was later to find out about a similar attempt to blame a police killing on a slightly larger than normal heart. Dalian Atkinson, a professional footballer who had played for Aston Villa, died in August 2016 after an officer repeatedly kicked and stamped on his head with such force he left imprints. I spoke to his girlfriend and she said they tried to use his 'abnormally large' heart as an excuse for his death, but again an expert rubbished the claim, saying it was almost certainly due to his fitness as a professional footballer.

Around the same time, we were told that the court proceedings were to be put off until January. This was so a decision could be made as to whether the inquest or the criminal proceedings would come first. The police were pressing for the criminal case to be delayed until after the inquest, while Ruth objected due to the emotional pain these delays were causing the family.

By now, Christopher's case had completely taken over my life. I was spending every minute I could either on the phone to the authorities, speaking at public events, or with my solicitor. I spent less and less time with my old circle of friends: they wanted to relax and have fun and I felt like I was becoming a weight around their necks. When I did speak to them, I often heard comments like 'you'd best be careful, you don't know what they could do to you'. This fuelled my anxiety, making me feel even more alienated from them. I had always been determined that the battle for justice would not change me, but without realising it, I *had* changed. It felt like I no longer had control over the direction of my life. It was only the campaigning that helped me feel a little more in control, along with meeting people who had some understanding, having seen cases like this before.

On 29 October 1999, Ruth wrote to Fleming again, following our discovery that the defence had received a copy of the CCTV footage of Christopher's death, before we had even been allowed to see it. Fleming replied that we would be able to see all the evidence, including the footage, but only once he had investigated the procedural precedence. It was now over eighteen months since Christopher's death and no one seemed to be in any hurry to end our torment as we considered the horrors that might be on that video. I was in constant apprehension and the CPS held my psyche in their hands, like a cat toying with a mouse. It felt so cruel and insensitive.

Meanwhile, I remained in touch with my local MP in Burnley, Peter Pike. He liaised with the various bodies involved in the case – the PCA, the CPS, the Home Office and Humberside Police – and would raise concerns with them on my behalf. I told him about how I had been followed by the police after leaving the station that day in Hull, and that I suspected I was still under surveillance. My mail repeatedly failed to arrive – including some important documents from Ruth – and I was also convinced that my phone was being tapped; during phone calls, people would often ask me what all the strange sounds were – clicks, echoes, and even breathing sounds. I didn't like to admit it, but I was scared. Peter Pike wrote to the PCA telling them of my concerns, but they wrote back telling him that I had not made an official complaint. He made sure to send copies of all the correspondence, keeping us informed of any progress as best he could, and even had some meetings with the PCA, but he was never told more than the minimum. It was clear that our MP had very little power or influence on his own.

In early November 1999, a meeting of the campaign had agreed that we would attend a surgery with Jack Straw at his constituency in Blackburn to raise our ongoing concerns about the police investigation. I didn't have a clue who he was, but on 20 November, Andy and I travelled to Blackburn to meet who I had by then learned was the home secretary, one of the highest positions in the British government, and the one responsible for policing. We made our way to the Audley Community Centre where he was to hold his surgery. It was a very cold, wet night and there were already around twenty-five supporters waiting for us outside with placards. Suddenly I felt a bright light blinding my vision and a man with an enormous video camera was asking me why I was there. I felt confused and embarrassed; it was all so foreign to me. But before I could answer, he and his camera suddenly swung around and he began running towards two big posh black cars that had just entered the grounds. Soon I was also running, along with the rest of the protesters, towards the cars as they came to a standstill. A door opened and out stepped Jack Straw in his dark Crombie coat, clearly recognisable from his oversized glasses and greying hair. Alongside him, his minders were keeping us all at a distance. I decided this was my chance: I wasn't getting a straight story from anyone; maybe I could get something from him? I approached him and began telling him about the case, and we were soon summoned into a small side room within the community centre. I faced him, flustered and very emotional, and told him that the police were telling me lies and I intended to cause such a stink. I was in tears as I spoke; all the pent-up fear and frustration came flooding out. His reply was, 'Leave it in my hands, I will look into this.' As I left, I saw there was a queue of people from Blackburn, all waiting to air their own dissatisfactions to their local MP.

On another occasion, I ran into Hull MP and deputy prime minister John Prescott, after a pre-trial hearing in Hull. I walked out of the court and there he was. It was around the time the Labour government was going hell for leather about the amount of traffic on the roads, and I suppose Prescott was trying to set an example, leaving his Jaguar at home that day and making his way on foot. It was quite surreal. I was with Andy and the Hull campaigners, who had been demonstrating outside the court earlier, so we ran up to Prescott demanding to know what he was going to do about Christopher Alder, who had died in a police station in his constituency. 'It's about time your government started telling the truth about what's going on in this country,' I told him. He became flustered and replied that he didn't know what I was talking about and quickly scurried on his way. Despite being Christopher's MP, and one of the highest profile politicians in the country, he had never publicly said anything to condemn what happened nor made any contact with the family.

The mental pressure at times made me wonder if I would be able to hold out. I seemed to shake for days after each event. The police and other public bodies wanted us to believe that they cared and had the family's interests at heart, but this was totally contradicted by what I was experiencing.

Back at home, I had stopped going upstairs to bed; I would just throw a quilt and pillow on the settee and spend my nights there, staying up all hours. One morning, I had just nodded off before being suddenly awoken around 4 a.m. The TV was still on and I had woken to a news story of yet another young Black man who had died in police custody, this time in Tottenham, north London. I just caught the end of the story, but I later found out it was a man called Roger Sylvester. In January 1999 the police received a report of a disturbance outside his mum's house; Roger, who suffered with psychiatric health issues, was handcuffed and restrained by police officers and later died from brain damage.

After Christopher's death, as time passed, I realised how I really hadn't had a clue what went on in others' lives until they affected my own. Now I was starting to see just how common these horrors really were.

All this time, Christopher's body was still in a deep freeze in the mortuary in Hull. Thinking about it troubled me. At times I felt confident enough to say to myself, 'That's just a shell in there; if he was six feet under the ground, the pain would still be the same.' But at other times, I would question myself and feel guilty, thinking, 'Shouldn't we have buried him by now?' Yet to do so before the inquest, when his body might have contained the only clues as to what happened to him that night, seemed wrong.

Travelling around the country campaigning gave me confidence in my thoughts and beliefs. I felt as if I had hit a brick wall with the authorities: I had still not seen the CCTV footage, and my brother's clothes had been burned without being tested. But when I said this at public meetings, no one seemed to negatively question me, and that confirmed to me that I was not going insane, that my suspicions, although not proved, were indeed strong possibilities. This support was definitely needed. Through all the pain and terror, meeting other families did help me see I was not alone. I could relate to their struggles and them to mine; we gave each other inspiration as well as the will to carry on. But the gory thoughts still haunted me and my moods grew as dark as the winter nights.

On 11 January 2000, another pre-inquest review was held. This was for the coroner and legal representatives of the 'interested parties' to agree how the inquest would be run. I was very anxious about it. When would it be held? Who were the witnesses going to be? Were they going to bring people in to do a character assassination of Christopher, with him not there to defend himself?

While we were sat in coroner's court, I noticed a tall lean man with grey hair, and realised it was Superintendent Holt from West Yorkshire Police. I had only met him once before, a few months after Christopher's death, when he'd told me he had dealt with plenty of Black and Irish deaths before. I attempted to avoid him, but he sidled over to me and Ruth. I gave him a piece of my mind, telling him he should be ashamed of what he'd said.

Jason Paul was also to be represented at the inquest. After the very serious charges that were brought against him, I think he was determined to look after his interests, especially as he had a civil case against Humberside Police in the pipeline.

The Hull coroner agreed to our request for full disclosure of all the relevant documents being held by the police and other authorities; I appreciated this and considered it crucial that the family should be able to see and discuss the evidence with our legal team. He also thought it important for me to view the CCTV footage, so that nothing would come as a traumatic surprise during the inquest. At last, the police would be forced to stop stonewalling our requests and allow us to view the video – or so we thought.

Then, in an unprecedented move, the coroner ordered funding to pay for a barrister for the bereaved. This was not standard practice, and we were elated. As always, Ruth came up trumps and within days of the hearing, had set up a meeting with the barrister Leslie Thomas.

The next move for the campaign was meeting with journalists. The local papers and TV channels in Hull and Lancashire covered the case quite extensively, and I filmed the interview with the BBC One regional news programme *Look North*. Then, on 14 December, I received the phone call from John McGee, a television producer from the company Just TV, who wanted to discuss making a short documentary about Christopher's death for Channel 4. By this time, I had become convinced the only way we could hope to get justice was through maximum public pressure, so I was in favour of anything that would bring the issue to a broader audience. I sent John the transcript of the video and the Home Office pathologist report and we arranged to meet at Andy and Maggie's cafe.

Shortly afterwards, Ruth, Andy and I travelled to London and met Leslie at his chambers, 2 Gardens Court. He was an extremely smartly dressed and very handsome Black man: intelligent, sharp and forthright. With his cornrowed hair he was nothing like his pin-striped older colleagues who looked like extras from *Rumpole of the Bailey*. Leslie listened intently as we outlined our case, and immediately agreed to represent the family. He had been involved in many death-in-custody cases in the past and had great experience. At last, I thought, we would have a chance to get our questions asked in a forum where they could not be simply brushed off.

Disclosed Documents

2000

The first tranche of disclosed documents began to arrive from the police about a month later. There was a phenomenal amount of documentation – including more than 150 witness statements from the nightclub, which the police knew at the time had nothing to do with Christopher's death. We couldn't believe they had dedicated so much police time and resources just to attempt to build a case against Jason Paul, when they hadn't even done the basic minimum in the investigation into Christopher's death, such as testing his clothing. As we trawled through it all, at times I began to suspect they were trying to simply overwhelm us with information. But that only made me more determined to continue, to find whatever it was they hoped would be lost in the mounds of irrelevant material.

As the inquest approached, Ruth and I were in constant communication about what we were finding. Among the documents were the interviews with the five Humberside officers involved in Christopher's death, conducted by the West Yorkshire investigation team. Ruth described these interviews as very weak, and noticed that what minimal investigation was done by this team appeared designed simply to accumulate material that would corroborate the officers' accounts.

Even more shocking was the discovery of a memo from social services noting that, shortly after Christopher's death, the police had requested copies of all the Alder family's care records, listing Christopher and all four of his siblings by name. For some reason, our family background seemed to be a priority for Humberside Police's investigation into a supposed GBH charge against Jason Paul. I began to wonder if they had also been on ancestry.com to research our long-lost ancestors in Nigeria. I failed to see what social workers' opinions of our childhood behaviour could possibly have to do with my brother being left gasping for his life on their cold stone floor. Did they believe his horrific mode of death was the hereditary behaviour of the Alder family? Why were they seeking all this information on us? I couldn't work it out.

They also seemed to have been digging for dirt on Christopher's adult life. Two days after Christopher's death, six officers raided his small, one-bedroom home. His computer, pager and Filofax were all seized, the computer hard drive analysed, and the flat sealed off for two weeks while the police laboriously itemised and mapped out every item in the home. The primary reason given for the search, as recorded in the police log, was that it 'may reveal drugs and/or steroids ... which may be of assistance to the pathologist in establishing course [*sic*] of death'. But at this point the police already knew from post-mortem tests that Christopher had no traces of any drugs in his system. Why were they treating him as a suspect rather than a victim, even when he was already dead? Was this a desperate attempt to find something to smear his name? They had even obtained all of Christopher's social security and work records.[1] How would any of this have helped their investigation?

The documentation was yielding more and more evidence of a cover-up. We already knew that Christopher's clothes had been destroyed without being tested, but now we discovered that the police officers' uniforms had also been dry cleaned before they could be tested.

Then came the bomb. I had long feared that CS gas had been used on Christopher, despite the possibility always having been brushed off by the PCA and the CPS. But there among all the documents, I found reference to a 'use of force' report completed shortly after Christopher's death – by PC Dawson, the officer who arrested Christopher. This document had been with the authorities all the time, and yet had never been mentioned to us before, even when I had specifically raised the issue. We had already heard in the medical reports that Dawson had threatened Christopher with a CS gas attack twice on the night of his arrest, and now we had this report. If gas had actually been used, this suggested at minimum a struggle and possibly a full-blown assault on Christopher by the officers that had never been acknowledged. No wonder they had been so keen to destroy his clothes.

I started to read up on the impact of CS gas. One of the main effects is inflammation of the upper airway passages. Christopher had been unable to breathe. Was CS gas the reason? As I ploughed on through the documents, my suspicions seemed to be confirmed. Among the many papers were the police officers' notebooks. PC Blakey's notebook clearly recorded that he had sent a CS gas canister for destruction on 3 April, just two days after Christopher's death. CS gas canisters must be sent for destruction if they have been used. For two solid years my head had been swimming with questions about the additional injuries Christopher had received after leaving the hospital. The early pathology reports had given no reason for Christopher's death, and I couldn't get my head around why he was no longer alive. Now things were starting to make a disturbing sort of sense.

More unpleasant revelations emerged from the police officers' notebooks. Dawson, one of the two officers who had arrested Christopher, recorded that he had gone to the hospital for a medical examination at 9.35 a.m. on 1 April, the morning after Christopher's death. This was corroborated in the notebook of DC Stephens, who wrote that both Dawson and Blakey (the other arresting officer) had attended Hull Royal Infirmary that morning, although the time he gave was 10.15, and a different doctor was mentioned.[2] My head started swimming with questions: why had the arresting officers gone for an examination within hours of Christopher's death? Were they being checked for injuries? I wondered if there had been some sort of a fight between the officers and Christopher while his hands were cuffed behind his back. Had he tried to defend himself and lashed out at the officers? And why had the officers not been asked about this examination when they were interviewed by the West Yorkshire investigators?

But the worst part of the disclosure was reading through the transcript of the CCTV footage from the custody suite on the night of Christopher's death. It began with the custody sergeant, Dunn, answering the phone to be told about Christopher's arrest 'to prevent a breach of the peace'.

'That's pathetic,' he says, before telling his colleague, 'We'll see what it is but, I mean – see what it is and then kick them straight back out again.' It seems even the police knew that Christopher should never have been arrested. A few more minutes of chatter were followed by the 'sound of doors' as Dawson and Blakey arrived with Christopher.

'Oh, for fuck's sake, what's this?' Dunn asked, adding 'take him to hospital' as soon as he saw Christopher.

But instead of doing this, Dawson and Blakey made excuses:

Dawson: 'He's just come from hospital.'

Blakey: 'They won't have him at all.'

I already knew this was a lie; the hospital had given very specific instructions that Christopher should be returned to the hospital immediately if there was any sign of deterioration.

'This is acting now,' PC Dawson told the others. 'Oh, he's right as rain', added Blakey, 'this is a show, this.' The more I read the deeper and darker the hole my head was falling into. I felt like a horror movie version of Alice in Wonderland, entering a different world, a frightening one that I did not understand.

'This is just an acting thing,' Dawson repeated, with Blakey adding that 'He kept doing dying swan acts, falling off the trolley.' The officers who arrested Christopher seemed desperate not to take him back to hospital and I wondered why. But the answer seemed horribly clear: the staff there would ask awkward questions about what had happened to him since he left.

Another officer, PC Barr, noticed that 'he's shit himself,' but no one was interested. Instead they discussed what they might be able to charge him with.

Barr says, 'Can we get him on his side, he's going to be restricted with them cuffs on.'

'We'll take the cuffs off,' Dawson replies, adding, seemingly to Blakey, 'You know it'll be your turn to take the cuffs off love, you've got the gloves on.' Why was he wearing gloves? And why did the transcript note several sneezes just when Blakey was struggling to get Christopher's cuffs off, when no one had been sneezing before?

At one point one of the officers again expressed concern about

Christopher's condition, but the two arresting officers made sure no action was taken.

'The trouble is,' said Blakey, 'he was not like this at his time of arrest.'

'I don't think we've got an option of taking him back to hospital, then, have we?' said Dawson.

'It's going nowhere,' Dawson concluded. I couldn't believe the way they were talking about my brother.

"Cause he was in a semi-dazed state, he's just had somebody who's pushed that [tooth down his throat].' I was stunned. Christopher's tooth had been knocked out outside the Waterfront. Who had pushed a tooth down his throat? The post-mortem had recorded a second tooth missing that had not been missing at the hospital. Had Blakey pushed it down his throat, is this what Dawson meant? The brackets in the transcript meant the recording was unclear. But I was alarmed.

'I'd rather do him for an offence than just have him laid there for a breach of the peace,' Dunn said, while Christopher lay dying. Clearly he was desperate to justify the arrest he had already admitted was 'pathetic'.

And then, eleven minutes after they dragged him in, PC Barr noticed that 'he's not making any of them noises anymore, lads. There's fucking blood coming out of his mouth as well'.

'Well, there's blood been coming out of his mouth since he's been in hospital,' said Dawson.

'We can't follow him around like minders, can we? This is the trouble,' chimed in Blakey.

'He's not fucking breathing, lads,' Barr said.

Dawson said, 'Get him in the recovery position.' So they obviously hadn't bothered to do this earlier.

'Try his pulse,' Dawson added.

'We've lost him, sarge. We've fucking lost him,' said Barr. I just couldn't believe the total lack of support they had given a dying man in obvious distress. The transcript continued as the police finally attempted to resuscitate him, and called an ambulance, all too late. And then, just after 4 a.m., Dawson explained to an inspector that 'he was fronting up outside and he was given the option to get up and go, so ... [inaudible] ... arrested him and then he started to ... [inaudible] ... but that's when we come in with the gas.'

Making the Documentary

2000

Early one morning, while my head was swimming with all these chilling discoveries, Magnus and John from Channel 4 pulled up to my house with their camera crew. They were in a massive six-seater silver transporter full of rucksacks, cameras, recording equipment, and wiring of all lengths, and had picked me up to do some filming for their documentary. As we drove to Hull my heart was pounding. Being in Hull always filled me with a deep sense of regret and I didn't know what to expect. But the crew made me feel relaxed; everybody seemed to chat away sympathetically and believed what I was telling them.

The car stopped at a hotel on the outskirts of Hull directly under the gigantic Humber Bridge. I remember, when I was about nine and the bridge was still being built, our house parents promised to take us to see it when it was finished, but for whatever reason, we never went. I had never been this far out of Hull when I was living there and standing underneath the bridge now was an overwhelming experience; the sheer size of it made me feel like one of the tiny pebbles on the stony beach.

We were shown to the hotel's function room, lunch was ordered, and I sat and ate while the camera crew set themselves up. When they were ready I was sat in a chair, with bright lights shining into my face. I was not at all comfortable behind the camera and I could feel my face burning in the heat of the lights, self-conscious as I felt pearls of sweat forming on my nose. John sat opposite me asking questions, and at times I felt fearful about what I should and shouldn't say, worrying if I needed to be a little more careful. I was scared and unsure of what would happen when it was put on air for the police to see, but at times I rambled on, not caring what they would think. Nothing much seemed to make sense to me at that time anyhow; my life felt like an ongoing nightmare.

After that, John wanted to do some filming on the beach. It was windy and very cold, and the beach wasn't easy to walk on. Then, as I walked towards the bridge, I saw a police car approach. My heart jumped. John and his crew had previously done some very open filming outside Queen's Gardens police station, and now someone obviously wanted to know what we were up to. It didn't seem to faze the camera people but I froze: now I'm really going to be seen as a troublemaker, I thought. After my childhood experiences, I felt sure I would be seen as a 'tell-tale'. Eventually they left, but it left me in a heightened state of alert for the remainder of the interview. Some of the questions seemed quite intrusive, and John's tone sometimes made me feel as though he didn't believe me. Some of my reactions got quite impassioned; I was feeling unsure and scared about my surroundings; I suppose he was trying to get a natural reaction. No doubt they had dealt with people like me a hundred times before and were sensitive to my sensitivity. I was beginning to feel drained from talking about what I had experienced, when John decided more shots should be taken of the police station and the hospital entrance before finishing for the day. Oh no, not directly outside the police station, I thought, as John and the crew set their cameras up right beside the automatic doors, beneath the Humberside Police logo that read 'to protect, help and reassure'. But seeing the bobbies being filmed on their way in and out seemed to give me my strength back in a strange sort of way; I suppose it made me feel like I was fighting back.

After the last click of the lens outside the hospital it was time to return home to motherhood. As it always did, it took me a while to rebalance, to get back to the point where I could cope with everyday living again. My time was absorbed in reading all the paperwork given to me – and sleep was rarely on the agenda as my mind could never settle for long.

The day after the programme aired, the newspapers started phoning asking for stories, wanting to meet me and take photographs. But my sudden launch into the public eye was making me feel more and more uncomfortable. I was battling against my own personality as essentially quite a closed, private person, and as the interest built, so too did my insecurity and the feeling that my privacy was being invaded. I had learned as a child to keep my emotions hidden and my feelings private, but now my mind was being prised open for all to see. While I was grateful for the abundance of publicity which was helping to keep the pressure on the authorities, on the other hand the attention could be suffocating. It would have been different if I was stood there because I'd broken the hundred-metre world record, but I hadn't: I was undergoing a slow-motion traumatisation that I was constantly reliving in real time.

At the same time, all the horrific things I was discovering about Christopher, which were troubling enough, were also bringing to the forefront some of the childhood skeletons I thought I had buried. My psychological pain was now beginning to show itself on a physical level too: my asthma returned to the point where I was getting hospitalised for the night increasingly frequently.

I spent a lot of my time at Andy's cafe. I felt safe there; it was the only place I felt comfortable. Andy and Maggie understood where I was coming from and would help me talk through the case, piecing together what we knew and didn't know before I returned home to continue trawling through the mountain of case documents.

All the while I felt surges of inner gut pain flooding over me as if my instincts were trying to tell me something. I could neither shake it off, nor explain why I was feeling it. Was it the anger and mistrust that was growing in me? I wanted to close my eyes and wake up and for everything to be back to normal. I began to blame myself for the way I was feeling. I couldn't stop thinking about the bad times in care, the treatment my family suffered, my mother ending up in psychiatric hospital: all of it came flooding back, cutting into me deeply. I began to relive all those moments I thought I had laid to rest, and became more and more angry. At the same time, I was wracked with guilt, privately beating myself up, asking myself, How can you sit there and read what has happened to your brother in full gory detail?

While I was sat at home one morning, a package came through my letterbox. My dog, Rocket, barked, and started to attack the thick white A4 envelope that had fallen to the floor. On picking it up and opening it, I saw lots of guys with shaved heads and angry faces on the front of a magazine. I froze; my immediate thought was, 'How do they know where I live and what have I done?' When I was young we got a lot of trouble from skinheads, but I wasn't expecting to be involved with any now. I quickly hid the package under the settee as my son, Nathan, was due home any moment and I was worried it would scare him. For days I worried about who had posted the literature; I even suspected the police, not knowing what lengths they would go to to intimidate me, and remembering people's comments about how I should be careful of what they might do to me. It wasn't until I had another look at the magazine that I saw it was an anti-fascist publication called *Searchlight*, which keeps an eye on how racism is affecting society.

The nights were running into days. I was staying up late into the night reading through all the documents that we were being sent, or just trying to piece things together in my head, fretful and scared. I would look out of the window, see the dawn break and hear the birds singing, and then try to get an hour or two of sleep before getting Nathan up for school. Before all this my children had been my main focus, but now I felt guilty because my mind was becoming absorbed with what I had read. It was hard to muster enough energy or enthusiasm to make tea at times, or to make sure Nathan did his homework. I knew it was essential to keep some form of normality going for my son and daughter amid the trauma, but this was far from straightforward. I felt my son was beginning to feel my every mood, which of course affected the way he was feeling and reacting. Campaigning was becoming my life, and my children were seeing less and less of me. Looking back, I was lucky that my daughter, Caroline, was a little older, and all credit to her for helping keep things together. It must have been difficult having a mum that went from organising everything down to the last detail to being unsure as to whether she was even in the same world as everyone else.

Viewing the Video

2000

On 25 January 2000, Ruth had received a letter from Superintendent Holt, finally agreeing to let us watch the CCTV footage from the police station on the night of Christopher's death. But the letter stipulated that I would have to view it on police premises, with a police officer stood outside the room. I refused. There was no way I was going to watch my brother surrounded by police as his life ebbed away, with police officers stood around me. Eventually Holt agreed to disclose it to Ruth and our barrister Leslie Thomas, but only on the condition that they signed a document declaring it wouldn't be copied or given to me. Ruth then made arrangements for me to watch it at her house. I don't know why they couldn't have let me watch it in the comfort of my own home, to allow me some privacy in a place where I felt comfortable and at ease. I wondered what they were frightened of.

When the video arrived, it contained just eleven harrowing minutes of the 108 hours of footage available. The whole incident had been captured on nine multiplex cameras, each one running for fourteen hours. I couldn't understand why the complete footage had not been provided.

As I prepared to view the video, I was edgy and apprehensive. I hoped it might provide some answers as to how Christopher had died. I had already read about his injuries, his laboured breathing, and that he had died with his trousers around his knees, but I hadn't seen it; all I had was my imagination, which had caused me enormous psychological stress. I had been suspended in emotional limbo, but now I was going to see and hear exactly how Christopher died on 1 April 1998. I was scared.

When the day came, Andy drove me to Leeds and dropped me at Ruth's house, agreeing to pick me up after I had seen it. When I arrived, Ruth made me a cup of tea and a sandwich, although I was so apprehensive I found it hard to eat. Her home was cosy, with a nice, calm atmosphere, and full of interesting trinkets from her travels to India and Africa. It was certainly more relaxed than a police station would have been.

Still, when the time came, I really didn't want to watch it. When I see something on television, I place myself in the moment, and every image of pain and suffering drains me. And now I was about to watch one of the most painful things imaginable – the death of a loved one. I knew I had to do it; I needed to know what happened. But my feelings were in conflict and I wanted to back out. These conflicting feelings and thoughts were going through my head constantly.

Leslie arrived, and we sat down in front of the television. I felt cold and rigid. Ruth pressed play, but the video seemed to take ages to start. The first thing that appeared on the screen was a police emblem, and the words, 'To protect, help and reassure. Property of Humberside Police. Any unauthorised usage of this material may be liable to prosecution.'

My brother Richard had already seen the video in the

presence of his own solicitor. Even though I had Ruth and Leslie with me, I felt alone. I was filled with such a toxic mix of emotions that it was hard to breathe. I wanted to get up out of my seat and run away. I was about to watch my brother die, with no one there to 'protect, help and reassure' him. Childhood memories started coming to me, of playfighting together, laughing and joking around, always somehow getting through any difficulties. My brother, who protected me so many times at school, and taught me to stand my ground, would never again be able to talk to me about our painful childhood or the bright future. Our own children's right to the warmth and wisdom of a loving father and uncle had been ripped away.

I had spent weeks trying to prepare myself for this moment. But I could never really have been prepared.

The video started. A buzzer sounded, followed by a doorbell, men's voices and loud shuffling sounds. The door banged open, there was more shuffling of feet and a cough, and two police officers moved through a corridor about three feet wide. My brother was hanging limp in between them, the lower half of his body dragging on the floor, an officer gripping him under each armpit, with his wrists clasped together behind his back by rigid handcuffs that seemed to have no leeway for movement. They entered the custody suite and left Christopher on the floor, chest down. I saw one of the officers raise his arm to wipe his brow while Christopher was lying on the floor there with blood oozing from his mouth, heaving for breath, unconscious and unable to roll over. I wanted to scream at the callous way my brother had been dumped, face down, on the cold stone floor. I wanted to go and comfort him, and to hit the officers; but it was all happening on screen, beyond my control. I felt his laboured breathing like the asthma attacks I've experienced so many times myself: the closing of the throat, the pain in the chest, the panic. I could feel it all now, watching him as I stared in shock at the screen.

One officer commented on the blood coming from Christopher's mouth, but no attempt was made to assess his condition. Dunn said that Christopher should be taken to hospital. Well take him then, you bastard! I thought, take him! But it didn't take two minutes for him to change his mind. None of the officers even bent down to see if he was OK, they just callously left him gasping for air. I couldn't understand their lack of natural concern. It was all happening in front of me and there were tears behind my eyes, but I couldn't do the natural thing and allow them to roll down my face. I was too angry.

I had never seen anyone die for real before, but there I was, forced to watch my brother dying in front of my eyes for reasons no one knew. It was clear that he was unable to breathe, that he was gasping for air. The video seemed to say it all. It felt like watching the television news from a war zone in a faraway place. But this had happened in a police station in Hull, and I couldn't do a thing to stop it. All those hopeless feelings from childhood, from seeing my family being demoralised and degraded, powerless to do anything about it, returned with a vengeance, coupled with anger and rage making me want to lash out at the TV.

At one point, the two officers who'd dragged Christopher in stood gazing at each other, as if they knew something the others didn't. It made me think there was more to the video than meets the eye. The smirking bravado and the dismissive sighs, the nodding in agreement; to my mind they formed a defensive moat which separated them from Christopher, while he lay struggling in pain.

All the while, Christopher was rasping, desperate to get just a tiny bit of air into his lungs, the gurgle of blood in his mouth echoing, unable to swallow, his reflexes gone. His laboured breathing made me feel choked; it sounded like water trying to run down a blocked sink. I wanted to catch his breath for him, clear his throat of whatever was obstructing it. I felt a well of anger; but all I managed to say was: 'look at them'. And all the while, the arresting officers insisted that this was all a show to gain attention, while they tried to figure out what they could possibly charge him with. Having to watch it felt like abuse.

No one tried to pull Christopher's trousers up; his buttocks were on full view. His dignity seemed to be of no consequence, although there were comments made to the female matron when she walked in, warning her to close her eyes to save her from embarrassment.

Nor were any attempts made to alleviate the gurgling in his throat, or any acknowledgement of the clear signs of his breathing difficulties. Eventually, one of them went in to take his cuffs off, and was overcome by sneezing as he leaned over him. Even then, no one bothered to put him in the recovery position; they just left him face down on the floor, his arm still twisted up behind his back, his breathing becoming ever more laboured, gurgling and rasping – and less and less frequent.

Finally, after eleven long minutes, one of the officers went to take Christopher's pulse. He was dead. The screen went black.

The room was silent. I could tell by their faces that Ruth and Leslie were as devastated as I was. They were very solemn and no one really said much. I just kept repeating, 'How could they do that?'

My head was battered, as if there had been an explosion; my psyche was in shards like shattered glass. I felt sick and enraged. Christopher had been a paratrooper for the British state, risking his life to serve its interests, and decorated for his service – but once he had served his purpose he did not even seem to count as a human being. I just couldn't understand the lack of compassion. I thought about the loneliness, the darkness, whether he could hear the mumbling of the voices, and wondered if any of the officers had given any thought as to what he was experiencing during those moments immediately before he died. He had no one around him who cared for him, and was denied the comfort of the presence of a loved one and the words of compassion they may have spoken, thanking him for his kindnesses, his good deeds, our shared experiences. Any last message he might have had for his family was gone. I couldn't help thinking that if I'd seen somebody lying on the floor in such discomfort, in a place of work, uncovered, unable to breathe, I would be concerned, and my instincts would be to find out if they were OK. I would not take the risk of assuming that they were play-acting; I would raise the alarm, or at least try to talk to them. And if I couldn't help I would try to find someone that could. And had I not taken these basic steps to check up on the safety of somebody in that condition in my care, I'd have been sacked, and if they'd gone on to die as a result, I'd have been charged with manslaughter. Wouldn't I?

I remained frozen. Only when Andy knocked on the door was I able to move. I needed to get back home, to be on my own. I said goodbye to Ruth and Leslie and got into Andy's car. I was numb, my emotions still pent up, like they were tied in a knot. There was a dull silence on the journey back home, my mind busy processing it all, questioning whether I had really seen what I thought I had – more than I was meant to see, perhaps. I felt a burning rage inside. Every little bit of confidence I might have once had in the police was now gone for ever. And the gurgling sound of Christopher's last breaths kept echoing through my mind.

Andy dropped me back at home, where my children were waiting. I didn't know how to explain what I'd seen without frightening them, so I kept it brief and general. I tried my best to carry on as normal. But once I'd got them settled and into bed, the images of Christopher came flooding back. I was plagued by questions – how did his trousers get to his knees? How did he get mud on his thighs? Why were Dawson and Blakey so determined that he should not be taken back to hospital? How did he get his additional injuries? Why was Blakey sneezing whenever he went near Christopher? Why did the police burn Christopher's clothes without testing them? Questions that have been haunting me ever since, along with the officers' total indifference to the danger he was in, his suffering, his dignity, his *humanity*. The casual disregard of those officers will remain with me for ever. Fury pulsed through my veins and I was more determined than ever to see these men brought to justice.

After the Video

2000

After viewing the video, I went into shock. I just collapsed inside. Throwing myself into preparation for the inquest, I tried to bury my feelings as I had done in childhood. I felt increasingly numb and cut off from the world, and reading through mountains of disturbing documents by myself increased my sense of isolation. I tried to keep up some semblance of normality, but with my head flooded by images of Christopher's dying breaths, and a growing mass of unanswered questions, it felt like a losing battle. In truth, I really wasn't coping. I kept apologising to Christopher, feeling that my weakness was letting him down.

As the inquest approached, I grew more and more apprehensive. I was not sleeping properly, and meals were not getting made on time. My health was deteriorating rapidly, and my kids were internalising my distress and acting out; Nathan, who had always been a loving and studious boy, began skipping school and coming home late. I hoped against hope that the inquest would bring some kind of clarity and closure and allow me to get my life back on track.

With the inquest weeks away, I braced myself to read

through the statements from the police. I wondered how they were possibly going to justify leaving him to die in the state he was in. I knew it would make upsetting reading, but what I found was both disgusting and ridiculous. Ellerington stated that he believed Christopher was 'feigning deep sleep', while Dunn explained that, although he was aware of the gurgling, he ignored it, believing Christopher was deliberately blowing through the blood to 'try and upset' the officers. PC Barr said he had believed the noises 'were intended for our attention, in other words he was putting it on, or he was unconscious'. But if he thought he may have been unconscious, why on earth did he not put him in the recovery position? Dunn said that he 'formed the opinion, from what he was told, that the man's behaviour at the present time may be play-acting or attention seeking'. I found it incredible that anyone at the inquest could believe that this fit, hardy paratrooper, who had lived through war and fought pitched battles, would lie on the floor and feign sleep, play-acting and attention seeking, by deliberately soiling himself with his trousers down, as some kind of dirty protest. What would be the point of craving attention, when it was absolutely clear he wouldn't get any from these officers? Christopher had soiled himself because his life was ebbing away. As far as I could see, there *was* feigning going on in the custody suite that day – but it wasn't coming from Christopher. My brother was treated like a delinquent who was making a nuisance of himself with his choking, and who had then caused further trouble by dying on the floor. I thought back to the video, and to my visit to the police station, and the reactions and mindsets of all the characters I had been dealing with, and wondered whether they were all so desensitised that Christopher's death was no more than an irritation, a problem they had to get rid of.

As I ploughed through the documents, I searched in vain for some investigation of what had happened to Christopher in the van to cause him to lose consciousness, his belt and a second tooth. The CPS argued that they could only bring manslaughter charges if it could be proved that Christopher would have survived had he been given medical attention; I guessed this was why they had been so desperate to find an expert willing to blame his death on his 'big lips' rather than his lack of treatment. They were acting as if the first contact the police had with Christopher was when he entered the custody suite, as if the possibility that the police themselves were in any way *responsible* for his condition was unthinkable. They never enquired into what had happened in the back of the van, never investigated the possibility that he had been assaulted by the arresting officers. The CPS had always claimed they were looking for the cause of death, but were refusing to ask obvious questions such as whether the officers had beaten Christopher. Instead they were desperate to find some mysterious natural phenomenon in Christopher's body, a physiological cause that was nothing to do with the police, and would probably have killed him anyway, even if they *had* treated him.

To me, it was an insult to Christopher's life and memory to keep asking the experts whether he would have survived if he had been given treatment. The only way to have found out would have been to have treated him, and what was clear to anyone is that no attempt was made to do so, robbing him of any chance of survival. I felt as if they were saying that the officers' failure to look after him didn't really matter as he might have died anyhow – all the while refusing to ask what had brought him so close to death in the first place.

I kept wondering how Christopher had lost another tooth

after leaving the hospital. And where had this thick, ragged laceration on his lower lip, which had not been recorded at the hospital, come from?

One truly bizarre document was the statement of a refuse collector called Keith Brown. He told the investigators that, the day after Christopher's death, he had come from Scunthorpe to Hull to do his daily rounds. I thought that was odd, as Scunthorpe is twenty-five miles from Hull, and I assumed Hull had its own refuse collection. And why were they interviewing a refuse collector in the first place? In his statement he claimed that he had collected the rubbish from the Waterfront nightclub on the morning after Christopher's death, but then, after emptying it at the landfill, he received a call from his boss telling him to stop. Apparently the police needed to search the rubbish to find Christopher's tooth, which had been thrown in the bin outside the club. So supposedly, between 16.45 and 18.10 on 1 April 1998, police officer DC Ward went to the local landfill site at Humberfield Quarry, located the refuse truck, and with Brown's assistance identified the exact spot where he had earlier dumped the crushed rubbish from his truck – and found Christopher's tooth! Had they enlisted the tooth fairy in this miraculous feat? I also couldn't understand why Humberside Police had committed so much manpower to finding a tooth in the middle of a rubbish tip, when they seem to have put no effort into finding the tooth that came out while Christopher was in their custody.

An Uphill Battle

2000

I was starting to realise what an uphill battle this was going to be. The CPS had seen the same evidence I had: they had seen the video; they had seen the obvious difference in Christopher's condition on leaving the hospital and arriving at the police station. They knew about his additional injuries. They had heard Dawson and Blakey's determination to resist taking him back to hospital at all costs, because 'the trouble is, he was not like this at his time of arrest.' They had seen his visible distress, his gasping for breath, the officers leaving him in prone position, Dawson's comment that 'that's when we come in with the gas'. Yet they had refused to investigate the possibility of an assault by the officers, or even to bring manslaughter charges against them for neglect. How could they not see what was so clear to me?

The more I learned about the CPS, the more my suspicions grew. Talking to other families I was meeting through the campaign, I became aware of the CPS's track record of extreme reluctance to prosecute police officers, or even those with connections to them. In the Stephen Lawrence case, the CPS and police between them failed to prosecute his murderers over multiple stabbings they had been involved in, and yet had been determined to press charges against Stephen's friend Duwayne Brooks over a trivial offence which was later thrown out.

As I looked more closely into the CPS, it was obvious where this reluctance came from. A relatively new institution, only formed in 1986, it was basically a re-organisation of the regional organisations that had conducted state prosecutions up until then. These institutions were simply the prosecuting arms of each police force. In other words, for a century and a half, up until barely a decade earlier, the CPS had essentially been a wing of the police – and even now, the CPS is divided into areas mirroring those covered by each force. The CPS was created in the 1980s by essentially amalgamating the prosecution arms of each separate police force. No wonder they identified with the police so strongly – they were effectively a *division* of the police. I began to see, though I resisted it for a long time, the sheer scale of the forces we were up against. It was not just the police who were committed to shielding their officers from accountability. It was the whole criminal justice system.

The Crane Report

2000

Luckily, Ruth and I had long since stopped relying on the CPS to collect the evidence that would be necessary for a successful prosecution, and just weeks before the inquest began, we received a report from Professor Crane. Crane had been recommended as a trustworthy and respected pathologist who was unafraid to speak the truth, even if it ruffled feathers. We had contacted him ourselves, requesting that he review the medical evidence on Christopher's death as we did not trust the independence of those commissioned by the state, whose conclusions seemed so often to be at odds with the evidence they had presented. It had been very uncomfortable to discover that the Chief Inspector of the force I considered to be responsible for my brother's death had been stood right beside the Home Office pathologist as Christopher's post-mortem was being carried out, before the family had even been informed of our right to be represented there. I wondered what else they were concealing from us.

Crane's report seemed to confirm our worst fears. He ruled out the suggestion that 'cardiac arrhythmia' or 'excited delirium' had been factors in Christopher's death, noting that 'there was no evidence of any significant natural disease which would have caused or accelerated his death' and that 'the mode of death is clearly not that associated with a sudden cardiac arrest.' But, he added, 'little consideration has been given to the possibility of Mr Alder having received another injury to his head either accidentally or deliberately at some point between his being placed in the van and his being dragged along the corridor in the station.' He went on: 'His scalp injury, which was not bleeding when he was examined at the hospital, would appear to have been bleeding in the van and to have caused a blood smear on the side panel.' He also noted the additional missing tooth and lip injury that had appeared after Christopher left the hospital, writing, 'Clearly if Dr Khan is confident that only the upper lip injury was present when he examined Alder [in hospital] then an explanation must be found for the more extensive injury to the lower lip, i.e. that this injury was sustained between his leaving hospital and being dragged into the police station. Whilst this lip injury could have been accidentally sustained in the back of the van, possibly due to his striking his lip on the edge of the bench seat, it would also be consistent with his having sustained a further blow e.g. a punch to his mouth. If this blow was inflicted whilst he was still sitting in the van then his head could have been thrown back and the back of his scalp made contact with the interior side panel causing the blood-stained mark. Also further bleeding from the mouth wound could have caused the drops of blood visible on the bench seat.' This was the first time the possibility of a police assault on Christopher had been spelled out so clearly – and it seemed to be the only theory that adequately explained the evidence. Neither the police nor the CPS had even tried to account for Christopher's additional injuries or the blood smears in the van, and their hypotheses as to the cause of his unconsciousness had no medical evidence whatsoever.

When it came to the cause of death, Crane concluded,

> I have no doubt that whatever the cause of his loss of consciousness his death was ultimately due to upper airway obstruction as a result of his airway being partially obstructed by his posture and secondly due to inhalation of blood from the gum lacerations and the bleeding tooth sockets. This respiratory obstruction was exacerbated by his posture on the floor whereby movement of his chest was reduced by his face-down position on the floor and the weight of his body interfering with expansion of the chest cage. There was clear evidence of blood in the upper air passages and having been inhaled deeply into the small air passages of the lungs. It was this obstruction of the upper air passages by blood which can be heard on the soundtrack of the video. Whatever the cause of Alder's loss of consciousness there would appear to be no reason to preclude his recovery had he received appropriate medical attention, if his airway had been cleared and he had been placed in a correct recovery position prior to his removal to hospital.

It was painful to read, but I felt vindicated. Christopher had not died of some hidden heart condition; he had died because he had been left face down on the floor choking on blood flowing from fresh wounds sustained after his arrest. At last, we had an independent medical report unafraid to follow the evidence. Crane's report gave me a renewed hope that justice could be done.

The Inquest

2000

The inquest was to be held in Hull, beginning on 3 July 2000, and was due to last four weeks.

Plans were made for me to stay in Hull during the week, leaving Nathan with a childminder or with Caroline and returning home for weekends. Ruggie Johnson from the Monitoring Group also left his home in Sheffield to stay in Hull on behalf of Christopher's children for the full length of the proceedings. It was agreed that because of the massive publicity given to the case, and the expected press and public interest, the coroner's court would not be big enough, and the most appropriate venue would be Hull Crown Court on Alfred Gelder Street.

The coroner's office offered to pay for our expenses and travel. After they had seen the video and the inhumane, degrading treatment it showed, it felt like an attempt by the state to ease their own minds, rather than to ease the pain of a grieving family. But what they were allowing us as ordinary citizens was nothing compared to the amount of taxpayers' money being spent to protect the state's position. All the family really wanted and needed was justice.

The first day of the inquest finally arrived. It was over two years since Christopher's death. I woke up hyperalert, tense to the point of nausea, before Andy and Maggie drove me the two and a half hours to Hull. The crown court was an intimidating building, and it didn't help to see a group of around half a dozen police officers outside, all dressed up in ribbons and stripes, watching our every move. I was relieved to see a small crowd of supporters gathered there, with banners and placards demanding justice. Several of the campaigners were there, as were several members of the United Families and Friends Campaign, a woman from the Hull Afro Caribbean Society,[1] Helen Shaw from Inquest (a charity that advises families of victims who have died in police custody), Ruggie and Ruth. Cars saw us and honked their horns in support. The press were there too; the case had quite a high profile and the inquest was going to be the first death in custody inquest in British legal history where the death had actually been captured on videotape. As we went in, the cameras clicked and flashed, and once inside, we faced the usual security procedures – going through metal detectors, emptying our bags and so on. I knew it was all standard practice but I couldn't help feeling intimidated, as if we were the suspects.

The courtroom itself was clinical and modern, with cream walls and a skylight. The family seating area was just to the side of the jury. Richard, Ruggie, Ruth, Andy, Helen and I were joined by other members of the United Families and Friends Campaign. Helen was a lovely woman, forthright in her manner of talking, but very supportive. Presiding over it all was the coroner, sat on a raised platform in front of a shield embossed with a coat-of-arms.

The room was full of people in black gowns and wigs shuffling papers. Their movements, language and demeanour seemed quite deliberate and rehearsed, and the sheer number of barristers for the police sent shockwaves through me. There was one for each of the five officers involved in Christopher's death, and one for the chief constable. On top of that was one for the Health Authority and one for the Ambulance Trust; in total, eight barristers were representing the state, along with their teams of juniors, all paid out of the public purse. Then there was Leslie Thomas, representing the family. Jason Paul was representing himself, having been denied legal aid for his own barrister. It was strange to consider how, for all these lawyers, Christopher's death was an opportunity to further their careers. Suitcases full of documents were being dragged around – and somewhere in those caskets was Christopher's life, reduced to pieces of paper. The formality of it all was stifling.

The jury was sworn in and the coroner went through the events of the night Christopher died.

The jury then withdrew for some procedural matters to be dealt with. The police barristers insisted that Leslie should be the first barrister to question the neutral witnesses[2] (after the coroner's initial questioning), which would obviously put him at a disadvantage, leaving him unable to counter any narrative created through any subsequent line of questioning. The police barristers seemed to imply it was my fault it had to be that way, pointing to the criticisms of the police I had made in the newspapers as evidence that the family had an axe to grind while the police were neutral and innocent.

This is when I first got to see Leslie in action. The police lawyers' arguments were 'quite frankly … nonsense,' he said, as he told the coroner to 'listen to what I am saying'. I was impressed. In the end, the coroner ruled in favour of the police barristers' request – although he said Leslie could come back with any supplementary questions after the other barristers had finished their examinations.

The inquest evidence was to be heard 'chronologically' – i.e. hearing from the nightclub witnesses first, then from ambulance and hospital staff, then from those at the police station, the West Yorkshire Police investigators, the medical experts and finally from the five officers themselves. I was called as the first witness to give some background about Christopher's life and upbringing, based on a statement I had written for the court. The coroner asked me a bit about our childhood, and then Leslie asked me about what I'd been told about how Christopher died. I explained the three different versions of events we'd been given – first, that he'd collapsed in the custody suite sat next to a police officer; then that he'd had a fight and died from his injuries; and then finally, months later, that he had already been unconscious when they pulled him out of the van. When I described how one of the officers had been chewing gum with his hands behind his head while telling me his version, the coroner interrupted and told Leslie I was 'straying from the purpose'. None of the other barristers had any questions.

There were two more witnesses after me on that first day, both describing the events at the Waterfront nightclub. Over the next few days, the court heard from several witnesses to the fight between Christopher and Jason Paul, and there seemed to be mixed opinions about who had thrown the first punch.[3] From the evidence that I'd read, it was very hard to judge who had started the fight. It was clear the impression the police were attempting to give: trying to incriminate Jason Paul, despite them having video evidence of Christopher dying on their own custody suite floor. But that got nowhere because there was just as much evidence to suggest that Christopher had started the fight. Personally, after reading and hearing all the evidence, I thought it was very hard to prove either way. Fights aren't uncommon on Friday and Saturday nights outside nightclubs. In any case, the post-mortem had shown that Christopher's injuries from the fight were not serious, and the punch had not killed him.

Trying to keep up with everything was difficult, so I was lucky to have Ruggie, Ruth and Helen there to help me to digest it and understand the process. Just having them there during the proceedings helped counteract the stuffy and intimidating atmosphere, and during the breaks they would help us to understand and process the evidence. Ruth in particular was always very sensitive to my feelings. Ruth and Helen were both very busy with other cases, but made sure that if one of them couldn't attend, the other one would be there. Ruggie attended every day, and stayed at the same hotel as me. Every morning at breakfast he would play classical music on the upright piano, which was soothing and calmed my nerves.

The nightclub witnesses took up most of the first five days of the inquest. After them came the hospital staff. A picture emerged of Christopher veering between periods of calm and periods of confusion and anger while he was at the hospital, but it was when the police arrived that his behaviour really began to deteriorate. Where the hospital staff had generally tried to calm him down by being patient and calm themselves, officers Dawson and Blakey seemed intent on escalation, virtually frog-marching him to the toilet almost as soon as they arrived, and then threatening him with CS gas when he objected.[4] Although they were there to take his statement as a complainant in an assault, it seemed that right from the start they treated him more as a perpetrator than a victim.

Dr Aamer Khan took to the witness stand on day eight. This was an important moment, as he had examined Christopher in the hospital and listed his wounds. It was the disparity between the injuries he had recorded with those found later at the post-mortem that had revealed the extent of the additional injuries Christopher received after leaving the hospital.

Responding to Leslie's questions, Dr Khan confirmed that Christopher's erratic behaviour was fairly common for someone suffering a head injury, and that his blood pressure and temperature were both normal, undermining the police barristers' attempts earlier in the inquest to suggest that Christopher might have simply died from 'excited delirium' – essentially that Christopher had got himself so excited that he died.[5]

Leslie then established that Dr Khan's examination had been very thorough. Christopher had been cooperative with him, and had not tried to shrug him off or resist in any way, and the doctor had been able to make a comprehensive and detailed list of his injuries. Leslie then went through each of the additional injuries in turn, identifying them on post-mortem photographs, to check they had not been present at the time of Dr Khan's examination: his eye injury, the injury to his lower lip, his additional missing tooth, an 'abrasion' on the top of his scalp, and the increased size and renewed bleeding of the haematoma on the back of his head. In every case, Dr Khan confirmed that the injuries had not been there at the time of Christopher's examination in hospital – and that he did not think he could have missed them.

Leslie then asked: 'If, on arrival at the police station ... he is unconscious, would you have expected Christopher to have been brought back to the hospital?'

'Well, yes, I would hope so. Yes.'

And then: 'Was there anything that Christopher did at the hospital that you saw that could give rise to an impression that Christopher was feigning or faking his condition?'

'At the hospital, no. I would not say so, no.'

By the time he had finished his questioning, Leslie had, it seemed to me, clearly established that Christopher had incurred a whole series of injuries *after* leaving the hospital, that the police's story about him 'faking' his condition was ridiculous, and that they had been grossly negligent – or had something to hide – by not bringing him back to the hospital.

Next it was the turn of the six police barristers to question Dr Khan, led by Mr Ferm, counsel for PC Dawson. He began by reading out a section of Dr Khan's statement where he referred to Christopher using the f-word when he was getting agitated by the police. I thought it was a pretty cheap trick to try to paint Christopher in a negative light and I hoped the jury would see through it. He carried on in this vein for a few more minutes, reading out other sections of Khan's statement that supposedly emphasised Christopher's obstreperous behaviour, such as how he 'would not allow the officers to walk him normally by resisting and slumping'. Finally, he came to the injuries. Dr Khan had described Christopher's haematoma as the size of a fifty-pence piece, whereas the pathologist at the post-mortem had described a bruise 8 cm in diameter. Ferm tried to suggest that perhaps the wound had not grown in size at all, but the pathologist at the post-mortem was measuring something else.

'An underlying bruise 8 cm in diameter is not the same thing as a haematoma, is it?'

Dr Khan gave him short thrift: 'Well, an underlying bruise – a haematoma is basically, can be classed as a bruise.'

When he came on to the facial injuries, he seemed to suggest that Dr Khan might have missed some of them because they weren't pointed out to him: 'When you are examining most patients who are cooperative and want to be treated for their injuries, very often the patient will tell you exactly what injuries he has got and point them out to you and so forth?'

'Mm hmm.'

'And it is a factor, is it not, in your examination that Christopher did not do that?'

'Well he did tell me that his tooth had been knocked out and he had a lump on the back of his head, but you know, yes.'

'But apart from that he at no point in your examination volunteered any verbal help to you to locate and consider his injuries. That is right, is it not?'

It was clear that Ferm was trying to discredit Dr Khan's evidence by suggesting that Christopher's injuries had been there all along but Khan simply hadn't noticed them.

Later on, he added: 'Injuries in a difficult patient that are plainly too minor to require any treatment or attention are less likely to be noted than injuries that are obvious and need attention?'

'I'd like to think I note all injuries down myself.'

Again, I thought the questioning was misleading: Khan had already explained that Christopher was *not* being 'difficult' when he was being examined, he was calm and cooperative. Again, I hoped the jury could see this.

Before he sat down, however, Ferm said something that made my ears prick up: 'Speaking medically and in terms of his medical condition without any outside interference, you never expected in a million years that there would be a sudden deterioration in his condition, did you?'

'No.'

'It was entirely unforeseeable to you and contrary to the diagnosis that you had made of his condition?'

'Yes.'

I thought to myself, if the chances of a medical event causing Christopher's deterioration were a million-to-one, surely that suggested that something else had caused it.

For his parting shot, he tried to pin the blame on Dr Khan for supposedly not telling the police to bring him back to hospital if he passed out: '[In your statement] you say this: ... "I gave verbal advice that he should return if he felt unwell"?'

'Yes.'

'But no reference to giving any advice to the police here about deterioration in his condition.'

Bearing in mind Christopher was at this time held by two officers on either side of him when the doctor was giving this advice, this seemed to be totally disingenuous. When one of the other barristers took a similar line, Khan spelled it out: 'I did feel I was talking to all three, but I always address the patient.' Had Christopher even had the appearance of becoming unconscious while in the care of the police, he said, his expectation was 'that he'd be brought straight back'.

In all, the whole line of questioning from the police barristers seemed to be clutching at straws, suggesting one minute that Christopher's additional injuries did not exist, the next that they'd been there all along.

Yet the thing that stood out for me from Khan's testimony was nothing to do with any of this. Right at the start of the questioning, Khan had mentioned, in passing, that Christopher had been wearing a belt in the hospital. If that was the case, what had happened to it? Where had it gone? And how had

Christopher's trousers ended up round his ankles if he was wearing a belt?

The police had said in their statements that the van left the hospital driven by Ellerington, with Dawson and Blakey following in a car close behind, and that Christopher was alone in the back of the van. They then entered the backyard of the police station before getting Christopher out of the van. Ruth had repeatedly requested an investigation into whether anything untoward happened in the yard at this point, and had been told that the yard was not covered by CCTV. However, there was a civilian gatekeeper in his box in the yard that night, Ken Crichton, and he was next up on the witness stand.

Crichton was particularly important as one of only two witnesses to events in the police station that night who were not police officers themselves[6] and the only person who had witnessed the officers removing Christopher from the van in the police yard; although the police yard was visible on the custody suite monitor, and the officers in there had seen the van drive in, they all claimed to have missed the moment the police opened the van doors and pulled Christopher out. We knew at least one of the three officers was wrong about the arrival in the yard, as their statements did not match up.[7] On top of that, Dawson and Blakey's claim that Christopher was sitting upright while asleep on arrival seemed totally implausible,[8] especially given the additional injuries we now knew about. But Crichton had seen it all on his monitor in the gatehouse at the entrance to the police station yard.

Most importantly, Crichton had said in his statement that he had only seen one police officer getting out of the car, one walking round from the front of the van and getting into the back, and then two officers 'emerging from the back of the police van'.⁹ This suggested there was something seriously wrong with the police's account of events. If one of the officers had been in the back of the police van with Christopher, why had the police claimed otherwise? What were they trying to hide? Despite – or perhaps because of – his crucial importance as a witness to Christopher's death in custody, Crichton was not interviewed by West Yorkshire Police until 5 June, nine weeks later. I wondered whether this was to give the officers time to 'lean on' him, and persuade him of what he *really* saw (or for Jason Paul to be charged with murder and the police's role quietly forgotten). Would he 'remember things differently' now?

Again, Leslie began by establishing the credibility of his testimony, making sure he couldn't have been mistaken. The lighting in the yard was 'very good … very bright', Crichton said, and the camera had a 'wide-angled lens and it will take in the whole of the yard'. But what he couldn't see was what or who was in the back of the van when the doors were opened, as this view was obscured by the doors themselves. Yet he stuck to his claim that he only ever saw one officer in the car. But he now added a strange caveat – 'I *think* there was two in the car,' he said, but 'I can only *remember* one.'¹⁰ If he only remembered one – and he was sure of this – why did he *think* there were two?

After the barristers' questioning was over, the jury made an important point: due to the narrowness of the parking area, any passenger in the car might have got out immediately after coming through the gate, before parking up. But Crichton explained that if this had happened, he would have seen them walking across the yard afterwards, and he had not.¹¹ Besides this, all three officers had stated that they parked before getting out of their vehicles. Something was still not adding up. I hoped against hope that the officers would be forced to explain.

On day twelve of the inquest, everything changed. It was the third week of full days in court, and my energy was depleted from more than two years of delays and frustrations. Each day's new evidence was draining me further; some days I didn't want to go, but I forced myself. I was becoming more and more nervous, finding the atmosphere stifling and oppressive, but trying my best to look and stay strong. At times my mind would drift, as I found myself just looking around at all the people that had been brought into my life against my will as a result of Christopher's death. While this whole process was life-shattering for us, it was clear that to most of the people in the courtroom it was no more than daily routine.

First up that day was PC Kane. Kane was part of the West Yorkshire force that was supposed to be investigating Christopher's death and had been given the role of reconstructing Christopher's journey in the police van from the hospital to the police station. He completed the route six times while handcuffed and sat in the back of the van; the idea was to see whether it was feasible that Christopher could have remained upright while unconscious or asleep, which is how the police claimed they found him when they opened the doors. The journeys were videoed and played to the court. Even on the slower journeys, Kane had to keep shuffling his feet to remain balanced, and at one point nearly fell off his seat. Under questioning, Kane confirmed to Leslie that it was 'obvious' that someone asleep in this position would not have been able to remain upright and 'would end up in a heap on the floor', and that was for journeys of an average of just over five minutes. According to the police who actually drove Christopher to the station, their journey was much faster, lasting between three and four minutes.[12] In the light of this evidence, PC Blakey's claims that Christopher was asleep and upright on arrival[13] seemed completely unfeasible. Kane then confirmed that, despite not being drowsy from alcohol, or suffering from a head injury, he had had another officer placed in the back of the van with him to 'prevent me causing injury to myself'. So why would they have left Christopher on his own, in a far worse state, and then driven at an apparently reckless speed to get to the station? It seemed that either the officers arresting Christopher had been incredibly negligent leaving him in the van on his own[14] – or they were lying that they had done so.

But it was what came next that really shook us.

Gillian Leak was the forensic scientist who had been brought in to examine the police van and the police station following Christopher's death. Her role, she later told the inquest, was to examine the custody suite and police van 'for blood and to interpret the distribution of any blood that I found'.[15]

She told the court about her findings. There had been a 'linear smear of blood' at shoulder height on the door into the police station from the yard, she said, followed by other smears and a fingerprint. It couldn't have come from Christopher, as he was unconscious with his hands cuffed behind his back. I also wondered how Christopher's blood had reached shoulder height if he was being dragged along the floor. Who carries an unconscious person at shoulder height? Or had the blood come from the police officers' clothing? And if so, how had it got there? She also said that there were other splashes of blood in the custody suite, but that these looked like they were old and pre-dated the night of Christopher's death. She took samples of blood and left the custody suite.

After extensive discussions between five or six senior police officers, she was allowed to see the van which had been used to transport Christopher from the hospital to the police station. There, she said, she found 'a heavy contact smear of blood approximately 5 cm by 10 cm,' that suggested someone 'with a head injury' had been 'slumped in the seat with their head in the corner.' This did not seem to fit with the police claims that Christopher was sat upright on arrival, in the same position he had been in when they left.[16] Yet, she said, she 'found no splashes of blood in the rear area of the van'.

Her findings, she explained, suggested that Christopher had been 'bleeding freely from his injuries'. Yet his head injury had not been bleeding at the hospital. What had caused it to start bleeding again?

Leslie began his questioning by asking whether the blood she thought was old had been tested to check it was not Christopher's. She explained that she had not tested it herself but had handed it to the police – and yet 'no samples were received at the laboratory to my knowledge'. This was the first I'd heard of any such samples, and we had not received test results from any blood samples in the pre-inquest disclosure.

During Leak's examination, Leslie referred to photographs of the blood in the van taken by the Scenes of Crime Officer shortly before Leak's arrival at the scene. But as his questioning continued, Leak interrupted: 'Before you go any further with this, can I make a comment, sir? I have got notes in relation to what I saw in the van and obviously I cannot confirm now whether or not this is blood, but there is additional staining in these photographs that were not there when I carried out my examination.'

There were audible gasps from across the courtroom.

This was how we learned that, prior to the forensic scientist's examination, and without her knowledge, crucial bloodstains had been removed from the scene of Christopher's sudden deterioration. The coroner called a break so that the lawyers could take instructions given what had just been revealed. We all wondered who had removed these apparent bloodstains – and why.

After the break, Leslie asked Leak about each of the 'new' stains in the photographs. One, she said, close to the 'heavy smear' on the van wall, showed what she described as 'bubbles', which is what you see when blood has come from someone's mouth. If this was so, Christopher could not have been sitting as described by the police, sat upright with his head slumped forward. Leslie put this to Leak, and she replied, 'No, he would have to be turned the other way.'

Leslie asked her whether the finding of these new bloodstains 'could have an impact as to whether an assault could have occurred in the van'? She said, 'This had an obvious impact on whether an assault occurred in the van,' and that, because of this, she could not rule out such an assault.

Then it emerged that Leak had not been told where the van had originally been parked, nor that it had been moved – a breach of the crime scene that Humberside were supposed to have established. This meant she did not get an opportunity – nor was she asked – to look for blood spots *between* the van and the custody suite: that is, in the very area which would have held evidence of any assault carried out during Christopher's removal from the van. She 'very much' agreed with Leslie that 'in considering whether Christopher was assaulted or possibly been assaulted, the place where Christopher was at would be very important' in terms of being able to do her job properly.

Leslie also asked about the blood smears on the police station wall, and whether they could have come from the hands of a police officer. 'I cannot rule that out,' she replied. She then confirmed that, as far as she knew, none of the police officers' clothing had been tested for blood. Asked by Leslie whether it was normal to test for the presence of blood on those in whose presence the alleged victim of an assault died, Ms Leak answered, 'it is very routine'. So why was it not done?

The energy in the courtroom was electric as Leak gave her evidence. At one point, while Leslie was questioning her, a flash of lightning lit up the court through the circular skylight in the roof, as giant hailstones pelted against the glass. There were cries of 'Go on, Chris!' from the public gallery, and it was a while before the coroner was able to regain control of the courtroom.

One of the photographs from the van showed what looked like a handprint surrounded by dust with blood around it on the Perspex screen separating the back of the van from the driver's cabin. There was no way this print could have been Christopher's as he was handcuffed behind his back. I wondered whether PC Blakey had accompanied Christopher on the journey to the police station, as Crichton's statement had suggested. I was desperate to know what had happened in that van. I hoped the police witnesses due the next day might be able to give us some answers.

The following day, it was the turn of Inspector Tolan to take the stand. Tolan was one of the West Yorkshire Police officers appointed to investigate Humberside Police's role in Christopher's death. The fact that there were only three on his team – two of whom had gone on annual leave a week into the investigation – was an early indication that they did not take the investigation seriously.[17] Still, I hoped to at least get some insight into their decision to allow important evidence to be cleaned away from the van and the officers' clothes.

Leslie started with questions about the three officers involved in Christopher's arrest. He began by asking whether any of the police officers' clothing was seized. Tolan replied, 'The clothing of PC Blakey and PC Dawson, the officers at the hospital, was seized on the 1 April 98, bagged and retained in police possession, but not Ellerington, the van driver.'

Leslie asked, 'Why wasn't Ellerington's clothing seized if both Dawson and Blakey's were?'

Tolan replied, 'The decision to seize the clothing had already been taken by the Humberside Police.'

This was ridiculous. It was Humberside Police who were under investigation! Why were they allowed to seize their own officers' uniforms, dry clean them without any tests being done and then return them the next day? Humberside were supposed to be investigating Jason Paul for allegedly assaulting Christopher outside the nightclub. Yet the officers whose clothes were seized had no connection at all with Jason. It was Inspector Tolan's force who were supposed to be investigating these particular officers. Did he not find the cleaning and returning of their clothes without testing a little suspicious?

Leslie then asked Inspector Tolan about the evidence the forensic scientist had given the day before, regarding possible blood on clothing. He said he didn't know about it.

I couldn't believe the casual impunity that seemed to be built into the system – involving another force seemed to be just pretence, a sham; police forces were apparently free to investigate themselves, destroy any evidence they chose, and then have the whole process approved by a supposedly 'independent' neighbouring force.

One of the things I had been desperate to hear explained at the inquest was why Dawson and Blakey had gone for a medical examination at the Hull Royal Infirmary a few hours after Christopher's death. One of the witnesses was Dr Gosnold, who worked at the hospital. Ferm, representing Dawson, confirmed that his client had seen Dr Knox on the day of Christopher's death, and asked Gosnold about the type of medical work performed by Knox. Gosnold replied that 'She was a full-time forces medical examiner for I think about five years, but she now deals with sexual abuse examinations and does not do general routine forces medical examiner work.' Hearing these words was like being hit by a truck. I couldn't bear to stay in the court.

Sitting in the family room, all I could think about was sexual abuse and Christopher's trousers round his knees with his belt missing. I found out later in the day that nothing else had emerged, and Gosnold could not explain why the officers had gone for examination by Knox. Neither West Yorkshire Police nor the PCA had done anything to find out, or even asked the officers about it. How could they possibly have the right to go to get the family's childhood social services' records, but do nothing to find out why these officers went to hospital to be examined by a sexual abuse specialist the day after a man had died in their custody? What the hell had been done to Christopher?

One of the medical experts called on at the inquest was toxicologist Dr Alexander Forrest, and Leslie questioned him about the effects of CS spray. He quoted what a police officer had told him during his training, that 'it is like having your face dipped in chip fat and having an asthma attack at the same time; it's an extremely unpleasant experience'. Dr Cooper's post-mortem report had noted that 'CS gas was not detected but this means little as the gas disappears very quickly from the body.' A statement by Dr Rice had explained that 'if the use of CS had actually occurred, not only would Mr Alder's clothing be contaminated but there is likely to have been some contamination of the inside of the back of the van in which he was transported.' Was this why the police had had Christopher's clothes destroyed, and those of their own officers dry-cleaned without testing any of it? Was this also why they had cleaned the van before the forensic examination took place? Dr Rice went on to say that 'the levels of irritating vapour ... would have been sufficient to cause effects in the police officers if the spray had been used only a few minutes previously.' So were Blakey's sneezes in the custody suite a result of lingering CS spray around Christopher's body? The use of gas would certainly help to explain his breathing difficulties, and perhaps even his death.[18] We know Dawson and Blakey had threatened to gas Christopher, and Blakey's notebooks had recorded that he sent his CS canister for destruction having supposedly discharged it two days after Christopher's death, while Dawson was on record saying he needed to file a Use of Force report on the night he died. Dr Rice had concluded that the use of gas was 'extremely unlikely', mainly because Dr Clark's autopsy report did not record inflammation of the throat and eyes, but I was still deeply suspicious. For one thing, many of the symptoms associated with CS are only detectable in white people; under questioning, Rice had agreed with Leslie that 'you would not necessarily get [the] reddening of the skin, particularly of the face [associated with a CS gas attack] in a person with black skin'. Leslie had then pointed out that Ibrahim Sey, whose inquest he had been involved in, also displayed none of the usual symptoms associated with CS gas, yet we know for a fact he *was* sprayed.

When Tolan took the stand, Leslie asked him about Dawson's 'Use of Force' report. But it seemed to have mysteriously disappeared. Wilcox, barrister for Humberside's chief constable, tried to make out that it had never existed – he confirmed that Dawson had *said* he needed to complete a Use of Force report, but said he had been incorrect – he did *not* need to complete one, Wilcox explained, because he had not used any force. It seemed a funny thing for Dawson to have been mistaken about. Tolan, however, claimed that Use of Force reports have to be completed whenever force is used *or threatened*.[19] The supposed drawing of the gas canister outside the hospital, he said, would have meant Dawson should have completed a form – but Tolan had been unable to find one. It was all very mysterious. But the hospital security guard, Malcolm Rogers, had been so adamant that the canister had *not* been drawn, despite Dawson and Blakey's claims. It made me wonder – did the officers simply invent this tale about drawing the canister in order to justify Dawson's recorded reference to needing to complete a Use of Force report?

Tolan claimed that Holt had 'made a decision to seize and retain' the CS canisters of Dawson, Blakey and Ellerington 'within the first couple of days of us being in Humberside'. He explained that they had made a request to Queen's Gardens police station for this to be done (again, putting the force under investigation in charge of doing the investigating) but that while this was done for Ellerington, 'it wasn't until August that I discovered that it hadn't been done for Dawson and Blakey'. Why had Humberside refused to comply with the request to seize and retain the canisters of the officers who had arrested Christopher?

Tolan said he then, on 4 August, took possession of Dawson, Blakey and Ellerington's canisters, had them measured, and found that they were all unused, although he admitted that the methodology for conducting these tests was flawed.[20] Either way, the fact that Blakey's canister was even available seemed very strange given that, according to his own notebook, his canister had been sent for destruction on 17 April, having been used, supposedly, on 3 April. Blakey seemed to be using his gas a lot.

This was when the explanations started to get really contorted. Dawson's lawyer claimed that Blakey's canister had been seized on 1 April 1998 after all, and that he had then had a new canister issued to him on 2 April. He then supposedly had his original canister returned to him on 3 April and was therefore in possession of two canisters, one of which was used that day, and then sent for destruction two weeks later, and the other later tested and found unused. But it got stranger still. Tolan then explained that just a few weeks before the inquest, and over two years since it was recorded as having been discharged, he had managed to actually locate Blakey's second canister at the Bradford stores, where he measured it, and found that it too was unused – despite having been scheduled for destruction on 22 July 1998.

It was impossible to make sense of it all, and the officers seemed to be contradicting each other all over the place.

During his testimony, Superintendent Holt confirmed that he had authorised the return of the officers' clothing, explaining that there was no suggestion at this stage of malpractice or criminal conduct by any of the officers involved and therefore to retain their clothing under these circumstances 'could have created unnecessary concerns among those involved and could be considered grossly unjust' to the police officers. It seemed that some of the most basic investigatory procedures had not been carried out because, as far as I could tell, Holt looked only for evidence that would exonerate the officers.[21] I was highly suspicious. If he really believed the officers were innocent, wouldn't he have tested the evidence which would have proved their innocence, rather than destroying it?

Holt then revealed that, yes, he had been aware that the officers had been checked by a doctor the day after Christopher's death, but that he had never followed up the reasons why. Nor did he order any analysis of the tooth so painstakingly retrieved from the landfill site.

Crucially, he also admitted that he had ordered the blood samples and fingerprints taken by Michael Gallagher, the Scenes of Crime Officer, and Gillian Leak, the forensics expert, to be destroyed without testing.[22] All of it was destroyed on 22 July 1998, along with Christopher's clothes and tooth, the same day that Blakey's canister was scheduled for destruction. It was a bonfire of all the forensic evidence relating to any possible assault on Christopher by the officers who arrested him, carried out by the force that I was convinced had killed him, and undertaken with the full support of the force in charge of the investigation. By the time Holt and Tolan had finished providing their evidence, it was clear that their investigation had been a total farce.

The police barristers tried to seize on the mental illness of my other brothers when – completely out of the blue – they brought in a psychiatrist. He took the stand and was instructed to consider why Christopher was the last to leave the club that night. The suggestion was made that this apprehensive behaviour had a psychological cause that might have caused him to fall unconscious in the back of the van, perhaps due to some form of panic attack.

It seemed to me a ridiculous suggestion. In the end it was left to the jury spokesman to put some rationality into what was being implied, asking the psychiatrist if he was talking about the same person who had served as a paratrooper, jumping out of aeroplanes into high-risk combat situations.

Stuttering and embarrassed, the psychiatrist admitted, 'If I had known that, I would have had to reconsider my opinion.' Rather than some sort of phobia, it seemed much more likely that the reason Christopher stayed late in the club was because he had correctly sensed there might be some fallout from his argument with Jason Ramm earlier in the night, and that it might be wise to give those outside time to disperse before making his way out.

They also, bizarrely, brought to the stand a woman with whom Christopher had had a fling fifteen years previously. It seemed to be another attempt by the police barristers to demonstrate that Christopher had some kind of phobia, in the hope, I suppose, of suggesting his death had been caused by a panic attack in the van. She said she remembered that he didn't like going in lifts, and that he didn't like anything around his neck, that she had once bought him a polo neck jumper and he refused to wear it. 'Is it possible,' Leslie asked her, 'that he just didn't like polo neck jumpers?' Everyone in the court laughed.

It was harrowing. Day in, day out I was in that court from 9 a.m., listening to the barristers carrying on, often in legalese, then having an hour's break for lunch before returning for more of the same until 4 p.m. The use of Latin throughout the inquest was particularly disorientating and made proceedings even more difficult and unaccommodating for the family. I did my best to catch the bits I could understand and note down the things I thought were important, but trying to make sense of it all was shattering. It was not only the strain and the tension of hearing evidence but of having to sit for so long among people who so patently resented me and wished I would just go away. Their faces made it plain.

After the day's proceedings were over, we would return to the hotel, have a drink and try to unwind. I had a nice surprise one particular evening when a very handsome man caught my eye across the hotel bar. He was with a friend, working in the area, and the two of them seemed to be getting quite a lot of attention from the girls in the bar. He looked across at me and we smiled coyly at each other; I can't hide it when I see someone pleasing to the eye. I felt my blood pressure rise. I got up from sitting with the supporters, went over to the bar and started chatting with him. I felt a real need for some tenderness, for someone to take me away from the doldrums of the court. He was gentle, kind, and – best of all – he knew nothing of the case. We laughed and giggled about nonsense, and he was just the tonic I needed. For the next three days, we met after court; then the weekend came and his contract finished: he was going home and so was I. Our love affair had been short lived, but much needed, helping to rid me of some of the frustration that had built up and reminding me that I was still human.

One morning I left the hotel with Ruggie and my cousin Tracy, who had come up to join us from London, and we began chatting to a local man who was passing by. It was a beautiful day and we had all noticed that the building across the road, an old warehouse, had an icon of a raven carved into the stone above the door. As we chatted, the man told us that the building used to be covered in ravens. We all exchanged glances at each other, as I had told them about my dream and Christopher's interest in the bird. The significance of the image just seemed to keep reasserting itself. I later discovered that ravens are considered mediator animals between life and death that represent ancient wisdom, intelligence and transformation, and are seen as spectral messengers and signs of an anguished soul.

And in the Celtic tradition, pipes in the shape of ravens were often carved out of the Alder tree, a tree sacred to the ancients as it appeared to bleed like humans.

Leslie Thomas was very sharp. He gave me the opportunity to pass him questions about the evidence I had read, and presented them on my behalf in front of the jury, weaving them into his overall strategy to get the verdict he sought. I was sat near enough to Leslie to pass him questions on pieces of paper, which of course did not please the police barristers at all, and they frequently complained to the coroner that I was disrupting the court.

I recognised the hierarchies within the inquest court. Each organisation was saying just enough to get themselves off the hook, but not enough to incriminate each other. The barristers representing the state formed a gang, looking after one another, while Leslie stood alone, trying to ask some uncomfortable questions on the family's behalf. Those in powerful positions, whether the hospital, the police, or the ambulance service, seemed to be working together, each with their interests to protect, while I was treated as a nuisance and a nothing. It didn't matter what the truth was, they did and said what they wanted with no shame, and we as a family couldn't do anything about it. When the police barristers started flicking through postmortem photographs in full view of the public gallery, it was as if we didn't exist, and certainly not as victims of trauma.

On another occasion, one of the police barristers made a comment comparing Christopher to a piece of dead wood. It was dehumanising. He then made an outburst accusing me of walking about like Hercule Poirot and said that I must have some sort of obsession. It was an inflammatory comment and I felt he was deliberately provoking me. He reminded me of Rigsby from *Rising Damp*, but, unlike him, I had to keep this comparison to myself. It ground my emotions, and I couldn't help but feel this was his intention. I wasn't going to sit there silently through all that, and I spoke out in no uncertain terms, leading to me being moved around the court like a child. Then they would casually turn on the video at will, replaying Christopher dying on the floor as though it was an episode of some lunchtime serial, expecting us to sit through the harrowing sounds of Christopher's suffering. I couldn't bear to sit and watch, and left the court whenever the footage was played, for which I was also accused of disrupting proceedings. Many of us in the public gallery sighed and gasped when we heard unexpected pieces of shocking evidence come out, but it always seemed to be me who would be reprimanded for any remarks made. As an ordinary working-class mother, a victim yet a survivor, it was clear that I was right at the bottom of their pecking order.

Another time, I was accused – in submissions made by a police barrister – of intimidating a witness, in order to bolster an application to excuse the police matron from giving her evidence of what happened on that night. She was the only independent witness of the events in the custody suite in the moments leading up to Christopher's death, and she was not well enough to give evidence, in part because I had supposedly intimidated her. I hadn't said a word to the matron; the only time I had even seen her was when we once passed each other in the court corridor.[23]

But it was easy to scapegoat me, as we were supposed to sit in the court saying nothing, no matter what indignities were thrown at us, and I refused to do so. In these situations, the barristers and the judges seem to have an understanding that they are right and the ordinary citizen is wrong, so of course when

I attempted to defend myself I was shot down. One barrister told the court I wasn't backward at coming forward, describing me as Mrs Alder 'that is, if she *is* a Mrs' in such a tone that I couldn't work out whether he was asking for my hand in marriage or insinuating that the very idea that I could be anyone's wife was ludicrous.

Finally, it was the turn of the five police officers who had been present at Christopher's death to give their evidence. One after the other, they stood in the dock, and Leslie asked them a total of more than 150 questions, giving them the chance to give their account of what happened on 1 April 1998. But none of them did: they would give their name and rank and then, to my horror, refuse to answer any further questions. After sitting day after day waiting for their explanation, we were now faced with them citing the Coroners' Rules that any response could provide self-incriminating evidence as they had an impending criminal misconduct trial. I was devastated. I couldn't help but believe this was a ploy by the officers and the CPS: deliberately charging them before the inquest but ensuring the trial was delayed until afterwards, in order to allow the officers to escape giving any explanation at all. Along with the matron's non-attendance, this meant that none of the six witnesses to Christopher's death gave evidence at his inquest, and the only people that could possibly have told us what had happened in the van said nothing. The sick feeling in the pit of my stomach remains with me to this day.

With the hearings over, it was time for the jury to deliberate on the eight weeks of evidence that had been put before them. The coroner left four conclusions for the jury to consider: accidental death, natural causes, unlawful killing on the basis of involuntary manslaughter, or an open verdict. For the unlawful killing verdict alone, the criminal standard of proof was required – beyond reasonable doubt – as it was legally equivalent to a manslaughter charge. We believed that Leslie had clearly demonstrated unlawful killing to this standard, establishing that the officers, through neglect or worse, had been responsible for Christopher's death. The police barristers, meanwhile, seemed to have been trying to argue that somehow Christopher had neglected himself, as if he had placed himself on the custody suite floor with his trousers round his knees, made himself unconscious and died, all of his own free will. Their entire case seemed little more than an attempt to elaborate PC Dawson's shocking comment on the night of Christopher's death: 'It was his own fault.'

On 24 August 2000, the jury came back with a unanimous verdict. Their conclusion read as follows: 'On the 1st April 1998 in Hull between 03.41 and 04.00 whilst in police custody, travelling in a police van from Hull Royal Infirmary and being placed on the floor in Queen's Gardens police station, Christopher Alder met his death. The cause of death was multifactorial leading to unconsciousness which resulted in upper airway obstruction and positional asphyxia. Christopher Alder was killed unlawfully.'[24]

As it was read out, the court was in uproar as the public gallery exploded in cheers. I, my brother and our supporters leaped to our feet, ecstatic, shouting 'yes!' I told the jury they were fantastic. The only people that didn't seem to be jumping about were the police and their small army of legal representatives.

I believe in every society there are people with a conscience. But I had not met many of them in positions of power, all of whom seemed only too willing to subordinate their consciences to their careers. Yet here we had a jury of eight ordinary people, prudent and intelligent, who were able to take an honest, logical and independent view of the evidence. They had been horrified when the CCTV footage of Christopher's death had been played, and shocked by the appalling evidence. They had listened intently to all the information available and drawn the only rational conclusion.

My faith in society had been restored, and their verdict gave me hope that the officers responsible would now be punished. It had been an emotional rollercoaster, but I now firmly believed that we were finally on the road to justice.

The Funeral

2000

With the inquest finally over, my thoughts turned to arrangements for Christopher's funeral. His body had been in the mortuary for over two years now, as burying him before the cause of death had been established had seemed unwise in case further examinations needed to be carried out. Now we were finally able to lay him to rest.

I met with Richard, his girlfriend Eleanor, Andy, Maggie and Pat, one of the Hull campaigners who had become a close friend, to discuss plans for the funeral. We decided he should have a really good send off, to which we could invite all those who had supported us in our battle for justice, followed by a private graveside ceremony for immediate family and friends. We launched an appeal for funds and managed to raise nearly £3,000. Pat came with me to the undertakers to make the arrangements.

It was a difficult time and my friends helped me with the preparations: buying flowers, contacting the undertakers, and even organising a horse and carriage. Arrangements were made with E W Brown & Son undertakers to collect Christopher from the mortuary and prepare him for burial and rest in their chapel until the day of the funeral. We met with a priest from

Holy Trinity church in Hull, discussed which supporters and friends we should invite, and things seemed to come together nicely. Ruggie advised me to request that Christopher's internal organs were available to be buried with him, something I had not even thought about. I had taken it for granted that all his body parts would be with him, but Ruggie said that it is a common occurrence for families to learn, years after a funeral, that their loved ones' organs had not been buried with them, having been removed during the post-mortem. He was right. I would later hear horror stories from other families in the UFFC who had lost loved ones before and after Christopher's case who had gone through very similar experiences. I asked Ruth about it and she wrote asking for Christopher's heart and other organs to be returned to his body.

With military service having been such a big part of Christopher's life, I phoned the army to request that they send someone to attend the service. When I mentioned Christopher's name, the lady on the end of the phone told me that they had had a visit from Humberside Police to collect Christopher's army medical records. I suppose this was another part of their attempt to shift the blame away from themselves by trying to pin his death on some pre-existing condition. But they had not informed the army that he had died; the woman told me that Christopher's name was still on the records for potential call-up in case he was needed to serve again in an emergency. She was as shocked as I had been when I told her of his death and the circumstances surrounding it. She said they had informed the police on their visit that Christopher had left the army with a good record, having been decorated for his services in Northern Ireland. I dread to think how the police would have used his history had it been any different.

So, on Saturday 25 November 2000, two and a half years after his death, Christopher's funeral finally took place at Holy Trinity Church in Hull. That morning it was raining like mad and I had had another sleepless night back at Kingston Hotel, where I had stayed during the inquest. Nathan, who was now nine, was with me, and this would be the first funeral he had ever been to. We went to the breakfast room and met with Ruth, Christopher's two sons and their mother, and Ruggie and his wife. After breakfast I got a surprise when a huge bunch of around forty red roses arrived at the hotel from an anonymous source. All the card said was 'care of Ruth Bundey'. It seemed someone had spared no expense to buy them, so we decided they would be placed on Christopher's grave, as we presumed that's what they must have been intended for. Part of me wondered if someone in their own way was saying sorry.

Christopher's funeral procession was to start from the memorial cenotaph in Hull city centre. When we arrived there, the atmosphere was muted, with people walking around chatting to each other in hushed tones. We all knew the circumstances that had brought us together, and you could feel the quiet, sombre ambience in the air. All three of my surviving brothers were there, Emmanuel and Stephen having been granted day release from the psychiatric hospitals in which they had spent most of their youth. It pained me to see the bloating of Stephen's body from years of medication and lack of exercise while in psychiatric care, and Emmanuel's grey sallow skin from the same. Knowing our shared past, I found it hard to look them in the eye without a feeling of guilt caused by my awareness of the childhood traumas that had compounded their state of illness. Beside them stood Nathan with Christopher's sons. Like a family of proud meerkats, they took centre stage at the front of the procession. Alongside them was David Hornby, a guy we'd grown up with in the children's home, as well as friends of Christopher's from his school days. The elderly couple who had been his neighbours on the Waterfront were also there. Two of my closest friends from Burnley, Andrea and Alex, came and supported me. I had always been able to talk openly with them about how I felt, but today all I could do was shake and linger, withdrawing to the back of the procession like the runt of the litter, unable to stop the trembling inside. Families I had met through the United Families and Friends Campaign, who had also lost loved ones in police custody, were there too, many having gone through the same experiences that we had; even though Christopher's funeral must have brought back the pain of burying their own family members, they had still come to stand side-by-side with us. Our cousin had travelled up from London to be there; Christopher's death brought us back together for the first time in many years. Lots of people had come from Hull, campaigners for justice who had been supporting us, as well as ordinary people that had been following the case and were appalled. People had come from all over the country to pay their respects and it felt like a great send off for Christopher: the presence of all these people giving him the respect he wasn't shown by the police or the state officials who had tried to make his death seem insignificant and sweep it under the carpet.

The procession began and we walked through Hull town centre in silence. Shoppers stood still as we passed, showing their respect. Unlike our previous vigils and meetings, there wasn't a police officer in sight, the procession being stewarded by what appeared to be traffic wardens. We came to the statue of William Wilberforce,[1] the anti-slave trade campaigner, which seemed momentously poignant as it towered over the Queen's

Gardens police station where Christopher had died, and stopped for a five-minute silent remembrance. Then the procession made its way to Holy Trinity Church, where the coffin was carried in by my brothers and David and laid at the front of the church. Nathan, Stephen, Emmanuel and Christopher's sons sat in the front pew. Richard was the first to speak and told the congregation how close he had been to Christopher. Just about holding back my tears, I could only manage to say that Christopher was part of our family. Then the congregation began to file past the coffin at the front of this grand church, as we sang hymns and said our last goodbyes.

After the service the coffin was carried out of the church and placed into the hearse. The family followed the horse and carriage in black cars towards the cemetery while the soldier representing Christopher's regiment played the emotive sounds of the 'Last Post' on his bugle. Finally, we arrived at the graveside to lay Christopher to rest for the final time on this earth. The priest said a prayer as we watched the coffin lowered into the ground, and then Christopher's two sons placed handfuls of earth on the grave. Nathan did so as well, and burst into tears, overwhelmed by the emotion in the air. Still it kept raining, shifting the ground under our feet.

Sometimes in grief and times of stress we look for signs and we like to think that our loved ones are still close. Back at the hotel, I looked for the raven carving again across the road. But it wasn't there.

The wake was held that evening in the Polar Bear pub. My barrister and others said a few words: we spoke about Christopher and how we had been successful in fighting for his name at the inquest by getting an unlawful killing verdict. As the day drew to a close, I felt we had given him the best send-off we could have done. But for me the funeral hadn't felt real. It was like I had been numb the whole day, unable to feel anything. It was so strange. Maybe somehow I had sensed it wasn't Christopher we were burying.

Just a few weeks after the funeral, I got a call from Ruth. She had been informed that Christopher's heart had not been buried; it was still in Sheffield, where he had been taken for his initial post-mortem the day he died. I was sickened. There seemed to be no let up with the emotional shocks, even after we thought Christopher had been buried. I had no idea how I was going to tell the rest of the family. I couldn't face the idea of having to disturb the grave all over again to add his heart to the coffin, so I decided I'd do it at the same time as adding a headstone, which I was planning to do as soon as I got the money together to buy one. I would put off telling the rest of the family until then. I felt that they had had enough to deal with for now. Now I am relieved that I didn't upset my family again to rebury Christopher's heart in the grave – as, little did we know in 2000, it wasn't Christopher in there.

Mr O'Doherty

2000–1

The inquest verdict had been a major victory, but Leslie had pre-warned us that the police were sure to appeal a ruling of unlawful killing. This is apparently standard procedure whenever an inquest decision goes against them, and they have unlimited funds to finance it. So it came as no surprise when, shortly after the verdict, the officers, backed by the Police Federation, sought to overturn it by means of judicial review.[1]

On 15 September 2000 I phoned Stephen O'Doherty at the CPS, who had taken over the prosecution case against the officers from Fleming following the inquest.[2] Leslie had explained to me that a verdict of unlawful killing was equivalent to manslaughter, so I had expected that this is what the police would now automatically be charged with. But apparently this was not the case; the trial was still to be solely for misconduct. O'Doherty told me that he had been brought in by the director of public prosecutions (DPP) to consider the case afresh in the light of the inquest verdict, in line with the recommendations of the Butler report, and that his mind remained open. Over the months that followed, however, that was not the impression I got at all. He was quick to dismiss the concerns Ruth and I raised with him regarding the new evidence that had come out at the inquest, telling me that the role of the CPS was limited to prosecuting, not investigating – despite the Butler report's clear stipulation that the CPS *did* have the power to require further investigation where necessary. It soon became clear that O'Doherty was simply offering us more of the same, attempting to give credence to the failed police investigation that the inquest had done so much to discredit. To top it off, he told me that he would not be reviewing the new inquest evidence at all until the police request for a judicial review of the verdict had been dealt with. But as he had not received the file from Fleming, he explained, he was not able to review the pre-inquest evidence either.

On 5 October 2000 I called him to ask if he had seen the CCTV footage yet. He said that first he had to find out whether the police were going to appeal the inquest verdict. I told him I wasn't happy with the charge of misconduct; the inquest had ruled that he was unlawfully killed, which was equivalent to manslaughter. But he said he was not there to give a second opinion and would follow Fleming's recommendations.

Around three weeks later, I called him to express my concerns about the original investigation and request that we meet. He refused. I explained that the inquest had revealed that blood stains had been removed from the police van before the forensic examination had taken place, that the blood swabs had been destroyed without being tested, and that the officers involved in Christopher's arrest had gone to the hospital for treatment the following day. I also mentioned that new evidence about the officers' CS gas had come out at the inquest, and that CCTV footage of the custody suite had picked up sneezing when Blakey went close to Christopher. Much later, when I got access to his written record of our conversation, part of the pre-trial disclosure for my civil case against the CPS, it appeared that he was mocking me. I had explained that when I had been exposed to CS gas once in a bar, the effects were so severe that everyone in the bar immediately fell about coughing and sneezing. I said that that experience had made me wonder whether CS gas had been the reason for the sneezing and coughing documented on the CCTV footage, given that Christopher had been threatened with gas, had unexplained breathing difficulties, and that Blakey had supposedly sent his canister for destruction the following day. O'Doherty's record of that conversation read as follows: 'She told me she had sniffed gas over the weekend and had sneezed and this reminded her that an officer could be heard sneezing.' It felt like he was insinuating I had just readily gone out and 'sniffed' CS gas. Just four weeks after taking over the case, and at our first meeting, he already seemed to feel contempt for me.

O'Doherty wrote to Ruth in January 2001, saying he had been asked by the DPP to reconsider the charge of manslaughter. I hoped against hope this would now come about.

On 6 February 2001, I phoned him again to see if we could have a meeting to discuss the possible causes of Christopher's unconsciousness. He refused, later explaining that in his view a meeting with my family would simply be a forum for us to vent our feelings of distress about Christopher's death. He said that while he did need to identify a reason for Christopher's unconsciousness, he totally dismissed the possibility that Humberside Police officers could have been responsible in some way, saying there was no positive evidence. This overlooked Humberside Police officers' *destruction* of all the potential evidence – Christopher's clothes, anything that was on their own clothes, the blood samples from the van – without testing it, in defiance of protocol. And still he refused to investigate the possibility of an assault in the van.

This is not to say, however, that he wasn't making any enquiries at all. Three days later we received a letter from him explaining that he was attempting to obtain yet another expert opinion as to whether Christopher suffered a heart disturbance in the van that might have caused him to die. No matter how many times this theory had been medically discredited, it seemed the CPS just couldn't give up on the idea.

Over the months that followed, we wrote repeatedly to O'Doherty to push for investigation into the possibility of an assault and the use of CS gas, raising the issue of the canister's destruction, the disposal of the clothes and the officer sneezing as he leaned over Christopher. But the CPS were simply not prepared to address the possibility of a completely skewed investigation or to conduct any independent review of it. O'Doherty wrote back saying that he had not heard any sneezing, and that was that. I questioned whether he had really listened to the tape or read the video transcript, in which the sneezes had been documented by phonetic experts. Later, O'Doherty insisted that the paramedics had not detected CS gas and that Christopher had no upper respiratory problems which would be associated with CS spray. How much more evidence was needed to show he was suffering breathing difficulties other than him gurgling for air and gasping for his life? And why would the paramedics be testing for CS gas when their role was to administer emergency first aid? It was the same circular logic the police employed from the start: there is no evidence, because there has never been an investigation, while the continued failure to investigate is justified by the lack of evidence.

What I still couldn't understand was why the CPS seemed to be so bent on ignoring the elephant in the room: the discrepancies[3] in the officers' explanations, their reported aggressive and threatening behaviour at the hospital, and the additional injuries Christopher received after they dragged him outside.[4] Ruth believed that the CCTV footage appears to have allowed attention to be focused on events in the custody suite, while what might have happened immediately beforehand was conveniently ignored. The CPS just did not want to know.

At one point, I asked O'Doherty why the officers who arrested Christopher should have gone for treatment with a doctor who specialised in sexual abuse the day after Christopher's death. But he just asked, in an indifferent tone, what inferences *I* drew from that. Of course, I felt totally incapable of relaying the gruesome inferences I drew. Exchanges like these started to make me question my sanity, leaving me with feelings of disgust and self-loathing for having these suspicions. But the uncertainty, the unanswered questions, the refusal to investigate what had happened in the van – all of it meant I couldn't stop wondering what had gone on and fearing the worst. He was quick to commission further medical evidence, so I couldn't see why he wouldn't enquire into the many concerns Ruth and I had raised.

In March 2001, we received papers informing us that the first hearing into the police appeal of the inquest verdict would begin at the High Court in London on 4 April, just over three years after Christopher's death. Andy and I travelled to London, where we were met by Ruth and Richard to hear the appeal, which lasted three days.

The case began with Judge Justice Jackson giving a detailed account of what had happened on the night of Christopher's death, and of his interactions with the police. He then summarised the medical evidence which had come out through the various post-mortems and examinations, and the testimony of the medical experts at the inquest. Finally, he recalled the possible verdicts that had been put before the jury, and the jury's decision.

After that, the counsel for the police made their case. They submitted that unlawful killing should not have been left for the inquest jury to consider, as the medical evidence was not sufficient to prove the cause of Christopher's death to the criminal standard, and the breaches of duty by the police officers could not be considered criminal. The police lawyers also argued that the jury had been biased and were trying to make out that the whole verdict should now be thrown out. To support their argument the police barristers then spent two hours going through the medical evidence, trying to claim that the views of Professor Crane were completely out of line with all the other pathologists.

After three days of these hearings, we then had to wait for the judge to consider all the arguments and make his ruling. It was nerve-wracking. I had no clue what to expect; my hopes and fears were all over the place, and while I couldn't see how he could possibly overturn the unanimous verdict of the entire jury, I had learned by now to temper my expectations.

On 10 April 2001, we received the judge's verdict. Justice Jackson noted that, although the evidence of Professor Crane alone would have been enough for the jury to convict, there were in fact four medical experts – Crane, Cary, Porter and Clark – in agreement that the blockage of Christopher's airways had, at the very least, hastened his death. He said that enough evidence had been placed before the inquest jury both to determine the cause of Christopher's death and to demonstrate gross negligence, and that an option of unlawful killing was therefore a verdict properly open to them. On the issue of jury bias, the judge ruled that there was no evidence of any undue influence. The appeal was dismissed and the officers' attempt to get the unlawful killing verdict overturned had failed.

I was elated. A High Court judge had ruled that the evidence existed to prove manslaughter to the criminal standard of proof. I hoped the CPS would take notice of the ruling, and finally bring manslaughter charges against the officers who left Christopher to die. But that was far from guaranteed; now began another wait, to see what the CPS decided to do.

Justice Jackson's appeal judgment is one of the many documents I have read again and again in the years since Christopher's death. Within the judgment, he noted that the coroner must not invite the jury to consider a particular verdict unless sufficient evidence has been presented to support the verdict. For an unlawful killing verdict to be considered the coroner had to identify the same three elements that constitute gross negligence manslaughter, namely: (1) breach of duty; (2) causation of death; and (3) gross negligence.[5] These three elements, noted the judge, had in fact been correctly identified by the coroner. He then said it was the coroner that should decide what verdicts are to be left to the jury, so long as they fulfil the necessary criteria, and that if the verdict under consideration involves a criminal offence then the jury must be satisfied to the criminal standard – that is 'beyond reasonable doubt' – that the verdict is correct. He said it was then up to the jury, not the coroner, to decide how and where Christopher had met his death.

The judge said that unlawful killing in this context meant involuntary manslaughter or gross negligence manslaughter. He was of the opinion that the ordinary law of negligence would reflect whether the police officers had been in breach of their duty of care towards Christopher, that whether or not the breach caused his death would determine whether this negligence was gross, and that this was for the jury to decide. Justice Jackson said that the coroner had been at pains to lay before the jury all the factors which could count against a finding of gross negligence, as well as the factors that counted towards such a finding – first and foremost the CCTV footage of Christopher lying unconscious on the floor in prone position. He said putting him in the recovery position and checking his airways may be regarded as basic matters of first aid which the officers should have been familiar with.

The judge did not accept the police officers' submissions that the breach of duty could not amount to gross negligence; in his view, it was up to the jury to decide. Given the verdict of several medical experts that they were sure the position in which Christopher was left by the police at least hastened his death, the judge came to the conclusion that the jury were entitled to be satisfied – to the criminal standard – both of the gross negligence and the cause of Christopher's death. He said the inquest jury had decided the breaches of duty were criminal and that the coroner had been correct to leave this for the jury to decide.[6]

Days later, Ruth received a letter from the CPS – not with their decision about manslaughter charges but with a reply to our queries. The predictability of the response made it no less distressing. O'Doherty simply stated that any further injuries Christopher received hadn't killed him – as if who inflicted them or how he got them was therefore of no consequence or importance.

It seemed to me as if O'Doherty wanted to have his cake

and eat it. On the one hand, he had been holding out against prosecuting for manslaughter on the grounds that – despite the jury's verdict and the clear High Court ruling – it supposedly couldn't be proved that Christopher would have survived if the police officers had looked after him. But at the same time he was trying to argue that Christopher had not been killed by something that had happened to him beforehand. So which was it? Was his death the unavoidable consequence of something that had happened to him? Or was it the result of his lack of treatment? The CPS appeared to want us to believe it was neither, that Christopher had just mysteriously died for no reason; his death had nothing to do with how he was treated or what had been done to him.

It was the same story with regard to a new piece of evidence that had come out at the inquest: Dr Khan had mentioned that Christopher had been wearing a belt on the night of his death – a belt which had seemingly disappeared, however, by the time he reached the police station. Yet these concerns were simply batted away as if they were of no importance. The following April, O'Doherty wrote to me to say there was no evidence as to how his trousers were fastened. I couldn't believe what I was hearing: the pathologists had clearly written in their post-mortem reports that Christopher's trousers had only two buttons opened, evidence had been provided by medical staff that he was wearing a belt, which was not documented later in the pathologist's record of his clothes, and then there was the CCTV from outside the nightclub, where Christopher is lying on the floor – the buckle of his belt was glinting in the lamplight. But despite my writing to the CPS about this, no further enquiries were made. O'Doherty's response to the issue, written with a definite air of finality, was that 'Mr Alder's clothes may well have been disturbed as a result of these actions [being dragged about by the police] but however it occurred, there is simply no evidence that they were in that position because of some unlawful act by the officers.' What had happened to Christopher's belt was never investigated.

Again I asked about the discrepancies between the hospital staff's statements that Christopher had been dragged backwards out of the hospital and those of the officers who claimed he'd walked out. My point was that if the police were lying about that aspect of their conduct, this could surely have relevance for what they claim happened afterwards. But O'Doherty asked me what charge such a discrepancy could relate to, as if I was supposed to be able to give him a page reference for a law book. I didn't have a reference; I just assumed that evidence of suspects lying in a formal statement to police would be considered significant.

These exchanges were excruciating. He could clearly see how distressed I was, yet he was still challenging me on my knowledge of the law. I thought he was the one who was supposed to be legally qualified; if he couldn't see why the possibility of Christopher receiving a beating by police should be investigated, then, as far as I was concerned, he was bloody stupid. I just couldn't understand his reluctance to make any further enquiries; it left a nagging, painful doubt in my mind.

As O'Doherty continued to brush off my concerns, I felt more and more that he viewed me as no more than an illiterate nuisance. I got the impression he thought taking steps to follow up my concerns was completely beneath him, that it would be demeaning for a man of his intellect, and that to do so would be a pointless pandering to my petty demands rather than a necessary part of any thorough investigation. And the idea that it might be worth doing simply to alleviate the mental anguish

I was feeling as a family member with unanswered questions? I doubt that even crossed his mind.

I know through my own experience of racism that it is not always explicitly expressed in racist words: it can be how someone deals with you, their perceptions and reactions. It can be a thought in the person's mind that makes them respond to you differently; O'Doherty's rebuffs made me feel I was being treated as such. I felt like anything I said to O'Doherty was being dismissed as no more than the ranting and raving of an angry Black woman.

With our correspondence going nowhere, Ruth began to make requests for face-to-face meetings with the CPS – all of which were declined. It felt like the gap between me and the institutions was widening.

It was from the *Daily Mirror* on 27 April 2001 that we first came to hear of the CPS's decision. Once again, their 'review' had decided that the officers would not be charged with manslaughter; Ruth and I received letters containing this information a few days later.

The letter claimed that 'to prosecute for manslaughter it is essential that Christopher would have lived if the officers had performed their duty of care to him'. But as Leslie had pointed out at the inquest, if you shot someone in the head while they were having a heart attack, you would still be tried for murder, even if it couldn't be proved that the victim would have lived. Leslie had explained to us – and Justice Jackson had confirmed – that the real test for gross negligence manslaughter was in fact that the negligence must have more than minimally contributed to or hastened the victim's death. He then specifically asked the medical experts whether the officers' failure to give Christopher medical attention and clear his airways had significantly contributed to or hastened his death. And their answer, time and again, was yes. But it seemed that the CPS were now asking a completely different question. They had seemingly moved the definition of gross negligence manslaughter from negligence *contributing* to death to failure to perform an action that would have *guaranteed* survival. It seemed to me this was an impossible test to meet: there was no way of knowing for sure he would have survived had he been treated; the only way to have found out would have been if they had tried. What was clear is that failing to treat him made his death certain, as Professor Crane had pointed out to the CPS. The goalposts had suddenly become so narrow you'd have had trouble fitting a ping pong ball through them.

Hearing about the CPS decision through the *Daily Mirror* had been a shock. I felt like I was purposely being sidelined again. The emotional rollercoaster I was on came crashing down; I was so upset that I phoned O'Doherty, telling him what a nasty surprise it had been to hear his decision from a newspaper before I had been told. I expressed to him my disbelief that, having seen the video of Christopher's death, he could possibly defend his decision. It was clearly visible on the CCTV: the officers stood around laughing while Christopher lay unconscious, bleeding and gasping for breath before dying just yards from their feet. How much more gross could you get? I told him that the inhumane lack of concern the officers showed for a human being in distress showed, I believed, discrimination against Christopher which could only have been due to the colour of his skin. It was agonising trying to get him or anyone else to respond with understanding and to see my point of view. I asked O'Doherty about his personal thoughts as to whether race could have played a part in Christopher's death.

But he simply dismissed the question and told me there was no evidence of racism.

I wondered if the denials were intentional, to make me feel as though I was using the race card. I was hoping the CPS would be able to see how this looked and felt to me as a Black woman, but they seemed to be incapable of empathy. Yet Ruth was white and she had no problem – for her, it was an obvious question to ask when you look at the video: white officers chatting and laughing while a Black man gasps for his life on the floor. I couldn't understand why the investigators were unable to take the same impartial approach and at least consider if the total disregard these officers had shown Christopher could have been down to racism. What happened to the critical thinking and open-mindedness of these professionals? Why could they not look at the race issue without apparently taking it as a personal attack?

Ruth wrote to Matrix barristers' chambers for an opinion on the test for gross negligence manslaughter, and on 23 May 2001 we received the following reply: 'The test adopted by the CPS is not, with respect, the appropriate test for determining causation in gross negligence manslaughter cases.' The correct test, they said, is that 'the negligence must have caused the death in the sense that it more than minimally, negligibly or trivially contributed to the death. This is the test which was adopted by the coroner in the inquest and approved by Justice Jackson and until this is applied the CPS will not be able to evaluate the result of the medical evidence in this case.' So there it was: Christopher's case met the standard test for gross negligence manslaughter as accepted by the coroner, upheld by a High Court judge and now verified by a barrister at one of the most prestigious criminal barristers' chambers in the country. But it wasn't enough for the CPS.[7] I now believed that they were wilfully blocking the path to justice.

O'Doherty had consistently refused to meet with me in person, but on 29 June 2001, at a court hearing for the officers, I spotted him with Nicholas Hilliard QC and requested a conversation. Reluctantly they agreed to talk but said we'd have to hurry as they were due in court shortly. They took me into a tiny side room where I tried to explain that the High Court had ruled that only one expert was needed to prove unlawful killing/manslaughter, and that we had such an expert, Professor Crane, who was willing to state categorically that Christopher's death was the result of neglect – even under the CPS's erroneous 'survivability' test. But O'Doherty kept insisting that he could not prosecute on Professor Crane's evidence alone, as the other medical experts said they were unsure what had ultimately caused Christopher's death. I was puzzled. I couldn't understand why, if Crane was the only expert that knew the cause of Christopher's death, O'Doherty was asking others who didn't. I said that if you had a bicycle that needed fixing and one shop was able to fix it while eleven others couldn't, you would go to the one that could, and not worry about the others. He accused me of raising my voice and being confrontational. I told him I felt the CPS were not doing anything to bring these officers to account, at which point he left the room saying he had to go into court for the committal and he wasn't prepared to have a meeting.

On 18 August 2001, I was invited to speak at the launch of the James Ashley justice campaign in Liverpool. James Ashley had been shot dead by PC Christopher Sherwood while he lay naked and unarmed in bed with his girlfriend in St Leonards in Sussex. Following the shooting, Sussex Police chief constable Paul Whitehouse wrongly told the press that Ashley had been wanted for attempted murder. Nevertheless, Sherwood ended up being charged with murder, making him only the second serving police officer in the UK ever to have been charged with a murder committed while on duty. Nevertheless, in May 2001, he had been acquitted at the Old Bailey, following the judge's instructions to the jury.

The meeting was addressed by James Ashley's sister Pauline and her younger brother, the driving forces behind the Ashley campaign. They explained that the CPS had announced that Whitehouse, who had been suspended while under investigation in connection with the events, would not face charges and had now returned to duty. Instead, he had been given 'strong written advice' over his role in the incident – although, explained the chairman of the police authority, Ken Bodfish, 'the advice will remain confidential'.

Here was yet another family denied justice, dragged through all the rigmarole of investigations that take years only to exonerate the police, their emotions launched onto a rollercoaster of hopes raised and dashed, with no justice or accountability at the end of it.

Battling the CPS

2001–2

I was weary. And my mind was in turmoil; I had an unwanted and uncontrollable urge to revisit the horror of 1 April 1998. The anger I felt convinced me I was doing the right thing, but at times I thought I was losing my mind. When my confidence was low, my feelings became conflicted and at times I started to see myself as the troublemaker the state perceived me to be.

Meanwhile, the CPS remained fixated on Christopher's heart. Ruth asked Professor Crane whether he knew a heart specialist who could clear the CPS's doubts about a possible arrhythmia. Christopher's heart was not an issue as far as Professor Crane was concerned, but nonetheless he suggested consulting the cardiologist Professor Jennifer Adgey, a top heart specialist. But the CPS instead insisted on instructing Professor Hall, who added nothing but further uncertainty. They seemed to be doing the defence's job for them: finding people to muddy the waters and resisting those who could help build a successful prosecution case.

Professor Hall said in his report that he couldn't determine the cause of Christopher's unconsciousness, and that even though there was no clear evidence to support it, a cardiac arrhythmia couldn't be ruled out. A conference was called between Professor Hall and the heart expert Dr Cary, who in 1998 had been sure Christopher's heart had nothing to do with his death. To our surprise, Dr Cary now suddenly reversed his opinion. Ruth was at a loss to understand why he had changed his mind, as Hall's report did nothing but postulate further theories with no new evidence. By bringing in Professor Hall, the CPS had cast a further element of doubt on the evidence already given at the inquest. It felt like confusion was being deliberately created to protect the officers – with Christopher's family just collateral damage.

With the CPS refusing to find evidence to support their case, it fell to us to do it for them. Ruth commissioned a report from Professor Adgey, who concluded that she did not believe Christopher's death was associated with cardiac arrhythmia as he wasn't an alcoholic. However, she said that even if he *had* had cardiac arrhythmia, her opinion was that with prompt medical attention his breathing could have been contained long enough to get him to the hospital for medical treatment. She said that with basic life support he would have lived – whether for hours, weeks or years was uncertain, but it was clear that the officers had prevented his initial survival. This report, along with Crane's conclusions, contained the evidence the CPS had been unable to find for four years.

Another boost came in August, when Ruth received an email from Dr Janet Porter, one of the doctors who had given evidence at Christopher's inquest. She had been horrified to find out that the officers were not to be charged with manslaughter, despite the unlawful killing verdict and all the evidence which had come out at the inquest. Ruth thanked her and asked that she put together a short report to pass on to the CPS, which she agreed to do.

With Dr Porter on board, there were now three experts whose

evidence all pointed towards a scenario where, with medical attention, Christopher would have survived, meeting the criminal standard that the CPS claimed was necessary to prove gross negligence manslaughter. Ruth referred all of them to the CPS in the hope that their evidence might finally lead to charges of manslaughter being brought against the officers involved.

On 9 January 2002, O'Doherty wrote to say he had finally applied to add a charge of manslaughter to that of misconduct in a public office via a voluntary bill of indictment.[1] This was the news we had been waiting for. I had no idea what a voluntary bill of indictment was, I was just happy that nearly four years after Christopher's death and eighteen months since the inquest finding of unlawful killing, the officers responsible were finally going to be charged. For the first time since I'd been involved with them, my confidence in the CPS started to return. Yet when I spoke to O'Doherty, I got a strange feeling that he was far from pleased with this new charge.

Ruth and I believed it would be helpful for me to see this application so that we could understand the evidence, so I asked O'Doherty if we could get a copy of the voluntary bill. I said that I understood that either the Butler report or the Stephen Lawrence report said that consideration should be given to reveal information to victims once a decision has been taken. He replied in a mocking tone that he knew of no such duty and that unless he was persuaded otherwise he would be providing this evidence to the police officers' defence solicitors only.[2] He appeared to view my request as some sort of threat to his authority, a sign of insubordination. My short-lived trust in the CPS collapsed once again.[3]

*

Just weeks later, I received another disturbing letter from O'Doherty. In it, he explained that the police officers and their representatives were concerned that I had unauthorised copies of the CCTV footage, which could prejudice the trial. He also wrote to Ruth, to confirm she had not made additional copies or given a copy to me. Ruth had already signed a document to say she would not release the video when it was first provided to her, and I found the accusations outlandish and insulting. There seemed to be more inquiries into my solicitor and me than into the officers who were supposed to be on trial.

By this time I was increasingly suspicious that the reason the CPS were not taking Christopher's death and my concerns about it seriously was because of racism. I reached out to a newly formed organisation called the National Black Crown Prosecution Association (NBCPA), whose aim was to 'promote equality and diversity within the CPS and the wider criminal justice system', and was astounded when one of their founders, Maria Bamieh, told me that O'Doherty himself had a finding of vicitmisation of an employee who had complained of racial discrimination against him upheld at an employment tribunal in December 1997, just months before Christopher's death. How could he possibly look at the race issue in Christopher's case with an open mind? I felt discouraged and began to see him as unqualified to continue in his role.[4]

Shortly before the trial was due to begin, we received notice that the proceedings were to be moved from Hull to Middlesbrough. This meant major disruption for the family and our supporters. Once again I would be forced to leave my home and children for eight weeks, plagued with guilt about neglecting my duties as a mother. Ruth could not see why it shouldn't be held nearer to Hull and the Yorkshire circuit; why not Leeds, Sheffield or Bradford? Not for the first time, the arbitrary decisions of the state had thrown me into inner turmoil; yet again, it was evident that, at best, no consideration had been taken of the needs of the family – and at worst, they were pursuing a vindictive agenda against us.[5]

Before the Trial

2002

On 14 March 2002 we received a letter from a director-caseworker for the CPS telling us that O'Doherty had, for personal reasons, asked to be taken off the case, and that, with reluctance, this request had been granted. He told us the future of the prosecution was to be handled by Christopher Enzor, head of the York division, and that Mary Clare Grant would be responsible for the day-to-day handling of the case under his leadership.

Ruth spoke to Enzor the same day, telling him how nice it was to make contact with him and asking if he had received the two pages of notes from me where I tried to piece together the discrepancies in the evidence. She told him of my concern that the trial was to start at the police station door, so anything that might have happened in the van beforehand, as well as in the hospital, would not be tested in court. Enzor explained that as he had only just been brought onto the team, his knowledge of the evidence was sketchy. He was aware of the case, however, because both he and O'Doherty had been involved in dealing with a number of police and prison custody deaths and as a result they had regularly discussed cases over the phone.

One of the first things he mentioned was the commissioning of the experts who had written the reports that secured the manslaughter charge. Once again, it seemed to me, they were questioning Ruth's integrity. Ruth had already written a several-page letter to O'Doherty, which she had hoped would provide sufficient explanation as to how the experts had come to be involved. Yet it still felt like a definite element of suspicion was coming from the CPS.

They discussed the timing of a conference that was planned for the next day, between me, Ruth and the CPS lawyers leading the prosecution. He understood that the solicitors for the five police officers were seeking further disclosure of documents and that this was one of the things we would need to discuss. Ruth agreed that it was important for us to have some method of communication with the prosecuting team, and emphasised that our priority was to have the voluntary bill and the proceedings explained to me, that I needed to be walked through the process so that I could be reassured that this was not just something being done for the sake of form.

Enzor agreed that he would inform us which witnesses the Crown would be calling, and Ruth asked if Peter Herbert QC could attend the meeting so he could explain things to me after the conference had finished. I found it really difficult to understand the legal aspects of what was happening in these kinds of discussions; my head was all over the place and I was totally disillusioned with the lack of willingness of the other CPS lawyers to meet and explain things. Ruth finished the conversation by telling Enzor of our concern that Christopher had been left the way he had because he was Black.

The following day, 15 March 2002, the conference took place. It was to be the first face-to-face meeting I had ever had with the CPS in four years of dealing with them, and it would also be the last. Up till then, all communication had been through telephone calls or letters – or if I was lucky I might catch the CPS lawyers walking in and out of court. It seemed to be done purposely; it's easier to make cold, calculated decisions when you are not forced to come face to face with those who are impacted.

The meeting was held at the chambers of the Prosecution QC. In attendance were Ruth, me, Ruggie, my brother Richard, Maria Bamieh, Inspector Tolan from West Yorkshire Police, Enzor, a junior CPS barrister called Gareth Patterson, Mary Clare Grant, and James Curtis, the prosecuting QC. I had contacted Maria before the trial began, and she agreed to attend when she could. She was a highly skilled CPS prosecutor and, though she had no role in this case, she had been given permission to attend both this hearing and the trial itself by CPS director of public prosecutions, David Calvert-Smith.

As we sat down, Curtis felt the need to tell me he had represented Black and white people, one of whom was Nigerian. It made me feel uncomfortable; I couldn't understand why he felt he had to point that out. Later, while discussing the need for a barrister with an understanding of the race issue to liaise with the family, he continued with patronising and racist stereotyping, referring to the appointment of a Black barrister to liaise with the family as more than a token gesture, not just a 'Black person there banging the drums'. I was stunned by this sickening comment, but none of the CPS lawyers said anything about the remark; they seemed to consider it acceptable. Enzor later claimed that while he understood what Curtis meant, he did realise this comment could have been taken in the wrong context by the family. But at the time he did not interject and did nothing to contact us afterwards to explain what was meant.

Embarrassed, I stood up to leave, and walked out of the meeting feeling totally humiliated. It took Ruggie to calm me down and explain that this was an opportunity to ask questions, so I went back into the meeting only to hear Curtis now telling my brother he knew a Black man in Birmingham and asking if he knew him. Even now, I can't decide whether this was pure ignorance or a deliberate attempt to inflame our feelings.

Curtis then introduced his choice of junior barrister to liaise with the family as someone who came from a deprived background, 'like you', as if a barrister from a poor background could relate to us but his own rich ignorance could not. Unfortunately, coming from my poor background I was only too able to understand where he was coming from. He then reminded us again that he had previously represented a Nigerian family. I couldn't see any reason why he should keep going out of his way to emphasise this. If that was his idea of making me feel comfortable it did the exact opposite; I felt it was a very clever way of implying that I was playing the race card when in truth, it was he who was doing so. Ruth believed the continued instruction of James Curtis QC was a disaster and he should never have been instructed in the first place. We had in fact suggested Courtenay Griffiths QC long ago as having the necessary insight as a senior Black member of the Bar, and Superintendent Holt had initially agreed, before we were told it would not be appropriate to go 'off circuit ...' So why was Curtis selected?

I raised my concern with Curtis that Christopher had met his death the way he had due to the colour of his skin. But the CPS QC was adamant there was no evidence of racism and totally refused to make race a part of his case against the police officers. He seemed to make nothing of the fact that the officers had stereotyped Christopher as a Black man, right from their first interaction with him in the hospital, where they saw him not as a victim displaying erratic behaviour symptomatic of a head injury, but as a trouble maker, and probably a drug user, in need of punitive sanctions – all the way through to their interpretation of his last desperate gasps for breath as nothing more than a ruse to gain their attention. In fact the way he later set his case strongly gave the impression that he shared the officers' belief that Christopher's behaviour was because he was aggressive rather than a man with a head injury. And the way he was dealing with me suggested that he had attached this label of 'Black troublemaker' to me as well.

As I discussed my concerns about the discrepancies in the evidence, he said that some of the matters were of such minute detail that they were not attractive to the prosecution. The trial was to start in a month.

After the meeting, I was concerned that Mr Curtis had said something about a promise having been made to the police that they would not be prosecuted for manslaughter. I phoned Enzor to ask him about it, and he was adamant that nothing of the sort had been said. But the police defence argued that such a promise *had* been made. Enzor explained that in light of the new evidence that had arisen, the prosecution did not accept this, and a manslaughter trial would go ahead. Shortly before the trial, Ruggie phoned Enzor on my behalf to get an update on how preparations were progressing. Enzor told him that it appeared that Christopher had been wearing a belt at the hospital and the Waterfront nightclub. This was what we had already concluded from the evidence at the inquest, but it was a significant development that the CPS had now accepted this conclusion. Yet I was shocked that the fact the belt was missing still hadn't led them to question whether this, and the dishevelled state of

Christopher's trousers, could have been caused by a possible struggle between Christopher and the officers. Despite all the unexplained issues that pointed in that direction,[1] the CPS still seemed set on refusing to even consider the possibility of a police assault on Christopher before his arrival at the police station.

A 2004 statement by the death-in-custody support/campaigning group Inquest accurately summarised the problems we were facing before the trial:

> The CPS was not prepared to address the racial issues inherent in the case during the preparation for the trial. They were asked to consider appointing Counsel, preferably Black Counsel, sensitive to and experienced in racial issues but announced that they were not prepared to go 'off circuit' and appoint anybody who was not from the North East of England. They were never prepared to address the possibility of a completely 'skewed' investigation and conducted no independent review of it. They were specifically requested by Janet Alder's solicitors in February 2001 why there had never been any investigation as to what else could have possibly happened between Mr Alder leaving the hospital and arriving at the Custody Suite. They made no effort to sit down with the family to learn of the family's concerns but treated the family as a complete nuisance and tried to use solicitors as a buffer.

Two weeks later, Ruggie and I attended a two-day court hearing for the application of the voluntary bill of indictment, held at Teesside Crown Court, Middlesbrough in front of the judge who was to oversee the criminal trial a fortnight later. We had still not actually been able to see the contents of the voluntary bill and, despite O'Doherty and Enzor's earlier promise, nothing was said at the hearing as to whether we could now have a copy. No one from the CPS was there, despite Ruth's request for one of the prosecution team to attend in order to explain the proceedings to us. On the second day I decided to call Enzor's office, but I was told he was tied up on another case in London and would not be back in the office until the following week. The lady on the other end of the phone told me she had tried to have a conversation with him, but his mobile phone reception was breaking up.

Much of the hearing went over my head, but I do remember the judge asking how the CPS were going to deal with the conflicting medical evidence. Being naive and under so much pressure, however, I was yet to understand the crucial significance of the point he was raising.

The Trial of the Officers

2002

The crux of the CPS's argument with us over the medical evidence had always been whether it could be proved that Christopher would have survived had he been given medical attention. Ruth and I had now found evidence to say that regardless of what caused Christopher to collapse, the officers contributed more than minimally to his death. The evidence the CPS found, however, said that because he collapsed for an unknown reason, he might not have survived even if the officers had given him proper medical care. It was with this in mind that, on 3 April, Ruth wrote to Enzor to inform him of the case law established in the Khan case just the previous month. A judgment had been handed down on 7 March 2002 directing – just as Leslie Thomas and Matrix Chambers had maintained all along – that the cause of death *could* be established without showing the individual would have survived, *if* it was shown that their death was hastened by the conduct in question. This is exactly what both Adgey and Crane had concluded in Christopher's case. I still could not understand why the CPS seemed to be so resistant to receiving information and evidence that would bolster the prosecution's case. Surely this is exactly what they were after. Wasn't it?

Another episode of the CPS's clear disregard for the needs of the family came with their decision to leave the appointment of Ms Jemma Ivens until just a day or so before the trial began. As a Black woman, Jemma was the only person on the case that I felt was able to understand our concerns on the issue of race. She was one of two junior barristers, and had been assigned the role of liaising with the family on behalf of the CPS. Her late appointment, however, had the effect of putting her in an untenable position in which nothing could be achieved, as she had no time to get to grips with the full scope of the case and was left playing catch-up.

The trial started on 15 April 2002, four years and two weeks after Christopher's death, at Teesside Crown Court in Middlesbrough. Each of the five officers present at Christopher's death faced charges of both misconduct in a public office and gross negligence manslaughter. Ruth and I arrived shortly before it was due to start, and a large queue had already formed at the entrance of the court, including members of the press. As we walked in to be security checked by the court staff, a police officer stood in the court foyer videoing everyone who entered the building.[1]

We were ushered into the court and I was allocated two seats in the public gallery for me and a supporter. We were sat behind a smoked-glass screen, behind which I was unable to clearly see the proceedings going on, hidden from the view of the jury and unable to see the centre of the court. I couldn't help but feel this was stage-managed, and right from the very start, the whole thing had the air of a theatrical performance.

Once we were seated, the QCs for the defence, their solicitors and the CPS prosecution team comprising James Curtis QC and his junior barristers strolled into court, dressed in those archaic outfits that were supposed to convey respectability, honour, truth and justice. They were followed by the investigating officers Holt and Tolan from West Yorkshire police. The officers on trial were already seated behind their mass of legal representatives, dressed in suits rather than their usual uniforms.

Directly behind us, the seats had been filled with the families of the officers on trial, along with other plain-clothes police from the Humberside force. It was deeply intimidating and uncomfortable to have them right behind me throughout the proceedings. They had obviously been given time off from their daily duties to support their colleagues throughout the eight weeks of evidence, and as the trial got underway, their continuous sniggering, comments and giggling left me feeling increasingly victimised. I wondered what the role of the CPS was as far as victims and witnesses were concerned; evidently no one had seen fit to ensure the family was protected from intimidation in the public gallery.

Just before the trial started, the prosecution QC told me that one of the medical experts had written to him expressing sympathy for the police officers, saying he believed they were being used as scapegoats. Scapegoats? A scapegoat is someone who is unfairly blamed for the misdeeds of others. What others? Who was responsible for Christopher's death at the hands of the police, if not the police? Christopher himself?

It was only much later that I discovered this was the same 'expert' who had argued that the reason Black people died of asphyxia in police custody was due to them having bigger lips and tongues. I had never heard anything so blatantly racist, or so crassly intended to get the police off the hook. Just like white people, Black people have different-sized features and tongues. Despite this bigoted comment, the CPS still decided to use him as a witness. I was greatly disheartened by this, as I would have thought that his comment would have disqualified him from giving evidence as an independent witness, not to mention undermining the prosecution case against the officers. Yet it seemed that undermining their own case was exactly what the CPS were determined to do.

There were tight restrictions on what could be published. As the press sat watching the proceedings, they asked the judge if they could report that Christopher was a paratrooper who had been decorated for his service in Northern Ireland, known facts which had long been in the public domain. The judge's view was that nothing should be printed that had not been mentioned during the trial. The prosecution had simply to mention the fact, therefore, and it could have been reported. Yet Curtis told the court that Christopher's history as a decorated paratrooper was not going to be part of his opening statement; instead, this information was totally set aside, and not mentioned to the jury at any point during the case.

As the prosecution case proceeded, things went from bad to worse. It was incredibly difficult having to listen to the prosecution QC describing Christopher as aggressive, never once mentioning the cerebral irritation brought on by the blow to his head that was the likely cause of his erratic behaviour in the hospital. He would repeat this description of Christopher time and time again, suggesting that this was probably the reason the officers thought he was play-acting or the reason why they were unaware of his condition. Why did he keep saying the officers were unaware? It had been made abundantly clear that, by the time he reached the police station, Christopher was unconscious, bleeding from the mouth and gasping for air. It was unbelievable.

Nor did the QC mention the officers' hostile treatment

of Christopher in the hospital: forcibly dragging him about, holding open the toilet door to deny him his privacy, and then unnecessarily removing him from the hospital before he had been treated. Instead, the prosecution QC kept repeating that there was ample evidence that the reason Christopher was unconscious was because of the blow to his head outside the Waterfront. I can't imagine that he didn't know that the Home Office-registered pathologist had ruled out the original blow to the head as a cause of death within twenty-four hours of Christopher's death. Why was he saying this?

At one point, the judge talked about the possibility of an assault and that the Crown might need to be prepared for the jury to reach this conclusion. I felt vindicated by this comment: it showed that my and Ruth's insistence that the CPS make enquiries into this possibility was a reasonable request after all. I wasn't mad; a further assault was a live issue that had come to the mind of the judge.

The prosecution QC said, 'It is bound to cross the jury's mind as to how the deceased had become so profoundly unconscious in that time. It is bound to cross their mind as to how he got into the condition he did, and how he sustained an extra cut to his lip, and I have dealt with this briefly in the opening with regards to the difference between the post-mortem examination and the hospital examination.'

Justice Evans replied, 'Yes, but there is an earlier issue, isn't there? There is the issue of how he became unconscious.'

'Yes, and that is unknown.'

'It is unknown but it is not alleged that that could be an assault?'

'There is no evidence upon which any medical person bases that and ...'

'Well, it goes further than that.'

'I was going to say it goes further than that apart from the split lip and missing tooth it is fair to say that Professor Crane goes some way towards suggesting that there might have been a trauma, a blow – there is no evidence of any blow sufficient to cause that deep unconsciousness.' To conclude, he said, 'it does not form part of the case.'

I was aghast. Why would the CPS ignore the possibility that the police had assaulted Christopher on the way to the police station if they wanted to make their case strong?

My mind reverted back to the evidence of the forensic scientist Gillian Leak at the inquest, when Leslie Thomas had shown her a series of photographs from inside the van. She explained that the scene had been changed, that there were blood spots in the photos that had been removed before she had done her investigation. She said that this had had an obvious impact on her ability to assess whether an assault had occurred in the van. None of this was part of the CPS criminal case. Why was the prosecution leaving out even evidence which had been referred to by the judge himself? I started to get very worried.

Instead, the CPS lawyers had made sure that their story began with Christopher's entry into the custody suite; the issue of what happened to Christopher between his walking into the van fully conscious and being dragged into the police station unconscious, and of how he sustained his additional injuries, played no part in the case. The question of what happened in the van remains unanswered to this day.

Even the language Curtis used seemed to be designed to whitewash the police's actions. Why did he describe Christopher as being 'carried' into the custody suite? Was he watching the same CCTV footage as me? I had seen Christopher being *dragged*, feet trailing, and legs sliding across the floor. Everything he said appeared to be aimed at painting the officers in the best possible light.

I became increasingly angry as I watched Curtis's performance. Time and again he referred to Christopher being 'aggressive' and 'abusive' but didn't once mention the cerebral irritation that was the most likely cause of this erratic behaviour in the hospital, as established at the inquest. He then said that this behaviour 'may set the scene for the subsequent behaviour of the defendants'. It was as if he was trying to excuse the police's treatment of Christopher, giving an only slightly more sophisticated version of Dawson's comment that 'it was his own fault'. On Christopher being dragged around the hospital, Curtis commented, 'Of course, it was now quite rightly a public order issue and right for the police to take over.' In fact, the Independent Police Complaints Commission (IPCC) later criticised the police for the way they treated him as a criminal rather than a patient in the hospital, and suggested it was due to racism.

He spoke of Christopher being 'knocked totally unconscious', outside the Waterfront, although there were conflicting reports on whether he was ever unconscious there. I felt Curtis was trying to play up the effect of the fight in order to exonerate the police.

He went on to say there was 'no medical evidence' of CS gas, without ever mentioning the police's wilful destruction, against all protocol, of any evidence they could have had, namely on Christopher and the officers' clothes, nor did he mention the officer sneezing as they leaned over Christopher in the custody suite. Even more shockingly, Curtis suggested that Malcolm Rogers, the security guard outside the hospital, 'saw Mr Alder kicking away and kicking off and resisting the officers' attempts to restrain him.' In fact, when asked at the inquest whether Christopher had poked one of the officers, Rogers's reply was 'definitely not. He didn't touch no police officers at all didn't Christopher.'

Another time Curtis spoke of the police being 'obliged' to threaten Christopher with gas, and then to arrest him. This was an arrest even Dunn, the custody sergeant, had described as 'pathetic', and about which the IPCC would later comment, 'the justification of arrest to prevent a breach of the peace was not going to avail the two [arresting] officers'.[2] Yet, Curtis was justifying it as if the officers had no choice. He even questioned the accuracy of Dr Khan's report on Christopher's injuries, as if he might have recorded a second missing tooth as one bent back by fifteen degrees!

On the possible assault in the van, Curtis brushed it off with the comment that 'there is no independent evidence as to what happened in that van'. He never mentioned the bloody handprint, nor the destruction of the blood samples that were taken, which the Scenes of Crime Officer had said left him 'flabbergasted'.

When it came to the medical evidence, things got even worse. Describing the conference of medical experts held in March 2001, Curtis claimed that 'all were agreed that it was not possible to prove to the criminal standard ... what it was that caused Christopher to become unconscious'. But this was totally irrelevant, as Christopher's unconsciousness was not what killed him; what killed him was his blocked airways. But instead of focusing on this, he went out of his way to highlight the lack of agreement over what had caused Christopher's unconsciousness.

It was unbearable to watch and I only managed to get through it thanks to the solidarity shown by all those who took time out of their lives to come to Middlesbrough and sit with me during the trial. As well as Ruth, there was Ruggie, who had been such a crucial presence for me during the inquest two years earlier, as well as the Black lawyers I had met through the National Black Crown Prosecution Association, Maria Bamieh and Peter Herbert. Maria was with me as the proceedings got underway and the CPS began to put their case across. Curtis explained to the jury that they were going to hear evidence from various medical experts and that the test for the jury was to be sure to a criminal standard that the officers' lack of care hastened Christopher's death. But Maria quickly became concerned that the CPS were calling *all* of the medical experts, even those that undermined the prosecution's argument, and explained that if they continued to do this they would not be able to prove their case. She told me that this was a most unusual practice and that in almost eighteen years as a state prosecutor she had never seen it before.[3] She then discussed the matter with some of her colleagues, including the QCs Peter Herbert and Courtenay Griffiths. All agreed that this was not sensible tactically, and that it clearly undermined the prosecution case. Ruth and I had worked so hard to get the manslaughter charge, but now it seemed that the evidence we had collected was being deliberately conflicted with contradictory evidence gathered by the CPS. The CPS, of course, had a legal duty not to withhold evidence from the defence. But surely the usual way to proceed would be to leave any evidence supporting the defence case for the defence themselves to present?

I was in total distress and told Maria that I was not going to attend the trial anymore. Maria did her best to calm me down and managed to persuade me to stay on board. But the more I talked to her, the more I began to believe that the case was a mockery. Even the judge seemed to share our misgivings, saying that he had never seen medical evidence put across in the way the prosecution were doing, and that it was confusing for him, let alone for the jury. At one stage he said that the case was more akin to a medical negligence case than one of murder or manslaughter. The prosecution QC kept saying that this was a unique case, but, in his directions to the jury, the judge queried this also. Years later, in their review of the case, the IPCC confirmed that the approach taken had been 'somewhat unusual'.[4]

I wrote to anyone and everyone that I thought might have some power to help. I wrote to Enzor and told him I believed the trial was being set to fail. I wrote to David Calvert-Smith, the director of public prosecutions and to the home secretary. I very nearly wrote to Tony Blair, though I am now glad that I didn't. In the early days I trusted those in positions of power, but I was devastated when I later saw more than 500,000 men, women and children killed by Blair's war in Iraq, a war that he had launched with next to no evidence of its necessity or legality. That's when I finally realised: why would people who are willing to kill hundreds of thousands of innocents be bothered about the death of my brother?

As the case ground on, the inconsistencies between the years of explanation we had been given by the CPS and what was actually being said in court became clearer. In a letter from 29 January 2002, for example, O'Doherty said that for a charge of misconduct in a public office, the Crown would have to show evidence of bad faith by that person in their action or inaction. So I was startled when Curtis told the judge that 'we submit that bad faith is a red herring' and that the prosecution was not alleging the officers were acting in bad faith. The judge responded, 'I think the defence agree with that.' Of course, the police lawyers seized on this own goal by the Crown. One of the defending QCs submitted that, four years on from Christopher's death, 'the prosecution still did not allege specifically bad faith. They say they do not have to prove bad faith.' He said that the CPS had been actively looking for evidence of bad faith for fifty months and had failed to find any.

To me it was obvious that the police officers had acted in bad faith. Barr had noted that Christopher was bleeding from the mouth and had soiled himself, whilst Dunn demanded he be taken to hospital from the moment he was dragged in, yet Dawson and Blakey stood in the way of that happening. If this isn't bad faith, I don't know what is.

It got worse. While the prosecution QC was making his submissions, he said that the Crown did not need to prove deliberateness, as apparently the 'Sheppard test'[5] did not require it. Again, and again, Curtis made reference to 'the defendant's unawareness of the risk to Christopher Alder's health'. It was unbelievable; the video proved without a shadow of a doubt that the officers were aware that Christopher was unconscious and in need of treatment. There was the officer who demanded he be taken to hospital as soon as he saw him, the comments that his breathing was being restricted, and the comments that he had 'shat himself'. Then there were the officers' statements, one of which states he thought Christopher 'was unconscious', another one that he was 'in no state' to give a statement. They even had the officers' notebooks, Barr's saying 'he needs the hospital' and Dunn's 'I think he needs the hospital'. The CCTV footage made it clear that, despite having commented on his need to be in hospital, the officers had made a conscious decision not to take him there, not to place him in the recovery position, and not to offer him first aid for his injuries. With all this, what could possibly have led Curtis to conclude that the officers were unaware Christopher needed help? In all our dealings with them, the CPS had not once said to me or Ruth that they believed the officers did not know the true nature of Christopher's condition or had not realised he needed hospital care. But now I found myself sitting in a trial where the CPS emphasised and repeated that the officers were unaware that Christopher needed help.

Looking back, I question how the officers could ever have been found guilty using Sheppard as the relevant case law. The Sheppard case gives a defence to those whose negligence results from a genuine ignorance of their charge's need for medical attention. This was a case in which a woman was unaware that her child needed medical attention and was subsequently found not guilty because her actions were not deliberate. Now the CPS were claiming, against all the evidence, that the officers too were unaware of Christopher's condition and their actions were not deliberate.

The Sheppard case was supposedly relevant due to its definition of the term 'neglect'. But to my mind, the word neglect, in this context, seems insultingly deficient from any real understanding of Christopher's critical position and agonising death, and absolutely inappropriate given the unlawful killing verdict delivered at his inquest. And on a psychological level, this comparison of Christopher with a neglected delinquent child felt doubly hurtful: not only was it demeaning and condescending in its own right, but it also felt like a vindictive reminder that we were, by any standards, neglected children ourselves. What a cruel circle of abuse the upholders of law and order were imposing on our family.

Feelings of horror began to well up in me yet again. To my eyes we had been invited to the court not to witness a criminal prosecution, but to witness the Crown proposing that the officers' actions were accidental.

Ruth and I had always questioned why the officers had just left Christopher to die as they did, and whether this degrading treatment was motivated by racism. We wondered whether anything that they had said in the hours before or after his death might reveal this. For months before the trial began, I had repeatedly asked the CPS whether they had viewed all of the CCTV footage and had anything relevant transcribed. But the West Yorkshire Police investigators told us they had looked at all the available footage, and the only material of any relevance was the eleven minutes I had already seen, and the CPS lawyer said he too had watched everything and found nothing of relevance.

We found this unlikely. Officers had referred in their statements to Christopher as being 'coloured' and 'of negroid appearance' – terms that suggested, at best, a limited understanding of the sensitivities around race, and were generally, even then, considered explicitly racist. We believed any evidence of racial prejudice should have been used in the prosecution as part of their case to demonstrate bad faith or malice, one of the ingredients of the crime of gross misconduct.

The CPS had always claimed that to demonstrate racism, it would be necessary to demonstrate 'differential treatment' of people of different racial backgrounds by the officers, and that they had no evidence of this. But we knew from witness testimony that, on the night of Christopher's death, there had been a white woman in one of the police cells who had been provided with a blanket by the officers, having complained of the cold.

This was in stark contrast to Christopher being left, exposed, on the cold stone floor with nothing to cover him. I couldn't see how you could get any more 'differential' than that.

The CPS said that while they did not intend to make racially motivated conduct a part of their case, the possibility of racial issues emerging during the case remained alive. Yet Ruth explained that the law does not work like this – the only way the issue of race could become part of the prosecution case was if it had been raised at the start, giving the officers time to prepare a defence. It could not simply be 'slipped in' after the case had begun.

In fact, far from the issue of race 'remaining alive', the CPS had done all they could to kill it. Not only was the officers' racially charged language not included in their case, but I later learned they had actually edited out the one part of the officers' interviews where they had been asked whether their treatment of Christopher had been influenced by race (to which they had simply answered 'no', and the questions had moved on). In so doing, they did their best to ensure that race was never mentioned in court and would not have been allowed as an option for the jury to consider.

So it was a total shock to find out that there had in fact been further evidence of racism on the CCTV footage, but the CPS had chosen to keep it out of the case. About two weeks into the trial, the junior barristers, Gareth and Jemma, called us into the family room and told us about a part of the video we had never seen or been told about before. In the hours after Christopher's death, as the officers stood around his dead body, they were having a good laugh about what sounded like 'banana boats'. This was a phrase which has often been used in a derogatory way in relation to African-heritage immigrants in Britain, with

Caribbeans described as having come 'straight off a banana boat' when racists wanted to demean them as culturally inferior. On hearing this phrase on the video six weeks before the trial began, Gareth had immediately requested a professional transcript by a court scribe. She agreed that an officer could be heard saying, 'I'm not going on that fucking boat sir, fucking banana boat, I'm not going on one.' Tolan verified these words and said they could be attributed to Barr. Just to be sure, a phonetics expert with twenty years' experience was also consulted, and she too confirmed the use of the phrase 'banana boat'. There then followed what the phonetics expert described as monkey or chimpanzee noises, followed by much laughter from the other officers, and comments about hoods with eyeholes cut out of them (like those worn by the KKK). Here, it seemed, was clear evidence of the officers' racism. It appeared that this was the first time anyone from the CPS had bothered to watch the full CCTV footage, four years after his death, and having told me repeatedly that no evidence of racism could be found.

As soon as the transcript had become available, it was served on the defence. It was then that Humberside Police produced their own version of the footage, denying what the experts had heard. The CPS accepted this new version of the transcript, despite the evidence from their own experts. It was decided not to present it as evidence in the case. And now it was too late to do so.

It was infuriating. I was so upset I just broke down there and then. I even wondered whether I had been shown this now deliberately, to break my spirit after I had begun complaining about the conduct of the trial.

Once again, the police were ignoring the explicit recommendations of the Macpherson report, which stated that 'police services and the CPS should ensure that particular care is taken at all stages of prosecution to recognise and to include reference to any evidence of racist motivation. In particular it should be the duty of the CPS to ensure that such evidence is referred to both at trial and in the sentencing process.'

The CPS claimed that the police were in fact referring to banana *boots*, which was, they said, a nickname for the yellow overshoes that were apparently given to officers if their clothes had been seized. As for the monkey noises, they said they could not be sure which officer had made the noises, and anyway they might have simply been an innocent reaction to the word banana. Their excuses were an insult; even leading politicians had condemned monkey chants at football matches. What is the difference between that and these police officers using the exact same type of mockery while Christopher's body was still lying uncovered in the custody suite in the police station? This interpretation of the monkey noises seemed to me a matter for the jury to decide, having seen the video for themselves, and having heard each side give their interpretation. What horrified me is that this evidence was simply kept from them altogether.

Peter Herbert was shocked when we told him. He subsequently wrote to the CPS explaining that the throwing of bananas at Black players was a commonplace occurrence at many football grounds, and gave an example from his own experience of an African-Caribbean woman being taunted with monkey noises by football fans on a recent train journey. He said that the association of Black people with bananas and monkeys were some of the most well-established forms of racial abuse in this country. Peter said that while this might appear a trivial issue to raise, it underlined the fact that any jury anywhere in the UK is well able to draw inferences that such behaviour is not solely attributable to wearing yellow overshoes and that the noises were directed at Christopher, rather than some innocent occurrence as the CPS seemed to believe. He said that this evidence should be put together with other aspects of Christopher's treatment by the officers, such as their stereotyping of him as aggressive, treating him as a criminal rather than a patient, constantly threatening to gas him when he was disorientated in the hospital, assuming he was intoxicated rather than ill, claiming that his unconsciousness was all an act, and so on. Peter suggested that there were primary facts from which the jury could draw inferences of racially aggravated behaviour, which would clearly aid the prosecution case by providing the ingredient of malice necessary for the misconduct charge, and suggesting the wilfulness necessary for manslaughter, and concluded that it would not be in the interests of justice if this evidence was hidden from the jury. Even the home secretary, Jack Straw, had written to me the previous year to say that he could well understand how prejudices and preconceptions might have affected the police officers' behaviour. But Peter's intervention had no effect. The CPS said the banana boat issue was now dysfunctional and had been disposed of with the judge's approval.

I began to give the lawyers names like the Sheriff of Nottingham, Mozart, Bungle and Big Bird, while the prosecution QC reminded me of no one so much as Kermit the Frog. Looking back, I think I must have adopted this tactic as a defence mechanism because I felt so alienated and disempowered by the experience. I was physically isolated, totally inexperienced in court procedures, and exhausted from trying to understand what was going on. Nobody from the CPS had explained how any of it was going to work before I entered.

Each day, the officers on trial would walk in and out of court as free men, able to mingle with friends, family and colleagues as they pleased. They would exchange greetings with witnesses about to give evidence with smirks on their faces and an air of knowing confidence that the trial was no more than an inconvenience from which there would be no final penalty.

As I sat there in despair, I became aware of being periodically stared at by those in the central arena, as if *I* was on trial. The 'respectable' ones, safely segregated from me as if from a venomous snake, would glance at me from the corner of their eyes before quickly returning their gaze back to the court. It was making me nervous – was I a laughing stock because of my lack of legal knowledge? Did the CPS and the QCs regard me as a source of entertainment?

Just as at the inquest, when the CCTV footage was played, I couldn't bear to stay in the court. I would remove myself from what I had come to call the 'showground' and wait in the family room outside; Ruggie would then come and get me when the video was over. It wasn't just the trauma of reliving my brother's death; I dreaded seeing the expressions on the faces of the police and court officers. Whether I caught them smirking or even laughing again or simply witnessed their cold indifference and apathy masquerading as objectivity, it would have used up all my reserves of resilience. And I knew that any emotions it triggered in me would only have given those responsible for Christopher's death a feeling of superiority, and would have given the lawyers another excuse to demand that the judge dismiss me from the courtroom. And then I would have been no good to Christopher at all.

I remember the tortured soul of a female member of the jury, who seemed to me to be particularly distressed after viewing the footage. I felt so sorry for her, but it did give me encouragement that at least there were members of the jury that felt deep compassion and who were just as appalled about what they had seen as I was.

At one point during the proceedings, Curtis suggested that Christopher would have been 'a cabbage' had he survived. It was extremely difficult to listen to such descriptions, and clear that the prosecution QC had absolutely no compassion towards Christopher's family members, who were forced to sit and listen to these heartless words.

The defence and prosecution QCs would sometimes break out into chortles of jolly laughter following clever little exchanges of wit and wisdom among themselves. At those moments it felt as though the rest of us present didn't matter and could simply be ignored. I became increasingly distressed, unsure of what the QCs kept laughing about.

On one occasion, for example, the prosecution QC relayed to the court that he had been challenged by a member of the defence to give the judge the phrase 'red herring' in Latin. '*Pisces rubra fumara*,' he revealed. What cleverness, what wit! Everyone laughed except me; I couldn't help wondering whether this was a deliberate tactic to isolate me further.

As I looked upon this scene, it was as if I had found myself in an eighteenth-century fish market, with everybody dressed up for the occasion and performing their party pieces. The prosecution QC was adorned with pink braces and lime green socks, bedazzling the court room every time he drew back his long black cloak to frame his jester's attire. Up till then, I had only ever seen court scenes depicted on TV, where the barristers were all soberly dressed. But here I was confronted by a man who seemed to have chosen his costume from a sweet shop rather than a tailor's. I kept thinking how insensitive it was that a court that was supposed to be seriously considering the circumstances of the most dreadful, protracted death of an innocent young man would keep bursting into peals of laughter – just as the officers had done while they stood around Christopher's body. But what could I do? However upsetting it was, I had little choice but to continue to watch this brightly coloured routine – even though it felt like a total mockery of my brother's life.

As the prosecution QC wittered on and on, quoting excerpts from one case after another, my perception was that he was just trying to kill time until the lunch hour, when both sides could go and chat, laugh and applaud each other for their cleverness and skill. I certainly didn't seem to be witnessing much in the way of forensic analysis of the evidence or intellectual rigour in pursuit of the truth. It felt like the motives, career ambitions and personalities of the court officials were regarded as being more important than the victims of crime or justice being done. But I didn't want to accept this and I pushed those thoughts away, still thinking that this was an English court of law and that my brother's suffering and brutal death would eventually count for something.

The Trial Takes Its Toll

2002

Just days into the trial, the defence made a request to Hull social services requesting the release to the defence of our family's care records from 1962 onwards. Social services objected, but their objections were overruled. I understand that nothing can be held from the defence, but what did my family's personal childhood records have to do with the trial against the five officers? I could see that Christopher's medical history might have some bearing on the case, but not the records from when he was in care, and especially not those of the rest of the family. Before the trial started, we had requested the release of the officers' medical records, suspecting they had assaulted Christopher and concerned by the revelation in their own notes that they had been to the hospital to get checked out the next day. But, despite their clear relevance to the case, the CPS told me they could not get the officers' medical documents for confidentiality reasons. Why didn't this same principle of confidentiality apply to me and my family when our documents were taken without our consent?

I was reminded of our time in the care home, when our rights were removed and our privacy was violated, with nothing we could do to stop it. Our personal childhood records were being passed around between my brother's killers behind our backs. It was like they were rubbing salt in our wounds. It just felt so wrong: as if we were the ones under investigation, that our rights meant nothing. To this day, no one from the CPS has given any explanation as to what information was disclosed.

The trial was taking its toll.

We were told at the inquest that the police were in possession of one of Christopher's missing teeth, which they claimed to have retrieved from the landfill site. Having now located Christopher's heart, we sought the return of the tooth as well, so that we could place them both with his body. So during the trial I approached Enzor and requested that my brother's tooth be returned to the family. He said he would get back to me.

A few days later, Enzor walked into the family room where we had been spending the morning break in the trial. He told me that he had spoken to Superintendent Holt, who had informed him that the tooth had been destroyed. I was in complete turmoil. It seemed that the very force whose own members were prime suspects in Christopher's death had taken it upon themselves to dispose of one of my brother's body parts – and yet neither the investigating force, nor the CPS – in fact, no one other than me and Ruth – seemed to be questioning why! I was so upset I stormed out of the meeting, went to the toilets and just sat and cried.

For me, the trial was an ordeal. I felt like I was being bullied and that any control I had over my life had been taken away. I developed constant nausea and bloating, and my digestion was totally messed up. Night after night I went back to the hotel terrified, often unable to join Ruggie and our supporters as I was mentally, emotionally and physically drained. Several times, Ruggie had to take me to hospital with severe asthma attacks – triggered, I believe, by trying to mask the trauma and suffering. On top of this, I was dealing with the guilt of being away from my home and children for eight weeks – not to mention the ongoing shock of witnessing what seemed to me like the woeful way the prosecution were conducting their case.

Following my complaint to Enzor about the way the trial was being conducted, he told me that my comments were unhelpful for my relationship with the prosecuting counsel team. He said that if I wanted to have continuing liaison with the prosecuting team then I should consider more carefully how I put my comments to them.

My unwillingness to compromise and accept what seemed to me absurd excuses for my brother's unexplained death made me very unpopular in court, and I soon learned that the CPS, the police lawyers and the investigating forces had been getting together to talk about me.

I was having my lunch in the family room one day when my phone rang; it was the junior CPS barrister. He told me that the prosecution, the defence, and West Yorkshire police had decided to make a complaint about me to the judge concerning the way I was reacting to some of the evidence. I was scared, and phoned a QC I knew to find out what this meant. He said I should be entitled to legal representation.

When I returned to the trial, I was summoned to stand in the dock. My family and supporters were vastly outnumbered by police officers and their families and I felt totally intimidated. I was aware that this was probably a provocation to aggravate my already fragile emotions and get me to react negatively in front of the judge. In an attempt to protect myself I simply said what I felt: that this was a witch-hunt. I felt like I was being punished for my refusal to accept the CPS's wilful bungling of the prosecution and that this was an attempt to break my will, put me back in my place and make a fool of me in front of the five officers on trial. All the lawyers were staring at the floor. I was the bottom of the pecking order and could be scapegoated at the will of the court.

None of the officers had ever stood in the dock and answered questions about what happened on the night of Christopher's death, either at the inquest or at the trial. But there I was, in the dock, when I had done nothing more than whimper in the corner and beg for an audience with the lawmakers.

But the judge seemed to have a tone of compassion in his voice when he stated he was not talking *to* me but *through* me to all those within the public gallery. I believe he was showing that he was aware of the inappropriate comments and giggles that had been coming from the family and police officers sat in the gallery behind me.

When it was over I had another asthma attack and was feeling so ill that Ruggie drove me to a doctor in Middlesbrough. The next day I stayed in the family room, still very raw and apprehensive about going back into the court's tense atmosphere. While I was sat there someone came into the room and told me I was being spoken about again in my absence. One of the police barristers had been complaining about me to the judge, requesting that I be dealt with more severely as I had plagued the police officers' lives for four years. When I entered the court and sat down, Ruggie told me to ask the judge for a transcript of the complaint. I did so, but the judge responded by asking me to come to the front of the court again before requesting that the police barrister repeat his complaint in my presence. The barrister, obviously embarrassed to confront me to my face, said, 'Your honour, I believe this is all just a distraction.' The whole thing felt like an engineered manoeuvre to break my spirit and humiliate me in front of the five police officers on trial.

Although no one had expected it to be, 21 June 2002 was the last day of the trial. The judge entered the court as normal, and everyone rose to their feet before sitting down again once he had taken his seat. My stomach was churning. The prosecution had completed their case – but the CPS team had given me no warning of what was about to happen. The air was like ice as the jury were called in.

It was now, I believed, the turn of the defence to make their case. But instead, the defence QC simply stood up and submitted that there was no case to answer. I was totally confused. I had been expecting to hear the defence and police officers give their version of events, their explanation of what had happened to Christopher on 1 April 1998, the answers they had refused to give the inquest on the grounds that this trial was forthcoming. What did he mean, no case to answer?

The defence QC sat back down. Then the judge began to speak: 'The prosecution have now called their evidence and the case is closed for the prosecution. Counsel on behalf of the defendants has submitted there is no case to be left to the jury. I do not intend that this ruling be a judgment on the detailed evidence I have heard during the prosecution case; it would be inappropriate for me to give such a judgment. I intend to give a ruling on the submissions that have been made to me. I shall do that in the presence of the jury.' I was in a cold sweat. Why did he not intend to give a judgment on the evidence put before him? I thought that was the job of a judge?

He continued: 'I do intend, having regard because of the

nature of this case and the level of interest in it, to set out in more detail than usual my reasons for reaching the conclusions I have.' The judge then recounted the events of 1 April 1998 – the altercation outside the Waterfront nightclub, Christopher being taken to hospital, his behaviour in the hospital – up to the point of the officers arresting him. He then noted how Christopher had been lucid and calm outside the hospital, but that within a five-minute journey he had become unconscious.

To prove the charge of manslaughter, the judge said the Crown had to establish that the officers owed Christopher a duty of care, that they had breached this duty, and that the breach was instrumental to his death; that is, that the officers' negligence was a significant contributing factor in Christopher's demise. I didn't understand what was going on. He was talking like he was summing the case up. But we still hadn't heard the defence! My heart was beating faster and faster; I felt like I was going to be sick.

The judge then talked about the medical experts, the inquest's unlawful killing verdict and the failure of the officers to overturn it. He explained how the Crown were not initially going to charge the officers with manslaughter, but that the family had, with great persistence and determination, found two experts to support the case, causing the Crown to change their mind. The judge then discussed how the Crown had presented experts who effectively contradicted their own case. I felt vindicated that he shared our concerns but remained anxious about where all this was leading.

He continued that everyone in the court had seen the officers put Christopher face down on the floor in front of the custody desk, and that all the police in the dock were present as Christopher breathed his last breath. He mentioned how all these events had been captured on CCTV, and that it was clear Christopher's level of consciousness was never assessed, that no medical help was summoned and that Christopher was not even put in the recovery position. He went on to say that first aid was only administered after it was realised that Christopher had stopped breathing and explained how the ambulance crew attended and attempted to revive him.

As he continued, the judge noted that 'the Prosecution has called medical witnesses ... whose evidence they knew did not support their case on manslaughter to the criminal standard of proof' and seemed to accept the Defence case that 'it is not open to the Prosecution to, in effect, invite the Jury to reject their evidence.' It all seemed to be heading in one direction.

The judge explained to the court that while he had in front of him the High Court judgment from Justice Jackson, he had not been able to refer to it during the trial as the CPS had not presented it as part of their voluntary bill application to add manslaughter to the charges.[1] It had not, therefore, been put in front of the jury and formed no part of the case. Yet Justice Jackson's judgment had shown that the evidence of Crane and Adgey would have been enough for the CPS to prove their case. In dismissing the officers' attempts to overturn the unlawful killing verdict of the inquest, Jackson had listed eight arguments as to why the verdict should be upheld; he said it was not only clear that there were breaches of duty by the officers but that the representatives of the officers at the inquest could not argue otherwise, and that the failure of the officers to get an ambulance, put Christopher in the recovery position, or check his airway and pulse until it was too late all 'militated towards' a finding of gross negligence.[2] Yet, to Judge Evans's bewilderment, the CPS had ensured that this damning judgment was never seen by the jury.

I was feeling so sick I thought I might faint. All that was going through my head was the vision of my brother being dumped face down on the cold stone floor with the five police officers stood around him, laughing as he lay dying. I couldn't face hearing what I could tell was going to be an acquittal. The thought of having to watch those officers walk out scot-free, with grins on their faces, without ever having had to open their mouths, was too much to bear. I left the court, ran to the family room and collapsed.

Later that day, the officers were cleared of all charges as the judge ordered the jury to acquit. The prosecution, he reasoned, had failed to make a case for either manslaughter or gross misconduct. The jury responded with loud gasps of disbelief.

I had had years of sleepless nights, having had to endure the horrific CCTV footage, trying again and again to challenge the CPS, followed by eight weeks sitting in court day in, day out, knowing that something was seriously wrong, and suffering with deteriorating health from the stress and trauma of it all. And in the end, the police officers walked free without having had to answer a single question about what happened to Christopher. What a terrible affront to Christopher, to me, to all of us.

After painfully going over this during the years that followed, I tried to comprehend the judge's reasoning, and did some research.

I now understand why the judge had to make the ruling he did on the evidence put forward. The CPS had simply failed to make a case; in fact, they had defended the officers by saying it was all an accident. Despite everything that could have been put to the court; all the comments, the evidence suggesting racism, the clear knowledge of Christopher's condition and clear refusal to do anything about it, the CPS had insisted there was no 'improper motive', destroying the chance of a misconduct conviction. And by both refusing to investigate what seemed to me like copious evidence of a police assault on Christopher, and failing to present clearly the medical evidence of death by neglect, they destroyed the chance of a manslaughter conviction. In essence, the CPS never even alleged that a crime had been committed.

In the guise of a 'prosecution', the CPS had effectively resuscitated the police's claim that their actions were not criminal, despite it having been so comprehensively demolished by the High Court. No wonder they sought to keep Justice Jackson's ruling away from the jury.

I found the whole court experience to be hugely damaging. It has only added to my lack of confidence in state institutions, which had already been instilled through our childhood maltreatment in care.

It seemed that the CPS preferred to spend their efforts getting me in the dock, a working-class mother who had already been rendered near to breaking point by their incompetence, rather than the five laughing police officers. Evidently, it didn't concern the CPS that those officers were able to avoid answering a single question regarding their involvement in the loss of Christopher's life, despite being the prime witnesses. No explanation was offered as to why Christopher was in the state he was in when they dragged him into the police station; nor was it asked for. To this day, they have never been made to divulge what they know.

I still couldn't understand what had gone on. Why had they called experts whose evidence flatly contradicted their own case?

Why did they choose to submit evidence that undermined their own key witnesses? Why didn't they leave that evidence to the defence and let the jury decide what they believed to be true?

Looking back on it, I think I suffered some kind of nervous breakdown after the officers' acquittal. I was already experiencing trauma and had been making emergency visits to the doctor's throughout the trial, with asthma attacks and palpitations. But adrenaline was keeping me going. Once the trial collapsed, everything caught up with me and I sank into a deep depression. There had been no justice for Christopher, and I felt like a failure for not having been able to hold anyone to account. My life began to slide away.

Christine and Herbert

c.1948–65

There was a knock on the door. My dad was at work and my three brothers were at school or nursery; my mum and I were the only ones in. We were dancing round the room, music blaring. I think it must have been winter as I remember a raging open fire; then again, the Hull climate was so much chillier than Nigeria that we could, I suppose, have had a fire going at any time. She answered the door to find a tall, smartly dressed, official-looking white man who told her he had come from Hull social services to see how she was coping. This is my earliest memory of my mum; I must have been about two.

Beyond fragments like these, what I know of my mum mainly comes from documents I received about ten years ago from the social services archives. My mother, Christine Alder (maiden name Christine Love), was described by social workers as a very attractive Black woman, feisty and full of energy. I don't remember her very well, but looking at the photocopied picture I have of her I can see that she was a beautiful, sophisticated-looking woman. She was born in a tiny village in Nigeria, and may well have lived there her whole life before coming to Great Britain. She and Herbert Alder, my father, came to England in, I believe, the early 1950s, at around the time of the *Empire Windrush*.[1]

Hull, the city my parents decided to make home, must have seemed very unfamiliar and disorientating. One of the social workers described my mum wearing a 'curtain' around her waist. It's reasonable to say that the 'curtain' Mum was accused of wearing could have been a beautiful batik African tribal wrap. I remember once looking through thick old leather belted cases at my dad's house – cases which had clearly not been touched for years and which my dad seemed to have forgotten about – and finding them full of these brightly coloured materials and gowns. Describing her dress this way shows just how much of a novelty Black people in Britain must have been to some people. This was the age when some B and Bs and hotels had signs on their doors openly declaring 'No Blacks, No Irish, No Dogs' and overt racism was part of the day-to-day experience of Black people. Even today, people of colour are a very small minority in Hull, unlike other major cities of a similar size like Leeds or Manchester; I can only imagine what it would have been like back in the fifties. While growing up I was aware that we were the only Black family on 12th Avenue; in fact, I think we were the only Black family on the whole of the North Hull estate. Moving so far across the world and then finding herself the only Black woman for miles must have been very lonely and isolating for my mum, something the social workers seem to have picked up on when describing her as the only coloured person in the district. I can only imagine the shock, disillusionment and feelings of homesickness she must have felt for her family, her lifestyle and everything she used to know.

For my dad, however, coming from Lagos, Hull must have

seemed like a slow-paced backwater. Lagos is the biggest city not only in Nigeria, but in the whole of Africa, bristling with people, traffic, businesses, and all the hustle and bustle of city life. The contrast with Mum's quiet village could not have been starker. Before coming to England, he had been a merchant seaman, so he would have been used to seeing new places, and had very likely been to England – and perhaps even Hull – several times in that role before finally coming to settle here.

My parents were never a traditional couple, even in Nigeria. For a start, they had broken the usual family traditions and rules of marriage by marrying across tribal lines: my father was of the Yoruba tribe and my mum from the Igbo. Such intermarriage was probably just as controversial, and with a similar stigma, to two people of different cultures being together in England in the 1950s. It was just not the done thing in those days, and I wonder whether that stigma, along with the dream of a happy prosperous life in the UK, could have been one of the reasons they decided to travel to England in the first place.

There was a roughly ten-year age gap between my parents, my father having been born in 1916 and my mum some time in the mid-1920s. Mum stayed at home and was left on her own quite a lot looking after us children while Dad worked long hours to keep his family. When he did have spare time, he spent a lot of it with friends he had got to know through work and settling in England, including other men that had migrated from Africa. Eventually, and with great difficulty, Mum started to make friends outside the family, and socialised with people on the estate. She seemed quite contented for a while, but at some point she started to disappear for days on end, going out on a Saturday night and not returning until Monday. She had got to know quite a few people, some from as far away as Liverpool.

As time went on, these problems with her staying away from home began to grow.

With the five of us children born between 1958 and 1965, my mum must have had years when she was pregnant almost all the time. They say it takes about two years for a woman's body to recover after birth. My mum never had time to get her hormones in balance before being pregnant again – and her unstable behaviour deteriorated as the years went by, either when pregnant or after each child.

I've often thought about my mum's experience of pregnancy and compared it to my own. I suffered postnatal depression after the birth of my son, which made me consider whether postnatal depression could also have been the cause of some of my mother's illness; studies have suggested it can be hereditary.[2] It was bad enough for me, but back in the fifties and early sixties it must have been even harder as the condition was virtually unrecognised.

By the time my older brothers were born, my mum's behaviour had become more and more erratic, and eventually she was diagnosed with schizophrenia. The records show that she picked up her tablets every week, but also that she was having some other kind of treatment as well, which was blacked out of the documents before they were handed to me. I can only guess this was electro-convulsive therapy. She must have missed her home, her village and the security of her extended family so much. I suspect that my experience was a fraction of what she suffered for years on end.

Mum spent more and more time hospitalised; she had been a very energetic, feisty woman, but now she was always heavily sedated and medicated. Social workers reported that you could tell she had not moved from the settee for days. At one point, she was seen on the stairs of the flats where we lived, with me in her arms, threatening to throw me down the stairs if social services didn't leave her alone. Violence and frustration seemed to go hand in hand with Mum's illness and my brothers, being older, remember being on the receiving end of it. I was too young to recall any of this. Once again she was shipped off to De la Pole Hospital in Hull, remaining there until after the birth of her last child, Stephen.

After the Trial

2002

Slowly but surely, my life began to fall apart. I was feeling dowdy, and my home was becoming a tip, with papers all over the place. The house was completely dark, as the hedge outside had grown sky high. My hair started to fall out and I became more and more of a recluse, only going out when I needed to do something for the campaign. I was an emotional and psychological mess. At the same time, I felt invisible, as if nobody could really see what was happening to me. Everybody thought that I was just soldiering on, but no one could see the damage being done.

Then there was the press. The phone calls began immediately after the trial, all wanting to know more about the collapse of the case. I was already devastated by the verdict, and talking to the press seemed to intensify it. I had to listen to them repeating again and again that the officers had been acquitted, they'd been found not guilty, none of the charges had been proven, and asking me how I felt about it all. The only word I could think of was 'sick'. Everything I had worked for had fallen apart and now it was all being thrown back at me, as if I was mad and they'd all been innocent all along. Although I put on a brave face, on the inside all those feelings of inadequacy came flooding back.

As I crumbled, I felt like I was neglecting my children. Before Christopher's death I would have the washing and ironing all done, with good home-cooked meals on the table every day, but all that seemed to be dwindling away. Caroline had moved out by this time – she was twenty-three – but I still had Nathan with me. I was trying my best but I was finding it hard to keep things together. I was still looking after him – I was very protective – but I was no longer the mother that I had been before. My experiences with state power had changed me. In this low emotional state, I was dangerously vulnerable – a sitting duck, really. It is clear to me now that I had lost all sense of my own self-worth. That was when I met Ben Almond.

It was about a month after the trial and I had finally gathered the strength to do something about the hedge. It was a beautiful day and the sun was shining, when a young man pulled up in his car and wound down the window. 'All right, Janet?' he said, and we started chatting. I had seen him around on the estate and we knew each other's names but not much more than that. He was wearing a Muslim prayer hat and, as this was the time of the war on terror, I thought this was his way of showing solidarity with Muslims under attack. A few days later he knocked on my door, and I invited him in for a brew. After that, he started coming over quite often; he was my release – a distraction from everything that was going on and all the pressure I was under. Like me, he seemed to be someone who asked questions, and didn't necessarily accept the authorities' answers. Unlike the other people around me at the time, Ben seemed to understand my vulnerability; he saw a side of me that nobody else seemed to be able to. While I hadn't cried in years, he would sometimes break down in tears, and it felt like he was connecting with my pain. It was a great relief and I felt understood.

Whatever faith I had left in social institutions had collapsed along with the trial. I needed to believe in something, and so I was looking to believe in the ordinary people around me. Ben spoke a lot about the loss of his father and how he had been emotionally abused, which had left him deeply scarred. But, as they had done with me and my brothers, the authorities had turned a blind eye. Both childhood victims of abuse and state neglect, we seemed to share a natural affinity. But my feet were far from the ground; my mind was far from clear.

Going into Care

1961–5

The long hours Dad worked at Smith & Nephew[1] meant he couldn't be at home with Mum. The social workers commented that our house was not being kept clean or to a standard they found acceptable, and soon my father was again summoned to court by the NSPCC. My three older brothers, Richard, Emmanuel and Christopher, had been taken before the juvenile courts in 1961 and briefly committed into state authority care. This happened again in 1962. Hessle Homes was a complex of separate houses donated and funded by the sailors and fishermen of Hull, originally for children that had lost parents at sea. Hull's main industry in those days was fishing, run from its bustling dockyards, but over time, the Hessle Homes orphanages were opened up to help other families with problems or suffering family breakdowns.

I was lucky as, being just over one at the time, I was considered too young to be taken away from my mother, who it was thought should be able to cope with one child. As my father was compelled to pay for the keep of my brothers in the children's home, however, this meant he needed to work extra hours, leaving Mum on her own for longer periods of time. Combined with her unfamiliarity with England, her lack of a support network, and her illness, this must have placed enormous pressures and strains on them both and I can only imagine how helpless they felt.

Social services had decided that it was essential for my older brothers to be kept together, and in around 1963 or '64, they were moved to a smaller, more close-knit children's home in Marlborough Avenue. Shortly afterwards, I too was taken to join my brothers in care. I went back and forth between the care home and my parents a few times before being eventually committed to the full-time care of the state in 1965, at the age of three.

Injustice

2002–3

Despite my emotional turmoil, I continued to campaign and address meetings; Andy would often arrange for me to go to two or three events per week or more and I felt I owed it to Christopher to take every opportunity I could to speak out.

At the time, Ken Fero's film *Injustice* was being shown by community groups around the country, and I would sometimes be asked to speak after a screening. It was at one of these screenings that I met Terry Stewart from the Harry Stanley campaign.

Harry Stanley was a Scottish man who had moved to London in his teens. On 22 September 1999 he was shot dead by the Metropolitan Police, who claimed to have thought he was Irish and that the table leg he was carrying was a gun. His inquest had returned an 'open verdict' on the same day that the officers in Christopher's case were acquitted. Terry told the meeting that the campaign would continue and that the family were appealing against the coroner's refusal to allow the jury to consider unlawful killing as a cause of death.[1]

I spoke to Terry afterwards and brought him up to date with what had happened at Christopher's trial. He explained to me that, as well as criminal prosecutions, it was also possible to bring private civil proceedings in cases like ours, and he recommended a solicitor – Jane Deighton – who could help. Back in Burnley, I got in touch with her and we started working on the case along with Christopher's children who were then still in their teens. We were determined to fight on. I also contacted the campaign group Liberty, and they offered to help me take the case to the European Court of Human Rights. Humberside Police had not heard the last of me yet.

In July 2003 I received a letter from the attorney general. He wrote that while the death of a person in custody is a tragedy for the family, any suspicions that the legal process had failed to provide justice had a negative impact that goes 'beyond those immediately bereaved'. He had come to the conclusion that the judge's decision not to allow the prosecution case to proceed raised legal issues that required clarification and he had, therefore, referred the issue of misconduct to the Court of Appeal. He hoped that this review would help make future prosecutions of deaths in custody more open and accountable.

I showed the letter to Ruth, who requested that we be allowed to attend the hearing and put forward our own submissions. It was refused. So much for openness and accountability.

I continued to travel around the country for the campaign. Later that year, I spoke at the National Black Police Association conference in Cardiff at the invitation of its chair, Ravi Chand. Put up in a hotel full of police officers, some of them dressed in full regalia, I couldn't help but feel intimidated. I went quickly to my room and locked the door for the night. When I arrived at the conference the next morning, the place was already full of police officers, most of them Black and Asian. I sat and heard stories of the difficulties they'd had gaining promotions to the higher ranks, many of which were truly shocking. Then David Blunkett, the home secretary, approached the platform and all I could think was, Yes! I will get the opportunity to tell him about Christopher! But by the time it was my turn to speak, he had gone. With pearls of sweat dripping from my brow, I walked up the stairs to the podium, behind which stood a massive TV screen beaming my face out across the crowd. It was a scary experience, but I'm glad I did it. I told that room full of police officers what their colleagues had done to Christopher.

The Goodhands

1965

My mum's illness was thrust onto my parents in circumstances they had no control over. The closeness of my mother's pregnancies had left her in a fragile state, and if my own experience of postnatal depression is anything to go by, she must at times have felt like she was in another world, the inhabitant of a distant planet with no name.

She had come from a small village in Africa, with its communal life and the support of an extended family, and she was completely isolated in Hull, with no one that resembled her or her lifestyle for miles around, having to deal with the racial prejudice of the time, the bodily and hormonal disruption of one pregnancy after another, her illness, being taken into hospital against her will and having electric probes strapped to her head. She must have been completely petrified; she very likely thought they were trying to kill her.

In November 1965, she returned to Nigeria. She had clearly been finding life in Britain very difficult, but it was never explained to us exactly why she went. We never saw her again. My brother Stephen came to live with us in the care home, at just four months old.

It must have been a very traumatic and painful time for my dad. When I read his letters begging the social services not to take his children away, I imagine him crying night after night, wondering where things had gone wrong. I know from my own experience as a parent that when things don't turn out as expected, it can feel like a meteor colliding with your world. Despite his many letters, ultimately he lost all control and choice over when and where he was allowed to see us, as well as any privacy over what he earned, how he spent his money, and with regard to any female relationships he might have in the future. For the rest of his life, he would be closely monitored and controlled by Hull social services and the courts. I'm sure he never imagined for one minute, when he came to Britain after marrying his beautiful bride, that this was to be the eventual outcome.

The care home was not free; my dad handed over half his wages to go towards our staying there. With his own rent, gas and electricity, and petrol for the car he used for work to pay for too, this didn't leave him with an awful lot to survive on. Yet if he ever missed a payment, they were immediately on his back with court orders. To pay the costs of our care, my father sought a better paid job, eventually finding one at Hawker Siddeley Aviation in Brough. This meant eleven-hour night shifts spraying aircrafts and aeroplanes, providing a weekly wage of £29, of which social services decided he should pay £12 for the keep of his children. I feel sad when I look back at the many letters from the social services administrators threatening to take him to court for default of payments. I now understand how the stresses and strains started to show on my father, whose health quickly began to deteriorate. He suffered from heart disease and high blood pressure, and I remember his breathing being very laboured at times, especially when he was asleep, exhausted after a full week of working nights. It was probably not helped by the spray paints he was exposed to on a daily basis, containing who-knows-what metals and chemicals in those days. I remember seeing paper masks dotted around the house, presumably for health and safety reasons – not a very advanced attempt to protect his lungs. Workplace health and safety was taken far less seriously back then.

My dad provided as best he could, with no idea he was paying for his children to be treated as cruelly as we were. He would have gone ballistic if he had found out about the abuse that was being inflicted on us; in fact, it would probably have killed him. Many a time he was in confrontation with Mrs Goodhand, the care home house parent, about the need to give us some understanding about our cultural background, but in no way was he aware of the rough treatment of his children he unknowingly worked so hard to provide.

Mrs Goodhand wasn't keen on my father and she wasn't shy about telling the social services her feelings about him. One social worker said she referred to him as 'Mr Hell' and would get hysterical when speaking about him. She showed him no compassion and was unsympathetic about him being forced to give up his children and having to watch us homed in a totally unfamiliar environment, his rights as a parent taken from him by the state. In fact, she seemed to despise him.

My father was a solemn man, but extremely handsome and very smartly dressed. He was in his time a bit of a ladies' man, I believe; I certainly remember seeing one or two other Mrs Alders around in Hull over the years. He was over six foot tall and always dressed in suits, with a trilby on his head and smart colourful ties with massive knots. He worked hard: he had been in the army and had various jobs in England and Nigeria, including fireman as well as merchant seaman. I recall him being an avid Labour Party supporter (in the days when you could easily differentiate Labour from any other party), and I remember the red and yellow leaflets and stickers that were fixed in his window at every election. He took his responsibilities seriously, both as a breadwinner and as a citizen, and took a great interest in the politics of both England and Nigeria.

I felt he did what he could under the circumstances he found himself in. I believe he genuinely thought that staying and being brought up in England was the best thing for us – that we would have a better chance in life than we would have done being brought up in poverty in Nigeria. Mrs Goodhand once said I would 'defend my dad and my brothers to the end', and she was right. I don't harbour any resentment for my mum or dad, and my experiences in life have only made me realise how difficult and how much harder it must have been for them both in the 1950s.

Police Disciplinary

2003–4

Soon after the acquittal, I had been contacted by a woman called Sally Hawkins who had taken over from Jim Elliott as caseworker at the PCA. She explained that she'd had a meeting with Chris Enzor from the CPS and that her role was now to look at the officers facing some sort of disciplinary action. This had been put off until after the criminal trial, but I knew where it would lead: a slap on the wrist and some extra training, at best. It's as though there is an unwritten law that the worst penalty that police officers involved in unexplained or suspicious deaths should ever have to face is a training programme. Actual *justice* is off limits. I told her I didn't want any involvement in a disciplinary hearing and that the only thing I would consider participating in was a full public inquiry into all the issues surrounding Christopher's death, the cover-up and the botched prosecution. I had nothing against her, but she had been given the unfortunate job of smoothing things over – and I wanted no part of it. I told her there was nothing more to say: the trial had, I believed, been set to fail, I had lost all faith in the British legal system and I was now looking into the possibility of taking the case to the European Court.

She replied by letter to Ruth and said that she appreciated our belief that a public inquiry would consider all aspects of the case in a coherent and open manner, but that if I wished to complain through the existing channels, she could lodge a complaint on my behalf to West Yorkshire Police about their investigation. I declined the offer. By then I was fully aware that complaining to one police force about another was like trying to quench your thirst by drinking a bucket of sand.

Despite Sally's efforts, my opinion of the PCA declined further when I attended one of their seminars in London in May 2003. I had arranged to go there with Terry Stewart.

As we walked in, the PCA were setting out their annual report and we were handed a copy. When I opened it, I couldn't believe my eyes: right there in the report was a photograph of me and some of our supporters walking into Teesside Crown Court. I wondered how they'd got hold of this picture and could only think it must have come from Cleveland Police, who had been standing outside the court and in the foyer taking photographs. But they had told us all their footage had been destroyed. My heart skipped a beat. This report went to all the police stations in Britain, and a picture taken of me and my solicitor without our consent had been placed in it. Were they setting me up to be stopped by every police officer in the country that didn't agree with me standing up to them? I found it rather eerie. When I got home, I complained about it to Ruth, who wrote to the PCA asking for an explanation. They responded with a feeble apology, which was too little, too late.

Sally Hawkins continued to be in contact, so I took the opportunity to ask her why the PCA had not discovered the monkey noises on the CCTV footage. I was told my solicitors hadn't noticed it either, but this was nonsense, as Leslie and Ruth had never been provided with this part of the footage.

In due course, Sally Hawkins wrote her report. For the first time consideration was given to whether the actions of the officers had been influenced by race; everyone else dealing with the case was still in denial – trying, for example, to pass off the monkey noises as no more than the matron laughing strangely. The report also noted the contradictions in what the officers had claimed about their awareness of Christopher's condition, and made these comments part of their application for the disciplinary process. However, when it came to action, the report was predictably weak, recommending simply that, as the officers with the primary duty of care for detainees in the police station, Dunn (the custody sergeant) and Barr (the cell warder) should be admonished, while all five of the officers involved should be seen by the chief constable and given advice regarding duty of care and receive remedial training in this area. And once again, what was not being investigated was what had caused Christopher to receive additional injuries and lose a second tooth and his belt. It felt like another whitewash. A man lay dead having become unconscious in a police van, with all the evidence of what happened in the van destroyed by the force that arrested him – and all that the Police Complaints Authority could recommend was training the officers in their duty of care.

The disciplinary hearing was conducted by the chief constable of Cleveland Police, Sean Price, behind closed doors on 19 June 2003. He swiftly concluded that there was no case to answer.[1] Again, I was sickened; however much you expect and prepare yourself for these outcomes, it never makes them any less crushing.

Concerned by the lack of disciplinary action, Ruth joined forces with Helen Shaw, co-director of Inquest, to write a public letter about the hearing:

As in all these cases, the Humberside Chief Constable must be brought to account over this death and the wider concerns it raises about police treatment of Black people and those with head injuries.

But in addition the systemic failures within the PCA, CPS and the whole investigation process must be urgently addressed. There is a disturbing pattern of cases where the police have failed to prevent deaths, and the criminal justice system has failed to bring those responsible to account. Christopher Alder's death once again brings the entire criminal justice system and the role of the CPS into disrepute.

The Government must take action so that when someone dies at the hands of the State the procedures that follow ensure accountability, openness, truth and justice. The failure of the current system denies bereaved families justice and sends a clear message that Black deaths in custody do not matter.

*Helen Shaw
Co-Director
Ruth Bundey
Harrison Bundey & Co
INQUEST 2004*

Sally Hawkins later told the IPCC that she had been very tense at the disciplinary hearing, facing officers who blamed her for initiating the proceedings against them. She said she felt bullied by the police. She also said that she felt the evidence should have been presented differently and more forcefully, and that it wasn't presented as powerfully as she thought it could have been. All I could think was, you and me both. It was exactly what I had felt at the criminal trial. And although I wasn't happy to hear she had been bullied, I did feel that at least there was now someone who could empathise with me, having suffered a little taste of the intimidating treatment I had received at the hands of police officers who cannot brook their impunity being challenged.

Care

1963–72

Our first care home was Hessle Homes, run by the NSPCC, where I went from the age of around two. But the one I remember most was 71 Marlborough Avenue, where we moved to about a year later. It had a large front bay, diamond-leaded windows, an arched glass door and an inner porch before the entrance to the grand house. The children entered the house at the back, via a big wooden gate that led to the garden. I loved that garden. It was massive, with a big horse chestnut tree; its conker shells were rather smooth compared to the spikey ones the other trees tended to produce, and in the spring it ornamented itself with an array of pink blossom rather than the usual white. Whenever I was sat 'in solitary' in my room, that tree would comfort me. I would look out of the window at the tree, eyeing up the biggest conker, making sure I kept my eye on it as it grew, ready to collect it before the other kids had a chance; as soon as it fell to the ground, I was out there, making sure I got it. The tree also taught me the seasons, as I watched the bare branches begin to sprout sticky buds, then flowers and flickers of greenery, before finally bursting into full bloom. Many a time I leaned out the window, praying to

God that things would change, before getting distracted as I watched big bumble bees and wasps busy at work in and out of the pink flowers.

The area was lovely. Westbourne, Marlborough and Victoria Avenue were all very similar: grand avenues with cast-iron fountains in the centre of the roads decorated with mermaids and herons. The council regularly filled the fountain basins with bedding plants, and in summer they were an array of bright colours. Trees of all types lined the grass verges from one end to the other, dividing the road from the houses.

When it was first built, in the years between 1875 and the outbreak of World War I, these avenues must have housed some of the richest and most affluent people in Hull. I used to imagine what the house was like when it had servants. I clearly remember the servants' bell system box fixed to the wall in the kitchen, still in its original form, although no longer working. It looked as if it must have been electric, with cords in each room to light up the bell box, showing the servants which room had requested them. Those early inhabitants would never have guessed that a load of children in care – or 'orphans' as we were described in those days – would one day be living among all this grandeur.

Ken and Jo Goodhand were our live-in 'house parents' – but it soon became clear that it was 'Auntie Jo' who ran the show. A well-proportioned woman, neither fat nor particularly thin, she always wore dark-coloured ski pants and thin, polyester jumpers in different pastel colours. To me, she seemed the type of woman that would spend her time pulling her husband down to gain control. After all, this was something she practised on us children on a daily basis. She would humiliate us by slapping us across the face and breaking us down to the point of feeling worthless. And when we were in trouble, she would scream in our faces until she was as red as the nail varnish she wore.

Those red nails came to me in my nightmares like red-hot flames. Witches would climb through the bedroom window to get me, their fingernails slowly coming closer and closer, causing me to scream out loud, waking up the whole household. No matter what I did, I could not stop these nightmares. As soon as I closed my eyes, I knew the same repeated nightmare was about to start. It was the only time I was unable to stop my feelings coming out.

Ken Goodhand did as he was told, and would do anything to please his wife. But he was vicious in the way he dealt out the beatings she ordered him to give us. And if we encountered him in a corridor, we had to swerve out of the way quickly as he routinely kicked us up our backsides with great force as we passed; I can still remember the thrust of the felt slippers he wore. I must have been about four when I saw him kick one of the older boys so hard that he was sent reeling into an outside drain, banging his face against the wall. I don't remember what he'd done to warrant this.

Ken would administer regular beatings with prongs of wood from dining chairs, though never without instruction from his wife. I still feel stunned when I think about those beatings. She regularly hen-pecked and humiliated him in front of people, and he seemed to take out his frustration and pent-up aggression on us. It was frightening to see how much control she had over him, and what she was able to make him do. We would be sent into a state of panic when she told us he would soon be home from work. But even when he returned, 'Auntie Jo' would make us wait until after our tea and then queue outside the dining room to 'get the stick'. We never knew how long we would have to wait – because that was decided by Mr Goodhand, who would let us know when he was good and ready.

One by one we would go into the dining room, while the rest were left standing outside, listening to the shrieks of agony from the child who had last gone in. Down with our pants, then we had to bend over the chair, fingers clinging tightly to the edges – as if that would help – as each stroke throbbed and smarted as he battered our bare behinds. Ken Goodhand dished out his ill-treatment with an aggression and coarseness that would leave us shaking, crying and distraught. I think the pain bonded the children in Marlborough Avenue; we had a kind of unspoken understanding based on shared trauma.

Ben Almond

2003–5

All throughout this period, I was drifting further and further away from my old friends. They were worried about my being with Ben, but instead of sitting me down to explain their concerns, they seemed to be getting angry with me. It was as if they'd lost respect for me because of my relationship. And my being in the public eye made things worse. On a night out, I suddenly realised that people I barely knew, or didn't know at all, were crowding round me. All these people started sitting next to us, trying to get close; it was really weird. It was as if, because I'd been on television, they were treating me like I'd become a celebrity. I couldn't cope with it; I felt like I was choking, gasping for air, and I just wanted to withdraw into myself. I found it hard to explain to anyone how I was feeling, and I wasn't even sure myself. I barely went out socially after that.

Then there was Ben's ex. Although she had wanted rid of him, she was still furious about us, and would send racist texts to him about me, calling me a monkey and other offensive terms. Nathan saw one of them on Ben's phone once by mistake. At other times she would come round to my house to have it out. I didn't want a confrontation, so I didn't tend to respond. But one day she came to the pub where I worked on a Friday and started being rude to me, swearing and calling me a nigger. I went to the toilet to escape but she followed me in and carried on. We ended up in a fist fight, and she came out worst. So she went to the police. Of course, Lancashire Police couldn't wait to get hold of me; they called me on the Saturday and I explained what had happened. They told me to go into the station the following day. I went in at noon and they held me until 8 p.m., with Nathan alone in the house all this time, wondering what was going on. Even then I was only released because Ruth had organised for a junior solicitor to come to the station to get me released on bail. It just seemed vindictive to me. Then, when the solicitor was signing the documents for my release, the copper said to him, 'She won't go to the papers about *me*, will she?'

When it went to court, the judge just threw it out. I was telling the truth and she was the aggrieved ex; he saw right through it. But for that Lancashire officer, it had just been an opportunity to detain me. I wouldn't be surprised if he had phoned Hull to tell them all about it as soon as he heard my name.

The shock, knock-backs and bullying were all taking their toll on me. After the collapse of the trial my expectations had been crushed, and this reinforced all those feelings of low self-esteem I thought I had laid to rest. I was becoming less aware of my own feelings, and stopped really caring for myself. But my worries about Nathan were magnified. He was in his teens now, starting to get strong and starting to rebel – and I felt he was at serious risk from the police. I knew they had been following me and I began to worry they would start targeting him too. Young Black boys seemed to be a particular focus of police violence and I knew all too well how that could end. I was terrified of what they might do to Nathan. They had already targeted my other brother Richard and I was determined not to let that happen to my son. But I didn't know how to protect him. I felt like he needed more than I could give; he was at a very susceptible age and I felt useless.

I was also starting to worry about how Ben's behaviour was affecting Nathan. Ben was still bursting into tears all the time, and it was hardly creating a very stable emotional environment. Then one day I walked through the kitchen to see that Ben had Nathan up against the door, supposedly playfighting with him. I just flipped; it's not how I wanted my son to be treated. I would never have a man in the house that would challenge my son. 'Oh no,' I said, 'that doesn't happen in my house.' They stopped, and that was the end of it, but it had rung an alarm bell for me.

But then one day, Nathan came running into the house all shook up. He had been in the front garden of his friend's house when a man came down the street with a baseball bat, apparently on his way to my house. 'Which one of you is Janet's son?' he had asked the group of boys in the garden. Nathan said he was, and this man punched him in the face. He was Ben's ex's brother. I was furious; I wanted to kill him. But I also felt guilty, because I had introduced these characters into Nathan's life.

That was when I knew I had totally lost control of what was happening and couldn't do anything to protect my son. I knew I had to get Nathan out of there, somewhere he would be protected, and away from the Hull police. So I decided to send him to Scotland to live with his dad. He was fifteen years old. It was the most painful decision I have ever had to make.

Taken but Unwanted

1963–77

I remember one Saturday after *Tarzan* had been on the TV, we were all doing the Tarzan call, jumping off the chairs with delirious excitement. The boys were arguing about who was the real Tarzan when one of my brothers put the poker in the fire. I had been playing his elephant – and now it was time for my branding. I put out my arm, but drew it away quickly as soon as the poker came out of the fire, shrieking 'Noooo!' 'You don't hear the horses cry, do you?' he said. I looked over at the poker, and it just looked grey, with no sign of it being red hot. Reluctantly, I put out my hand. He touched me with the poker and my skin just seemed to unravel in front of my eyes, peeling backwards off my hand and starting to bleed. I screamed.

'Don't say I did it!' my brother begged me.

'I won't,' I sobbed.

I don't think he had any idea that the poker might have still been hot or of the pain it would have caused. The house mother came dashing in and I told her I had caught it on the chair. She told me to shut up and took me out of the room. She put my hand under the cold tap, causing it to sting even more, then placed a plaster on it and sent me back into the playroom. This was about as much empathy as could be expected by the children in Marlborough Avenue: there was certainly no chance of a cuddle or a soothing word. It was clear from our social care records that Mrs Goodhand had no love for me and my siblings, even to the point of threatening to leave her role if we stayed there any longer.

We all had to endure a beating from Mr Goodhand whenever it was believed we had done something wrong, but my beatings were daily because I wet the bed. Every night after dinner I was summoned by the house father for punishment, but I never knew exactly when the moment would come. The wait was excruciating. Sat copying out chapters from the Bible, I'd listen for Mr Goodhand to arrive home from work. On his return he would set about making tea for himself and his wife. My mouth would be watering at the smell of lamb chops, liver and onions – food that we children were never fortunate enough to taste – but at the same time my heart was racing like the clappers, as I waited in apprehension for the inevitable. It was the sound of his footsteps coming down the corridor that finally braced me for what was coming. He would summon me into the dining room with just one word: 'Through.' As I entered the room, he pulled out a dining chair. I had to pull down my pants and crouch over it, knees not quite touching the floor as I wasn't big enough, and grip the seating area with my hands. Then came the whacks, over and over again sometimes; I never knew quite how many there would be. I cried a lot at first, but eventually the overwhelming humiliation led me to force back the tears, denying him his 'victory', but also denying myself the chance to express my pain. Sometimes I wonder if all the sporting activity I engaged in after school was a subconscious attempt to dull the pain and impact, firming up my gluteus maximus, and building up enough endorphins to numb the pain and block out the trauma. After a time I stopped crying altogether, the humiliation lodged as a lump in my throat. The memory still brings unflowing tears to my eyes. And even today, when I get a strong feeling of empathy, especially if I see or hear of others subjected to physical pain, I experience a pain running through my legs. Any suffering sends what seems like an electric current through my sympathetic nervous system, and I feel guilt for that pain. My nightly beatings continued for many years.

After Christopher's death, I received a letter from one of the boys we had grown up with in Marlborough Avenue, reflecting on our experiences there. He described me being held up by the heels, naked, and thrashed with a stick by Mr Goodhand in front of the other children, and said it was the sickest scene he had ever witnessed. He said that my brothers 'also received special attention' but this is the kind of treatment that all the children were subjected to at Marlborough Avenue.

Eventually I was taken to the doctor about my bedwetting. He diagnosed the cause as laziness, and provided the Goodhands with a wire mesh to place under my sheets. A wire attached the mesh to a buzzer box which stood in the middle of the room and would sound an alarm and emit a bright red circle of light whenever it detected moisture. Obviously this didn't help; it was supposed to train my mind to wake me up to go to the toilet, but all it did was send me into a panic once it was already too late. Alarm blaring, red light flashing, and my head still full of nightmares, Mr Goodhand would storm into the room and scream at me for waking everyone up. Then I would need to strip the bed and get clean sheets from the airing cupboard, knowing that I would be beaten in punishment the next day. I would climb back into bed, petrified of going back to sleep, as I knew it risked more nightmares, more bedwetting and a repeat of the whole horrific scene.

If by some miracle I wet the bed without waking the house parents, I would do whatever I could to stop them finding out. Many a time I would beg an older girl to help me creep past the Goodhands' room to find the clean linen from the airing cupboard, and then hide the wet sheets, usually in the most obvious of places. I even took to sneaking out of the fire exit to the dustbin to dispose of them. The only time I could relax was when I was at school. School was great, as it meant an escape from all this for seven hours, but as time ticked by, and it got nearer and nearer to home time, my instincts usually told me I'd been caught, that the hidden wet sheets had been found. A few times I got away with it, but this was unusual. And if I'd been caught, a beating awaited.

For some unknown reason, Mrs Goodhand was convinced that I didn't wet the bed at my father's house, and that that was because he smacked me. In fact, I wet the bed there too, but my father wasn't one for checking; week after week I slept on the same crusted, yellow, ammonia-smelling sheets. But the social service records show that one minute Mrs Goodhand said I didn't wet the bed at my father's, the next she was complaining that I was returning from weekends at my dad's with my nightie stiff with dried urine. I honestly believe she thought I did it on purpose, to get on her nerves and seek attention.

One of Mrs Goodhand's therapies for my bedwetting was for me to wash, dry and polish all the cutlery in the kitchen drawer, and then to sit at the kitchen table and copy chapters out of the New Testament while the other children watched TV in the playroom next door. But the words I was writing, about love, kindness and forgiveness, seemed to be in total contradiction to the kind of life we lived at 71 Marlborough Avenue.

When the social workers paid their visits to the home, my brothers and I attempted to tell them of the cruelty we were being subjected to, and requested to be sent back to Hessle Homes, where the staff had been very kind. They'd seem to listen to us and empathise, but the next minute they'd have a meeting with the house parents, and we'd never hear anything more about it. The social workers were aware I wet the bed at least once a night, but Mrs Goodhand had managed to convince them that this was something I did only while in the children's home, and could therefore only be down to sheer laziness. The social workers also knew that I had been caught going to the airing cupboard for clean sheets and throwing the wet ones in the dustbins outside in the middle of the night; she told them there was no excuse for that, as all I needed to do was bring them downstairs in the morning to be washed and then have a bath. She neglected to tell them that I had to wait for everyone else to use the bathroom first, making me miss my breakfast and arrive late to school. Nor did she tell them that the bath had to be stone cold, as part of my punishment. Nor, of course, did she tell them about the beatings that I received every time I wet the bed.

Wetting the bed every night was something I didn't grow out of until I was around fifteen or sixteen, and up until around the age of twelve it meant mental punishment and daily physical beatings. If we should ever go to bed early, I was filled with fear and dread because it gave me more opportunity to wet the bed, perhaps twice. Even hearing the blackbird's song triggered an onset of anxiety, as I knew it was the last song at dusk, and meant that the night and its horrors was nearing.

The CPS

2003–5

I carried on as best I could, saying nothing to anyone and trying to keep a smile on my face, just like I had done as a child. The whole experience in the years that followed Christopher's death had traumatised me, and after Nathan left, all of a sudden the constant adrenaline surge I had been on for six years stopped with an almighty crash. I missed my son terribly; we had been very close before this had happened, and the guilt ate away at me. He resented being sent away, especially as there was turmoil between his dad and his dad's partner. But at least I knew that he wasn't in danger there. His dad was a good bloke. Whereas Ben, I was starting to learn, could be extremely violent. He had hit people with hammers. I'd got Nathan out of that madness, but I was still deep in it myself. I just couldn't find a way to get away from the constant tension and dread. The atmosphere was nerve-wracking.

Throughout all of this I was still attempting to get to the truth of what had happened to Christopher and why the CPS had sabotaged the trial. I got hold of the trial transcript and documents and started trying to make sense of what had gone on.

The judge in the officers' trial had recognised that among all the contradictory information presented by the CPS, there was evidence that was favourable to the prosecution – namely the independent medical experts tracked down by me and Ruth. Those experts had categorically stated that it could be proven to a criminal standard that the actions of the officers contributed to Christopher's death, and it was this that had enabled the voluntary bill to be granted. Yet the experts connected to the state, such as those commissioned by the Home Office and the CPS, said they could *not* be absolutely certain that the officers' actions had hastened his death. A letter from the director of public prosecutions to my MP on 4 October 2001, which noted that the conflicting medical evidence was being reviewed, revealed how early the CPS were aware of the contradictions. Standard practice would have been for the prosecution to call the witnesses who supported their case, leaving any contradictory evidence to the defence.

We wrote to the CPS, raising a formal complaint that the trial had been set to fail. On 7 November 2002, Ruth received a reply from Chris Enzor, expressing surprise that I had complained some three-and-a-half months after the trial had ended. Obviously, the CPS's goldfish memory was kicking in again, conveniently forgetting that I had already written to him about this issue on 8 May, not to mention expressing my concern that the prosecution case was being deliberately thrown in numerous conversations around the trial itself.

It's hard to believe that the CPS had not anticipated that their presentation of conflicting medical evidence would result in an acquittal for the officers. How many successful murder or manslaughter cases had the Crown actually won by presenting conflicting evidence that undermined their own case? As the campaigning charity Inquest later put it, 'Following the successful application for a voluntary bill, the Crown at every stage was generous to the Defence and chose to call all the medical experts as part of the prosecution case, instead of presenting at that stage to the jury only experts who were clear, credible and certain.' It seemed clear to me that their mixing of the evidence in this way was done purposely, in order to achieve the result it did – the case being thrown out before the officers could be questioned. The CPS had, after all, been forced to mount a prosecution they had never wanted, having refused for years to bring charges of manslaughter. Bringing the prosecution had been a concession in the face of huge public anger; they had never meant it to actually succeed.

In 2003, the year after the collapse of the trial, the CPS issued their own report into what had happened. The author, Chris Enzor, concluded, among other things, that 'it is unlikely that there are any significant lessons to be learned from calling the experts in the Alder case'.[1] The audacity of these people never ceased to astound me. The prosecution's presentation of conflicting medical evidence, in stark contrast to the centuries-old practice of presenting evidence that supports the prosecution, and leaving the rest to the defence, had resulted in the collapse of the case. And now Enzor appeared to be saying he'd do the same again, every time. I'm sure that's true when it comes to prosecuting police officers, but was this to be the new standard for all future prosecutions? I seriously doubted it; if so, no one would ever be found guilty again.

'Perhaps the most obvious point,' he went on, 'is where there is conflicting medical evidence, it will always be difficult to persuade a court that there is a sound basis for conviction.' This seemed to me to be completely missing the point. The point is to let the jury decide, after *both* sides have made their case. By suggesting that the officers would have probably got off either way, Enzor was deliberately conflating outcome with process, as if the process was irrelevant, because – *in his view* – the outcome would have been the same either way. It felt like the Crown were playing judge and jury; that they had taken no notice of the ordinary people at the inquest who concluded that Christopher had been unlawfully killed, and were intent on ensuring the jury did not get the chance to make the same 'mistake' at the trial.

What I did learn from the report was that the CPS had actually been preparing for the outcome they achieved. 'In anticipation that the judge might direct an acquittal on all charges, a draft press statement and question and answer briefing were prepared,' the report stated, adding that this 'turned out to be a valuable investment.' Nobody from the CPS had thought fit to inform us that the trial could end as it did, or even bothered to explain why it had. Their priority was obviously to control the press narrative: 'We were able to move swiftly to issue the statement within minutes of the judge's ruling being given,' the report noted, going on to proudly report that many newspapers had quoted from their press release, and adding that the follow-up interviews that resulted 'allowed the CPS to put forward positive aspects about the case and to correct what in our view were misleading comments made by Miss Alder'.[2]

That press release had given a completely misleading impression of what had gone on. It stated that the CPS had been 'unable to prove that the officers' actions were deliberate and reckless'. But the truth is they had never tried; Curtis explicitly stated that he did not have to prove their actions were deliberate, and did not claim that they were. The press release went on to say that the CPS were 'disappointed' that the jury had not had the opportunity to hear the case in full. But the case *would* have been heard in full had the CPS not deliberately presented conflicting medical evidence, and then insisted there was no 'bad faith' on the part of the officers, a key ingredient of the misconduct offence.

The most insulting part of the report, however, related to the CPS's failure to allege racism. To prove racial discrimination in British courts, differential treatment must be demonstrated. We had clear evidence of such treatment with the white woman who was given a blanket in her cell to keep her warm, just hours before those same officers left Christopher bleeding, dying and half naked on the cold stone floor. The CPS's excuses for dismissing this evidence were ridiculous. Enzor claimed that this was not a valid comparison because the circumstances were different: firstly, because the woman was conscious, whereas Christopher was not (as if that meant he somehow needed less attention, rather than more!) and secondly, because Christopher had not been booked in, whereas the woman had.[3] What possible relevance that could have was never explained. The argument was breathtaking: an insult not just to Christopher's family, but to reason itself. It felt like he was sticking two fingers up at us.

In 2003, the same year the CPS report came out, Jason Paul mounted a civil case against Humberside Police for false imprisonment and wrongful arrest. At first, there was bad news for Jason when Judge Heppel decided to dismiss his claim in the County Court. But Jason and his solicitors took that decision to the Court of Appeal. In the Court of Appeal, Jason's QC argued that the police had been motivated in their dealings with Jason by the wish to distract public attention from the fact a young

Black man had died while lying on the floor of the custody suite with his hands cuffed behind his back. He said, 'had the behaviour of the police not been in question they would not have acted as they did' and suggested that DI Brookes of Humberside Police, who was leading the investigation into Jason Paul, would have felt a loyalty to the officers at the police station involved in Christopher's death.

On 17 March 2004, at the end of the hearing, the Court of Appeal overturned the County Court's dismissal, allowing Jason's case to go ahead. In his summing up, the judge ruled that there *was* evidence from which the jury could conclude that the police charged Jason Paul to draw public attention from their own role in Christopher's death and that the jury should, therefore, have been allowed to reach a finding in fact as to whether the police had acted in bad faith. A fresh trial was ordered.

Life in the House

1963–77

The garden at 71 Marlborough Avenue was divided by a small yellow privet hedge around two feet in height. The main area – 70 per cent of the space – was well-cut lush green grass, with a cherry tree at the edge. A rockery with stones of different shapes and sizes stood above primula plants and pansies of all colours and roses edged the footpath, with irises and other plants standing tall towards the rear of the garden. This part of the garden belonged to Mr and Mrs Goodhand, Vista the poodle and Tommy the tortoise.

The remaining third of the garden, used by the children, was covered in stones and the roots of the giant conker tree, whose elongated branches blocked both rain and sun, ensuring no grass could survive. We played under the window of the dining room and kitchen, feeling restrained as we were in full view of the house parents. If the other children needed a drink they could use the outside tap, the one we used to wash Vista's dog bowls. I was barred from having drinks because I wet the bed.

We children were strictly forbidden from entering the parents' side of the garden. But of course that didn't stop us, now and again, when the staff were not watching, from jumping the hedge to practise hurdles or escape from each other when playing tig. I remember one day I had fallen out with Christopher and he was goading me from the house parents' side of the garden. I don't know why I was chasing him, but all of a sudden I ran as fast I could, jumped over the hedge and hit him right on the nose. I was startled and expected him to chase me and hit me back, but he didn't retaliate, he just stood there holding his nose with his eyes wide open, as shocked as I was.

On her days off, Mrs Goodhand would lounge on the freshly cut grass in the sun. Being sent out to play while she was sunbathing made it difficult for us kids to let off a bit of steam as we were expected to play quietly; there was a definite air of 'children should be seen and not heard' at Marlborough Avenue: no shouting and absolutely no laughing too loud or we'd get in big trouble. We would try to whisper but when we were excited it was almost impossible not to make too much noise. Anyone who was heard was made to sit on the red brick seat in the shaded corner; being one of the louder children I sat there quite a lot, and I remember it being freezing, the sun blocked out by the huge Victorian house.

At the back of the house, there was another door that led straight to the laundry room, which I visited every morning after stripping the wet sheets from my bed. Sometimes I used it in the middle of the night, as it afforded quick, easy access to the dustbins, the hideaway I had found so it would look like I had dry sheets that night. For a while I got away without being caught; above the dustbins was the cast iron fire escape, which we clambered down in the dark in all weathers for fire drills. But eventually they realised what was up, and the beatings would begin again.

*

Before Stephen joined us, I was the youngest in the home and for a time the only one not at school. The house seemed big, empty and cold in the days without the sound of my brothers and the other children laughing, arguing and chasing each other around the furniture; the hours dragged on as I longed for them to come home. I spent the days alone in the playroom, playing house with whatever I could salvage of its broken dolls and toys, until I fell asleep in front of the fire, sometimes not waking up until dinner, a time I dreaded. Dinners were served at the huge pink Formica table, with as many as eleven of us sat round it; I was a skinny child and found eating far from pleasurable. I think the constant stress of anticipating my nightly punishment for wetting the bed meant I felt constantly full. Besides, what was served was not the best; it tended to be the cheapest food available. I especially detested sandwiches, which I seemed to have every day; Marlborough Avenue wasn't a place where you had any say over what you ate: the options were either eat it or sit there until you do, and be as thankful as you claimed you were when saying grace.

I really disliked bread, but I found cheese the most disgusting: it made me feel physically sick. Once I had been sat for what seemed like hours chomping on the same quarter of a cheese sandwich when the doorbell rang. As soon as Auntie Joyce – Mrs Goodhand's sister – went to answer it, I ran straight to the toilet and flung the cursed thing right down it. Well, I *hoped* it would go down, but, of course, the laws of physics meant the bread just floated around on top of the water. I had no time to do anything but return to my seat. Auntie Joyce returned to see my empty plate, and was immediately suspicious.

'Have you eaten them all?' she asked.

'Yes, they were very nice,' I replied.

She knew from experience that the one place those sandwiches were *not* was in my stomach, and went straight to check the toilet. Luckily Auntie Joyce was far less vicious than her sister. I got a good telling off and was told to go back to the playroom.

Auntie Joyce was more motherly than Mrs Goodhand. Slightly plump, she wore glasses, and tended to prefer dresses to the slacks favoured by her sister. Her body language was more relaxed and she seemed to have more empathy and compassion. She could raise her voice if she wasn't happy, but I don't remember her really making big issues out of things. She was married to Uncle Norman, who was a really nice guy – when he came to pick her up, he would always take the time to sit and talk with us, and we'd have a bit of a laugh. They didn't live in the children's home but worked there on Fridays and the occasional Monday. Auntie Joyce did most of the cooking and every Christmas she baked all the buns and cakes: jam tarts, fairy cakes and, my favourite, coconut buns with jam in the middle.

Auntie Joyce would sit and watch me do the splits on the kitchen floor after I told her I dreamed of being a ballerina, acting out the moves in my bedroom or down the avenue on my way home from the shops. I had convinced myself I was either going to be a ballerina or a gymnast like Olga Korbut, but although I was thin, I wasn't very graceful. I was built more for hurling myself over a high jump bar with no great technique; forget the Fosbury flop where you scale the bar backwards with an artistic arch of the body, or the Western roll where you curl your body elegantly around the bar – any old lurch would do for me as long as I got over. I also loved tumbling off the high horse suspended in the air, back somersaulting with no hands onto the gym floor. As a child that was used to being caned with a stick every night, I was hardly going to turn out a dainty little dancer; the more daredevil the event, the more I relished it.

It was good waking up on Fridays – and sometimes on Mondays as well – as it meant Auntie Joyce would be there. She'd spend the day doing all the week's ironing, washing and changing the beds – though she didn't have to bother with mine, as one of my punishments for wetting it was to make it myself. Fridays and Mondays were a lot more relaxed and I loved it. She tended to treat us with humility and kindness – although if we did mess around, as when we were jumping off furniture in the playroom, for example, she would come down on us like a tonne of bricks. Fridays and Mondays seemed so different from the rest of the week and I escaped my daily beating until after she had gone home. Mrs Goodhand said I would need the guidance of a woman, but the last thing I wanted was to pick up her controlling, manipulative ways; I would like to think some of Auntie Joyce's good points rubbed off on me though.

Staff came and left Marlborough Avenue, but it seemed no one wanted to say anything about what was happening to us – perhaps for fear of losing their jobs and comfortable lifestyles, or of being singled out as troublemakers. You could tell by Auntie Joyce's reactions to the children that she was far from content with the way her sister and brother-in-law treated us, but I don't know if she ever said anything to them behind closed doors. We would get monthly visits from social services, but these were private discussions with the house parents in which we had no involvement. Nevertheless, I chatted quite readily to my social worker about things in the home; he saw me as an open book, quick to make friends, forward, and very trusting. I must have been, as his reports described how I would sit on his knee, probably reflecting a craving for cuddles – the human contact

I so badly needed. Inside was a shy, fragile little girl – but he found me cheerful, intelligent, talkative, bright, bubbly and both sharp witted and sharp tongued, concluding that I was a child with great potential hiding behind a tough exterior, and that I was in need of firm, kind guidance.

Mrs Goodhand's perception of me, however, was somewhat different. Her notes referred to me as a lazy, cheeky, bossy telltale and troublemaker, with no pride in my appearance and unpopular even with my brothers. I can now accept that these were elements of my personality, but there was more to me than Mrs Goodhand's labels. I may well have embraced some of the traits she so negatively identified in order to survive and deal with the things that developed through my life. Even today, I can be very self-critical in certain areas of my life, and I wonder how much of her influence I took on board.

Our cultural identity was something the social workers did eventually recognise, but only after my dad's repeated insistence on the need for us to have some knowledge of our heritage. For him, this was not so much a racial issue as a social one: as Black children in a predominantly white society we could, of course, see that we were different from the other kids, but for my dad it was essential that we learned *why* this was so, and what our origins were. They told him they would try to find a Nigerian society for us to attend, but as far as I know, nothing was done to follow this through, and we certainly never attended one. Mrs Goodhand's idea of treating us with some cultural understanding meant sending the Alder children to school with a coconut instead of sandwiches and crisps. When I read about this in the care documents, it brought back memories of me running across the school playground, a boy chasing me for some of my coconut. I think of my naivety as I ran away laughing, unaware of the racist association between Black people and coconuts. Mrs Christie, the headmistress from Thoresby Infant School, was so concerned about this that she contacted social services. Speaking in confidence, she discussed me and my brothers and her dealings with us, strongly expressing her views on Mrs Goodhand and the childcare services. She said that Stephen was a kind and helpful, if mischievous, boy who needed constant supervision and told them that the bad treatment of us had to stop.

There was a clear distinction between the way my dad felt we should be brought up and the methods of the Goodhands. Both had sturdy views of the environment in which they believed we should be raised, and my father's main concern was that as Black children we should know of our cultural identity and Nigerian heritage. It was something he challenged Mrs Goodhand about with vigour. Mrs Goodhand was far from happy about this, as one incident in particular clearly revealed.

When I started senior school, there was a Black family whose gate I would pass every morning and evening on my way to and from school. They were a Ghanaian family, with a son and a daughter a little younger than me. Over time I got to know them and started to stop off at their house on my way home from school, if only for ten minutes, even if I was already late from after-school sports. I felt a connection with them: they looked like me, and I felt accepted. The mother would always ask me to come in and often I'd have some African food with them. I would sit and do some colouring with the kids, and the whole atmosphere felt homely.

Her daughter's hair was the same texture as mine, but looked nothing like it: hers was dark, shiny, long and curly, worn in braids and ribbons of different colours and styles. It looked healthy and soft. Mine, on the other hand, was always cut short to my head, it was scanty, dry and brittle, and always unkempt.[1] Her skin, too, was bright, moist and glossy, while mine looked dull, dry and ashy grey. On one of these visits, her mum decided she would plait my hair. It was excruciatingly painful. I wasn't used to having my hair combed daily and my scalp quickly became sore and tender. I shuffled about while she twisted and coiled it, the agony making it hard to sit still or even to hold back my tears. But despite all the suffering, when it was over I was really happy with the outcome: she had oiled it and bound it in cotton to loosen the curl, and I thought it looked great. I felt good and admired myself in every window I passed as I waltzed down the street to the children's home. I had enjoyed having a little bit of attention from a woman who could relate to my needs; I wasn't used to it, but she made me feel comfortable, and I skipped down the avenue, beaming. That feeling drained away the minute I stepped through the door of the home: Mrs Goodhand ridiculed my new hairstyle and sent me straight back out the door, demanding I get it taken out and put back to how it was immediately. Embarrassed and deflated, I trudged back to my friend's house and knocked on the door. I explained what Mrs Goodhand had said and, with tears in my soul, sat down while my hair was uncoiled and put back to its usual state. That was the last time I saw that family: from then on when I knocked on the door, nobody ever answered.

Death on Camera

2004–5

In late 2003 I received a phone call from Simon Ford, producer of the BBC series *Rough Justice*. He wanted to discuss making a documentary examining the circumstances around Christopher's death. We met several times and I talked him and his team through the evidence. Simon wondered whether the CCTV footage of Christopher's death could be screened as part of the documentary. It was a decision I agonised over: the images are very difficult to watch and I knew it would revive the pain felt by my family, as well as other families in the same position. Yet justice has always been my goal, and after a criminal trial in which no one was held accountable, I felt I had to do what was right and bring this to the attention of the public. I thought it was important for people to see the evidence for themselves so they could make up their own minds about what had happened, and I felt sure that, after watching the video, any decent human being would come to the same conclusions I had: that Christopher was unlawfully killed and that justice had been denied to him and his family. Time and time again, in case after case, the authorities tell grieving families that 'lessons will be learned', but the truth is, nothing can be learned until wrongdoing has been admitted; if the legal process has been blocked, only public pressure can bring this about. Painful though it was, I believed it was essential that Christopher's death should be shown. It was one of the hardest decisions I have ever had to make.

When I showed the footage to Simon, he agreed that it was in the public interest to screen it. No one had been punished or held accountable, the officers had never been cross-examined, and the criminal justice system had failed. It was important for the public to see with their own eyes the evidence for the crime that was being denied. Humberside Police were very edgy when they found out it was going to be broadcast, stating that they believed the film was not for public viewing. But I felt that it was not for hiding either.

The documentary, *Death on Camera*, was shown on 14 April 2004. It was the first time a real death had intentionally been broadcast on British TV.[1]

I knew that the programme would provoke knee-jerk reactions from those in power, but these were completely outweighed by the sympathetic reactions we got from the public at large, who were disgusted by what they had seen. We received phone calls and letters from all over the country from people saying how shocked and appalled they were that the officers had got off scot-free. The legal system may have been manoeuvred into getting the police off the hook, but the court of public opinion had definitely found them guilty. The pressure was mounting.

That same month, however, brought disappointing news from the home secretary, David Blunkett: he had ruled out the holding of a public inquiry into the handling of Christopher's death, despite pressure from me, my MP, the public and several campaign groups who supported our call. In defence of his decision,

Blunkett argued, 'Public inquiries in such circumstances cannot be triggered by TV footage of material which had already been shown, during judicial and inquiry investigations. However,' he added, 'I am asking the new Independent Police Complaints Commission to have another look at this and to report back.'[2]

The IPCC had just been established following longstanding calls for the abolition of the Police Complaints Authority (PCA) because of their manifest failure to hold officers to account. Again and again, they had failed to assure families that they were able to provide any kind of justice for the vast numbers of people who had lost loved ones at the hands of the state. Years of dedicated and tenacious campaigning from the families of Brian Douglas, Sean Rigg, Ricky Bishop, David 'Rocky' Bennett, Ibrahima Sey, Shiji Lapite, James Ashley, Harry Stanley, Jason McPherson and our own, along with many others, eventually succeeded in getting the PCA recognised as not fit for purpose, and disbanded, with the new IPCC brought in to replace them. Although this was clearly a victory, I remained suspicious of this new body. After all, the Home Office – the same state institution that controlled the police – controlled the new IPCC. It still felt like the police policing themselves – especially when so many members of the IPCC were, it emerged, former police officers, with a lifetime of institutional loyalty behind them. I decided not to participate in their review.

The Court of Appeal's judgment on the 'ingredients' of misconduct arrived in 2004. It confirmed what, despite the denials of the prosecution team, we had suspected all along: that the key ingredient in the proof of misconduct in a public office was indeed 'bad faith'. So it hadn't been a 'red herring' as Curtis had claimed; and his absurd suggestion that the police were 'unaware' Christopher needed attention had indeed served to directly destroy his own case. This was hardly the first time the CPS had mounted misconduct prosecutions – yet we were supposed to believe that on this occasion they had suddenly forgotten what they were supposed to prove, only for the Court of Appeal to restate the obvious when it was all too late.

I was by this time extremely worn out by the brick walls and perpetual denials of those supposedly responsible for investigating Christopher's death, with all remnants of the trust I had once had in them now shattered for ever. I had never allowed myself to be deluded into expecting a new body to come in and criticise all those that had failed over the years. I believed we needed a public inquiry in front of a High Court judge to air how Christopher's death had been dealt with, as well as those of many others that have died at the hands of the police without accountability. I met with members of the IPCC but I told them I was not prepared to engage with something I had no belief in. Not involving myself with the IPCC review enabled me to remain focused on exposing what I had found out and experienced rather than getting sidelined into what appeared to be an attempt to neutralise the growing anger.

The day after the *Death on Camera* programme was broadcast, the newspapers had been phoning, hoping to meet up, take photographs and get a story. The interest was building but so were my uncertainty and concerns about invasion of privacy. While I was grateful for the opportunity to publicise the case, as quite a closed, private person I found the constant exposure and attention overwhelming. It was as if, alongside my battle with the police and the authorities, I was having an internal battle against my own personality. The press had been very respectful to me, but after the emotional onslaught of the trial, all I really wanted to do was withdraw and heal my wounds.

One call I received, however, was different. In October 2004 I was phoned by Michael Nicholas and Lud Ramsey, the national secretary and chair of the Black and Ethnic Minority section of the Fire Brigades Union.[3] They told me they had seen the programme and wanted to support the fight for justice for Christopher in any way they could. They said they deplored the decision of David Blunkett to refer the circumstances of Christopher's death to the IPCC, and believed, as I did, that in light of the graphic evidence, it was quite clear a public inquiry should have been held to report on the actions of the police officers involved as well as the actions of the CPS, Humberside Police and the PCA. They expressed their concern that there had been two hundred deaths of Black and minority men in custody with no accountability, and said they would be raising funds for our campaign. At the end of the conversation, they invited me to address their annual conference in Torquay, offering to pay my travel and accommodation costs. I accepted their offer and gave a speech to their conference later that year. For the next two days I stood in the foyer selling T-shirts and badges and I couldn't believe it when on the final day I looked up to see around two hundred Black and ethnic minority firefighters coming down the stairs all wearing our Black Justice T-shirts emblazoned with Christopher's picture and the slogan 'stop the cover-up'. I was proud that my efforts to ensure that Christopher would be more than just a statistic that could be swept under the carpet had not been in vain. I felt boosted and re-energised, for the first time in a long while.

In December 2004 we found out that four of the five police officers involved in Christopher's death had been granted early retirement on stress-related medical grounds, receiving lump-sum compensation payments of between £44,000 and £66,000 on top of their pensions. The other, one of the two arresting officers, remained at work employed by Humberside Police.

Coming after their being cleared of all charges in court, and then being found with 'no case to answer' at an internal disciplinary, this felt like yet another slap in the face. Here they were, being allowed to retire on full pension in their early forties, and given an additional lump sum into the bargain, on the grounds of ill health caused by the stress of the case. Escaping justice, it seems, was not enough – the officers who stood by while Christopher died had to be compensated for the fact that their actions had even been questioned. Yet no one had considered the impact this all had on Christopher's family. The contrast between the officers' situation and mine couldn't have been starker. Having been determined at an inquest to have unlawfully killed my brother, they were patted on the back, given golden handshakes, and sent peacefully on their way; it was as if they were being rewarded for what they'd done. Whereas throughout the pain and anguish they had caused, I had lost my job, was living on £60 a week, and had even had to send my son away for his own safety.

Jane Deighton, the solicitor recommended by Terry Stewart, agreed to take on a case against Humberside police, the PCA and the CPS on behalf of me and Christopher's sons. Our case against the CPS had two aspects: firstly, the woeful way they had handled the prosecution, and secondly, the way they had dealt with me personally. The first part of the claim was based on how they had resisted bringing manslaughter charges, obstructed developing the race aspect of the prosecution, and, it seemed, failed to fully watch the video evidence in their possession for almost four years[4] and then bungled the prosecution. The second was based on their rude and dismissive treatment of me and how they had failed to pay any heed to my concerns and complaints regarding the manner of the prosecution and matters requiring further investigation, such as Christopher's additional injuries and missing belt. Our contention was that all these issues were rooted in the fact that both Christopher and I are Black.

This was apparently the first time the CPS had ever been taken to court, and of course they were not happy about it. Their first response was to try to prevent as much of our claim as possible from being heard. So in early December 2005 they applied to the lower courts to strike out those parts of the claim that dealt with the manner of the prosecution. The judge initially ruled in their favour, but also gave our solicitors permission to appeal his decision, and on 18 December, the Court of Appeal reinstated the full claim.

School

1966–77

School was an escape for me, away from tensions in the home. I would usually be in trouble as soon as I arrived, as having to change my wet sheets and take a cold bath every morning meant that I was generally late. Punctuality was something our headmaster was strict about, and I was continuously made fun of by the other children in the morning for wetting the bed. But I would always try to make the most of the rest of the day – and being away from Marlborough Avenue. I performed like the class clown, making light of the daily load I was carrying, but never pushing it too far. I tried hard in my academic subjects, contributed in class discussions, and was not slow to question things I didn't understand. I got on well with my form teachers and they seemed to warm to me. I was not seen as a child who caused trouble or was hard to control; the social worker observed that I did not mind authority as long as it was explained to me.

I was a thinker, but did not always have the confidence to express what was in my mind. I would often instinctively understand the correct answer to a mathematical question, but then start to doubt myself, question myself and convince myself I'd made a mistake. My confidence would ebb, arguing the original answer away and eventually getting it wrong.

Religious education was the subject I took the most interest in. Marlborough Avenue had given me an advantage here, as I *had* to believe in something. Many's the time I'd stood looking out of the bedroom window, staring up at the sky, praying to God to get me out of that place and end my nightly beatings. I enjoyed being able to contribute in RE, and with the added knowledge of the subject I had acquired at Sunday school – not to mention the countless times I'd been made to sit and copy out parts of the Bible for wetting the bed – I did rather well.

Handwriting was another favourite. I would practise writing like my dad, as his writing was the neatest I had ever seen. But, like most kids, there were some subjects I didn't enjoy. I wasn't keen on the sciences; I saw chemistry in particular as being of no value whatsoever.

As for boys – yuck. I had no interest at all – they didn't fancy me and I certainly didn't fancy them. My love was sport. Sport was my true escape: it didn't matter if my confidence was being hammered daily; sport made me popular, and I was good at it. And as a bonus, it was an opportunity to rid my body of the pent-up feelings of dread and adrenaline that would ravage my nerves as home time drew near.

Donna was my best friend, and sport was our shared passion. We were born just days apart and we got on really well. She seemed to have everything: she was great at sports, a good all-round athlete, and went out with the best-looking boys in school. We were very close and entered most activities together, although we excelled in different events. I spent a lot of my time at Donna's house: when we finished our after-school activities, her mum and dad would always welcome me into their home with a cup of tea and a chocolate biscuit. Nobody from the home would come to watch when we were in gymnastic competitions, but I used to get very excited when her parents attended; they made such a fuss over us both. Her mum tied our hair up like Olga Korbut's, which I loved, even though at that time my uncombed Afro hair was in no state for it. I thought the pigtails made me look like a real gymnast. Although I was in every team and had won many inter-school competitions, Donna always seemed to win sportswoman of the year. I can't say I didn't feel a little bit envious.

I don't remember having run-ins with any teachers except for the headmaster. I had got on well with the head at infant school, but at senior school it was another story; I remember feeling his cane across my fingers on more than one occasion. But what hurt more was his unwillingness to see how the racist taunts I received were causing me real psychological pain, chipping away at my sense of self-esteem, which was already under attack. I found it hard to understand why, whenever I got into an argument with a friend, the first thing they would use to hurt me was the colour of my skin. Colour was not something I thought about when choosing friends, so you can imagine how disillusioned I felt when bigoted comments spilled from their mouths when we fell out. Sometimes my pent-up frustrations would spill over and I would lash out at someone who had called me nigger, Sambo, golliwog or some other racist taunt. Inevitably, I would be the one sent to the headmaster's office to be caned, treated like an aggressor who had lashed out for no reason, with them seen as the victim. The school would then report the incident back to the Goodhands, ensuring I got another beating when I got home. Nobody taught us how to deal with this barrage of name-calling; it seemed my brothers and I were just expected to accept the insults that were being thrown at us, as if what was being said was somehow the truth. There weren't any Black or ethnic minority teachers in the school to sympathise with how we felt; there was no one who could walk in our shoes for a few minutes to imagine how isolated and worthless we were being made to feel. There seemed to be no comprehension that, to a small child, those words hurt just as much as the stick, delivering an emotional beating.

What's more, everything bad or scary seemed to be described as black or dark: you had to be careful going out in the dark, moods were dark, even a bruised eye which was in reality likely to be purple or red was a 'black eye'. When I was growing up, the libraries stocked books like Helen Bannerman's *The Story of Little Black Sambo*, and the television showed cartoons like *Tom and Jerry*, where the only Black person was a twenty-stone woman who wore a turban on her head and ran shrieking about the house in a shrill voice, chasing a cat with a broom.[1] *Gone with the Wind*, one of the biggest blockbuster movies ever, featured a similar caricature of a big fat Black woman, eyes popping out of her head, answering 'yes ma'am' to the wealthy and beautifully dressed white female plantation owner. Black slaves doing the manual labour were expected to be thankful for the little they were allowed. *Tarzan* was another popular television series at the time. Kids at school would imitate Tarzan's call to the monkeys and animals in the jungle when playing in the playground, and soon came to use it to taunt us as being like monkeys or gorillas. From a very young age my brothers and I unknowingly became fighters against racism, fighters for equality of treatment and survival.

We were one of only two Black families at Kelvin Hall High School, and my two eldest brothers had left by the time I started. This left three Black pupils in a school of around eight hundred: me, my brother Christopher, and Roland Gift, later the lead singer of Fine Young Cannibals, who left the year after I arrived. There were also, in my form, two Asian boys, but I was the only female of colour in the school, and I was pretty self-conscious about the way I looked. I've learned in life that some people fear anything different from what they see as the norm, and I don't believe many of the pupils at school knew or had even met any other Black people. As a minority, we were seen as either something curious or something to be feared; we were being challenged on a daily basis, either by racists with intentions to demean and degrade, or simply in testosterone-fuelled brawls. It felt like we were fighting simply for survival, for the right to exist and to be who we were, and for others to accept our difference. Those without genuine understanding and friendship were afraid of us, but there were also pupils who respected us for standing up for ourselves. In one way I was fortunate, as in each of the schools I attended, my older brothers paved the way for me before I arrived, and, as I've mentioned before, many a time I would run to Christopher if someone had upset me by calling me 'nigger' or 'rubber lips'. No one else would help; in those days nothing was admitted or really said about race discrimination and the only challenge coming from the teachers was to us, if we dared to react to the name calling.

Despite all this, I would always stay at school as late as I could. I would do whatever was in my power to delay the dreaded return home and the beating that awaited me there, even if this meant a cold tea on my return. I never got back before about 6.30. Instead, I would be tumbling gymnastics, hurling myself around in athletics, jumping and grabbing the netball. Over time I got very good at the majority of sports I was involved in, and won medals and certificates in gymnastics, high jump and sprinting. I even attempted cricket training from time to time when the boys would let me, but they drew a line when it came to girls doing rugby. I would have done any sport to stave off going back to the home for my flogging. Sport was my escape, and I loved it. Christopher was the same.

Elections

2005

On 6 April 2005, Tony Blair announced that he was calling a general election, to take place on 5 May. George Galloway's Respect Party had just formed in opposition to the Iraq war of 2003, and Andy and some of the other campaigners had joined. I didn't know much about the politics of the Iraq war but I knew it was bad. Going to kill people on the other side of the world just didn't sit right with me, and watching all the powerful states ganging up to attack a small country was horrifying. I could certainly relate. It felt like a global version of what they'd done to Christopher. Now the Respect Party were looking for candidates to stand in the election, especially people who had had personal experiences of injustice. A few days after Blair's announcement, I got a call from Andy asking me to be the party's candidate in Tottenham, north London. He said it would be a good place for me to stand because it had quite a large and politically astute Black community.

It was now seven years since Christopher's death, five years since the inquest and three years since the collapse of the criminal trial. I had long since committed myself to using any platform available to fight for justice for Christopher and challenge the Labour government, who were in power at the time of Christopher's death and many other deaths in custody. Years had gone by and not one member of Parliament from any of the three main parties had ever publicly condemned what the police had done to Christopher, even after it had been aired on the BBC. So I agreed to stand. For me this was a golden opportunity to raise the profile of the deaths in custody issue, which I felt I could not turn down.

At the time, however, I was very ill. I was sweating constantly and in a lot of distress; looking back on it, I think I was probably going through some kind of breakdown. But I was in the habit of ignoring my feelings and ploughing on, so that's what I did.

Within a couple of days I was on the train to London with Ben and my little dog. The campaigners had organised a flat for us to stay in for the month running up to the election, but when we arrived at the Respect Party's Tottenham HQ I got a shock. There was a big lorry parked outside with 'Vote Janet Alder' in huge letters on the side, and the office itself was plastered with posters of my name and face. I felt so embarrassed; I just wanted to melt away. Psychologically, I found this level of public attention really difficult, especially when my life had always been so private. True, as a girl doing cartwheels down the avenue, I used to dream of one day achieving stardom for my gymnastics. But I never wanted to be famous for this, for being the sister of a man killed by the police. It's very hard to accept recognition when it's over something so horrific; it was unwanted attention that had come on the back of my brother's death. But I had no option. Once you've made a decision to open your mouth, you can't go back.

As far as the election itself was concerned, I didn't really know what I was supposed to be doing. But the party organisers from the Tottenham community showed me the ropes and took me canvassing, knocking on people's doors and discussing the issues that concerned them. People were worried about things like Labour's attacks on public sector pensions and the privatisation of the Tube and, with foundation hospitals, of the NHS. I'd never lived in London, but I could see that the issues in Tottenham were the same as those faced by ordinary people in towns and cities across the country; and as a working-class mother I shared those concerns. Bringing my own children up on a council estate I knew how hard it was to get a property and find a job in a place with affordable childcare. Now my children were older I worried about them having to pay fees to go to university and being left with a lifetime of debt. I spoke to people about how unfair it was that while their parents had paid for Blair and his cabinet to go to university, his government was now forcing their kids to pay for themselves.

Deaths in custody was also an issue in Tottenham. Christopher's case was very similar to that of Roger Sylvester, who died after he was restrained – supposedly 'for his own safety' – by eight police officers outside his house in Tottenham. I had met the Sylvester family at some of the marches and film screenings, where Roger's dad explained that Roger had been thrown naked and handcuffed into the back of a van and taken to the local hospital. The family lawyers said he was left naked on the hospital floor where he suffered a seizure and was rushed to intensive care. 'Roger was swollen, battered and bruised,' his father told me, with an indentation on his right cheek bone and along his forehead. 'He had bruising all over his body. I'm still horrified. It looked like he was hit by a bulldozer.'

The Black community in Tottenham were very concerned about the issue of deaths in custody and I brought it up at all the hustings I spoke at. As far as I can recall, David Lammy, the sitting Labour MP and a junior minister in Blair's government, did not mention the issue once.

The Respect campaigners were on the streets knocking door to door every day, leafleting and talking to people, explaining that I was standing as a candidate and that my brother had died in similar circumstances to Roger. We got a good reception; I got the feeling that people desperately wanted an alternative to the Labour Party, as well as justice for those who had died at the hands of the state.

Even though we were doing really well, the stress was constant. But I carried on, living on adrenaline, unable to see the toll it was all taking on my health. I was still very poorly, suffering from high blood pressure, and constantly on edge; the upsurges and comedowns of adrenaline in my body meant I began to suffer hormonally, with sweats and dehydration and feeling generally unwell. Those around me would not have been able to see I was suffering because my upbringing in care had taught me from an early age to hide all signs of it, but when I was alone in the flat it would come out in floods of anguished tears. I once overheard some of the campaigners speaking about me, resentful that I had come out of nowhere to be the candidate and believing it should have been one of them. I felt awful and guilty and broke down there and then. At times I thought I was losing the plot, and perhaps others did as well – but now I see that I was simply experiencing total exhaustion because of the stress I was feeling. Somehow I seemed to be able to carry on and do what was needed at the time. I held firm to my convictions, and my inner strength – along with the support of many people around me – kept me going.

Standing in the elections gave me some unexpected

experiences. Until then, I had never attended an electoral ballot count, or sat at a hustings debating members of Parliament, or knocked on strangers' doors to talk about politics. But there I was, in Tottenham, meeting other people who were not prepared to sit and accept what they saw as the abuse of power and neglect of important issues that affected them and their families. Like me, they could not be silent in the face of injustice without getting up and saying how they felt.

Humberside Police superintendent Ken Bates later accused me of using Christopher as a vehicle to further my own political views and career. It was galling: over the years, every figure in authority who has dealt with my brother's case has done whatever they've needed to do to protect and enhance their careers – ignoring or destroying evidence, not rocking the boat, not making their colleagues and superiors look bad. And yet Bates projected all that careerism onto me – someone with no career to protect. As for my political views, I simply believe that the only way to give the public confidence in the police, and to ensure people who join the police can be proud of themselves, is to hold them accountable like the rest of us. And I am absolutely unrepentant about pushing that view.

I liked Tottenham. I felt I could relate to the people there, and I enjoyed walking up and down Tottenham High Road and Seven Sisters with their vast number of fresh fruit and veg shops and places to eat. I didn't have to cook once while I was there; I'd never seen so many Turkish and Polish restaurants offering all types of delicious food. I wasn't used to seeing so much variety; the little town of Burnley only had Indian, Chinese or fish and chips.

The Tottenham campaigners introduced me to some of the shop owners who, after a few days, began to recognise me and greet me, sometimes stopping in the street for a chat. Little did I know that by then, 40,000 leaflets with my face on them had gone through letterboxes; initially I thought nothing of it, but the attention this brought me was not always welcome. The majority of those I met around Tottenham were really good people, of all different races and from all different walks of life. But one man unnerved me. There was a knock on the door of our first-floor flat one morning, so I looked out and saw a face peering through the downstairs window. I asked if he needed help and he asked if a Polish family lived downstairs. I told him I didn't know, and he proceeded to tell me that he was a police officer, 'well, not a police officer, but kind of a police officer – I kind of work for the police' and that he had seen a guy enter my flat and take something. My immediate thought was, If you are some kind of police officer, why didn't you stop him? He then said the man was a known aggravated burglar. I became very suspicious; I wondered whether perhaps he had seen my face on a leaflet and followed me home, and that *he* was the 'aggravated burglar'. But I never noticed anything missing.

At that moment, one of the campaigners came by to pick me up. It was Sue Caldwell, who I got on really well with. So I asked her to give him a copy of the *Death on Camera* DVD and told him to return it to the Respect HQ when he had watched it. I thought if he really did work for the police and was trying to find out what I was doing, then I'll show him. But the incident was frightening; I was already nervous, and I got quite upset at the party because they hadn't prepared me for the possibility of things like this happening. I didn't feel comfortable staying there anymore and I told them I had to get out. Luckily a couple from the campaign invited me to stay with them instead. They looked after me very well.

Finally, election day came, and I ended up winning 6.4 per cent of the votes: around 2,000 in total. As I had only been there a month, and it was a new party, I thought this was pretty good. The campaign had given me the opportunity to raise the profile of Christopher's case as well as the confidence to stand up and air my concerns in front of politicians – even if, like the others I had met over the years, they always seemed to hide behind the usual excuse that 'while this or that is going on, I can't say anything'. I had carried on, despite my anxieties, and kept going till the end of the campaign – but through it all I was a nervous wreck; I didn't realise until much later, when I stopped for a while, just how damaged I was.

Holidays

1963–77

Christmas was surprisingly good at Marlborough Avenue. We didn't tend to spend it with our parents, so it meant eight or nine kids or more, all getting excited and looking forward to eating turkey, mince pies, Auntie Joyce's baking and opening our presents. The tree was put up a week before: around five foot tall, it was decorated with bright, multicoloured flashing lights and chocolate Santas which none of us dared touch until Christmas day. All the children would sit together and make colourful paper-chain decorations to hang from the ceiling; there was elation in the air.

Every year the house parents invited two sets of couples, friends of theirs who we got to know over the years, and the Goodhands were always on their best behaviour when they were around. The guests came to the playroom when they arrived, and I remember feeling a kind of relief when I saw them; I think it was because I knew there was no chance of us getting the stick while they were in the house.

On Christmas Eve, we went to bed early and there was no resistance from any us; we understood that the earlier we went to sleep, the sooner Christmas morning would arrive. Whoever woke first woke everyone else; we'd go running from bedroom to bedroom, jumping on each other's beds, laughing and giggling freely. Mr and Mrs Goodhand and their friends wished us good morning and when we got downstairs, the playroom was full of brightly wrapped presents.

Every year we got a brand-new dressing gown and slippers, a colouring book and felt tips, bubble bath or bath crystals, a game, a selection box and a clementine.[1] Many of these had been donated by the church, but we didn't care where they'd come from; we were in our element. We would even dive into our selection boxes and eat our clementines before dinner! As the smell of the enormous turkey began to fill the air, it was the job of the older boys to wash and rinse the potatoes that they had spent hours peeling the previous day, and to get rid of the piece of coal that had been put in with the potatoes to stop them going soft and brown. Christmas at Marlborough Avenue was full of colour and gorgeous smells. After our main course of turkey and numerous vegetables, we stuffed our faces with mince pies and Christmas pudding, all hoping to be the one to bite down on the foil-wrapped threepenny bit that we knew was hidden in one of the pieces. Later, Mrs Goodhand would show off her theatrical skills, singing and playing piano while we children joined in the choruses, singing 'The Holly and the Ivy', 'Good King Wenceslas' and other carols to entertain her friends. Looking out of the window, there always seemed to be a white, glittering blanket of snow. It reminded me of the Christmas cards with snow on all the branches of the trees. I can't remember one Christmas without snow. How I loved Christmas!

Summer holidays were bittersweet. The part I dreaded was that, for five of the six weeks, Mrs Goodhand's mum looked after us while the Goodhands were on holiday abroad. She was an old lady who didn't seem to like any of the children, though I felt she despised me most of all. If there was any noise coming from the playroom – and, being children, it would often get rowdy – she would storm in and I would be one of the first she dragged out by the scruff of my neck, often scratching me with her long fingernails in the process. My Saturday afternoons tended to be spent sat behind the couch as punishment, usually when my favourite Elvis Presley films were on. I would try to peep out round the corner of the couch, but the other kids – knowing I loved Elvis – teased me by blocking my view with their hands. I would then protest loudly, and Mrs Goodhand's mum would drag me out again. She would make me stand in the cold stone downstairs toilet; whenever the other children needed the toilet I had to come out and go back in when they had finished. I remember Christopher once leaving such a foul smell that I stood there holding my breath and pinching my nose until it bled. I had such a fear of this woman, despite her age, that I wondered whether she inspired my recurring nightmare of a witch with pointed red fingernails climbing through the window. But Mrs Goodhand always had highly polished nails covered in red varnish. Perhaps the witch was a horrifying combination of them both.

There was one week of the holidays we did look forward to, though: the one when we went away. It was either a week at Butlin's or day trips to the seaside: places like Scarborough, Bridlington, Withernsea and Hornsea. Beverley Westwood was one of our favourite destinations. It was like a forest: we could run wild and free, playing hide and seek and building dens, and on our way home we always stopped for a creamy vanilla ice-cream cone at Burgess, the best little ice-cream shop in the world.

I also enjoyed Hornsea, where we visited the potteries and the Robert Thompson wood-carving factory. We would race to find the little carved mouse on each piece of furniture, which was the factory's unique trademark. It was fascinating searching for them on the tables and chairs; they were never in the same place. Those were great days that I'll never forget; nothing is all doom and gloom. It made a difference that we children were all together as well, all facing similar trials and tribulations. Sticking together got us through most things, and our relationships with each other were strong. In a care home you meet lots of other children, including some who stay for such a short period that they've left before you've even discovered why they were there; but for a few years, it stayed quite stable, which enabled us to get to know each other and form a stronger bond. No matter why each of us were there, we knew that we were all in the same position and, surprisingly, the mixture of personalities got on relatively well. We didn't fall out very often or for very long. And if we did argue, I never once remember the white kids resorting to any racism against me and my siblings – a total contrast to my experiences at school.

The years we went to Butlin's – in Filey – we stayed in self-catering accommodation, the children split between three or four chalets with one house parent or other member of staff in each. Before we left, we would help fill boxes full of tinned food, bread, milk and cheese, as well as our holiday clothes. It was a time of great excitement and trepidation. We were left to our own devices on the camp complex; all entertainments were included in the entrance fee, so we were given the opportunity to decide for ourselves what to do with our time. The majority of my days were spent at the swimming pool or seeing shows, with evenings at the disco: my favourite place, because it was where Christopher and I would show off our dance skills. I was proud of Christopher as a dancer; he always attracted crowds of people who stood and admired his agility and strength as he performed backflips and somersaults to loud rock and roll. I was in awe of him.

Having an open, trusting character, I found it easy when I was young to make new friends, and every year I would meet another family from outside our group of children in care. I found it fascinating to see how ordinary families worked: it was all pretty alien to me, and very different from the way we'd been brought up.

Wherever we'd been for the day, we always had to be back in the chalets by 10 p.m. Leaving the disco one night, I had a terrifying experience when three older boys followed me out and dragged me into an empty chalet which was used to store clean sheets and blankets. They gagged my mouth, ripped my tights off and raped me. I was scared and had a feeling I'd done something wrong. I knew what had happened wasn't right, but for the fear of me getting into trouble, I told no one. I could not explain how my tights had been ripped; I probably just said that I'd fallen over. I felt awful, sick to the pit of my stomach.

Days later, as we were sat at the table having our sandwiches, Stephen started laughing and blurted out, 'those boys said that you had nipples like Jelly Tots'. Oh my god. My face was boiling and I could feel my toes curling, but to my surprise Mrs Goodhand said nothing. By the age of twelve, this type of exploitation was nothing new for me; I'd had many similar experiences before. But I couldn't understand why Mrs Goodhand didn't even question it. I was at an age where my body, and especially my breasts, were in the early stage of development. But the subject of this incident stopped dead at my brother's comment; nothing more was said.

For the rest of the holidays, if we were allowed and we weren't visiting my dad, we were let loose on Pearson Park. Eight, nine or sometimes ten of us would run down Marlborough Avenue, past all the huge old Victorian houses, racing to see who would be the first to get to the swings. As often as not, I would be doing cartwheels, my head full of grandiose thoughts of being spotted and signed up for a national gymnastics team and becoming the next Olga Korbut or Nellie Kim. The boys, meanwhile, would be playing Robin Hood, making bows and arrows with fallen branches; piggyback racing down the road, trying to push each other off; or throwing sticks up at the trees to knock down conkers. Every autumn, as the leaves on the trees turned rust-like colours, it was a competition to see who would find the biggest and strongest conkers. We had an advantage because our avenue must have had some of the best horse chestnut trees for miles, winning the boys many a game at school. At the park, we'd play rounders, cricket and football, or the games organised by the council, who ran activities which drew kids from all walks of life.

In the park was a massive pond where young children and their parents, as well as older people, tended to congregate to feed the birds. There were always ducks and sometimes swans and geese; if you were lucky, you might get to see ducks with their young waddling along the footpath. In the centre of the park stood the Victorian Conservatory, a giant tropical hot house full of exotic flowers and banana trees. Everything about the park and its location was grand, the houses that surrounded it a stark contrast to the council estate where our dad lived.

Something always seemed to go wrong when the Goodhands were abroad. One day we had all gone out to Pearson Park. We did all the usual stuff – went on the swings, round the pond, played some rounders – but then we ran into a group of skinheads, who appeared to be a lot older than us. They were wearing skinny drainpipe trousers with turn-ups, Doc Marten boots, T-shirts and braces, with close-shaven crewcut hairstyles. They called us niggers and golliwogs – there were white children in our group as well, but of course we knew it was our family they were targeting. Sometimes, in these situations, we would fight, but on that day we just ran. We raced through the park and eventually ended up ducking down an alley. Once we thought we were safely away from them, our attention was drawn to the fruit trees reaching out from the large rear gardens of the grand houses backing on to the alley, laden with apples and pears. This was too good an opportunity to pass by, so we started picking them, trying to knock them down with sticks. But, of course, the really big ones were out of reach. That was when someone had the bright idea of us all climbing up onto a garage roof. Little did we know it was made of fibreglass; as you can imagine, we crashed right through it. Immediately, panic struck – we knew we were in big trouble. We bolted from the scene of the crime, and once we'd got a safe distance away, we started to walk apprehensively towards the home, overcome by that feeling of dread when you know that punishment is coming but are completely powerless to do anything about it.

We said nothing, but the owners of the garage came to the house later that day and told the staff exactly what had gone on. Among ourselves, we tried to make light of it, laughing and jumping about on the furniture as much as we possibly could – but we knew that as soon as the Goodhands returned, all hell was going to break loose.

As soon as they walked in the door, you could feel the change in the atmosphere. A hush came over the house and we began whispering to each other about what was going to happen and whose fault it was. It wasn't long before Mrs Goodhand, sat in her usual comfy chair in the kitchen by a roaring fire, had us all lined up in front of her. Then the interrogation started. It felt like a military court. We were stripped down emotionally and psychologically. Some of us were crying before she had even opened her mouth; in that house, when you cried you were seen as guilty. Not one of us said anything; like many kids, we had a strict code of honour regarding snitching. Instead we just stood there crying out a chorus of 'I didn't do it, it wasn't me!' as Mrs Goodhand screamed at us that we would not get our tea until we admitted who was responsible. We were made to stand in separate corners along the corridor, nobody daring to say a thing. In those situations, we would just go into denial mode. We all knew we were in trouble, but none of us would say anything; very much as the police and other state authorities do in such situations, I suppose.

As it got later and later, to take the pressure off the situation, we started trying to make each other laugh and get each other into trouble. Each of us was reluctant to take responsibility, purely because we were aware, chapter and verse, of what was to come next; in the end, I think we all got the stick that day.

One way or another, whether it was climbing on the roof, losing the dog's ball or smashing the greenhouse window, we always managed to do something wrong when the Goodhands went on holiday. When we smashed the greenhouse window, it was the same procedure: we were lined up against the wall, grilled about who was responsible and made to stand for hours without our tea until someone owned up. As it got closer to bedtime, Mrs Goodhand got us all together again and told us, this time in a much quieter, more sympathetic tone of voice – that all she wanted to know was who had smashed the window. She said that if it was an accident it didn't matter, and that as soon as she knew, we could all get our tea. It was like she was now playing the 'good cop', trying to convince us that if we told the truth, we would somehow get something out of it, that our bravery in telling the truth would be recognised. In the end, it was decided that I would say I did it, because we were convinced she wasn't going to do anything, as it had been an accident. I thought I was being clever when I told her I did it, but she went absolutely mad, shouting at me for wasting everybody's time, keeping everybody standing there for no reason. She sent me straight to her husband for a beating and then I had to go to bed with no tea. I had thought I was being good. I went upstairs and this time there was no more standing at the window praying to God. That didn't seem to have helped, so instead I wrote a letter expressing how much I hated the house, hated her, hated her mum, and hated her husband, so much so that I often wished I was dead. I left it on the dressing table before I went to school. I didn't have the courage to tell her to her face, and I knew I could never have got the words out anyway. When I arrived back, the letter wasn't mentioned and I don't believe I got the stick that night. I thought this was strange, because, as always, I'd wet the bed. But things reverted to normal the next day. It was traumatic, both mentally and physically; this kind of treatment was dished out to us all for years.

The IPCC Report

2006

The IPCC report into Christopher's death came out in March 2006. After the IPCC had been set up to replace the discredited Police Complaints Authority in April 2004, the review into Christopher's death was one of its first jobs. I did not have high hopes. Whatever they found out, the IPCC had no power to hold anybody to account: they could only make recommendations, and there was no mechanism to ensure these were followed up. They could not even compel witnesses to attend – so, of course, all the police involved refused to speak, just as they had at the inquest. On top of this, the IPCC had worked very closely with the CPS, who, as far as I was concerned, had got the officers off the hook in the first place with their bungled prosecution. It certainly didn't seem very impartial. Besides, I had enough experience now to know that these state institutions protected each other. It was a damage limitation exercise, triggered by the public outrage that followed the *Death on Camera* documentary.

The report was more than four hundred pages long, and I read it from cover to cover. In many ways, I felt vindicated by the report, but in others, I thought it was continuing the whitewash, albeit in a more sophisticated fashion than before. Certainly, the report proved that the harsh treatment my family had received as victims by the PCA, Humberside Police and West Yorkshire Police was not all in my head. But it didn't go nearly far enough.

One thing the IPCC report did bring out was the duplicity of the police officers. After reading the officers' explanations as to why they had left Christopher in the position they had, the IPCC concluded that they must have been either deluded or simply lying in order to present themselves in a better light.[1] Clearly the IPCC had found their explanations just as difficult to accept as I had. Dawson said he thought Christopher was asleep, despite describing him as 'refusing to walk' when they brought him out of the van.[2] If the IPCC were able to see that these were not the comments of people who were telling the truth, I did wonder how West Yorkshire Police and the CPS had been unable to see that too.

Another thing I learned from the report was that not long after voicing my concern about Beatrice's appointment, she was withdrawn from the case after the meeting with Superintendent Ken Bates, at what she described as very short notice. She later said she was shocked at being withdrawn so abruptly without explanation, and felt she had been used. She believed her relationship with the African-Caribbean community had been strained by being put in the position she was without being given any knowledge of the case, leaving her unable to answer the community's concerns or to reassure them in any way. Bates had accused me of not liking Beatrice. This was typical deflection from the police; I didn't even know Beatrice. What I didn't like was the fact that she hadn't been briefed properly and wasn't able to help us. But according to Bates, I didn't like the fact she was Black, I was being racist towards her, and I was 'playing the race card'.³ He accused me of calling Beatrice a coconut, which he told the IPCC meant brown on the outside and white on the inside – clearly a term he had heard bandied about somewhere and thought he could use to smear me. Bates was obviously not aware that I lived in a predominantly white community, that my children are of mixed race, and that 'coconut' is the type of term that has often been used to describe people precisely like me. I believe that Bates was projecting his own mindset onto me; after all, he was surely well aware by this stage that many suspected Christopher's unlawful killing, as the inquest called it, at the hands of his police colleagues was motivated by the very racism of which he accused me.⁴

The report also commented on how the CPS had produced evidence that contradicted the evidence they were to rely on during the trial. The IPCC noted that the normal practice would have been for the CPS to present only the evidence it would rely on, while disclosing to the defence any evidence that was in material conflict with it, just as Maria and Peter had said at the time. For me, this showed that the trial had been set up to fail, as the CPS could never have proved their case by putting the evidence forward in this way. But the IPCC, despite noting that the approach was 'somewhat unusual', then rowed back to spend several pages uncritically quoting Enzor's convoluted rationalisations for the CPS's bizarre approach, concluding the section by suggesting that perhaps the coroner should never have allowed the inquest jury to consider unlawful killing in the first place.⁵

Elsewhere in the report, the IPCC commented that all the arguments and hearings that had taken place clouded the simple truth that these officers had, for whatever reason, dismissed Christopher's obvious distress. It was the first time this had been acknowledged by any representative of the state.

But I felt let down by the report. In one part, they wrote about PC Barr making two telephone calls to the station as an April Fool's joke. They didn't go into exactly what was said but noted that it was a joke about a death in custody. The IPCC claimed that these calls had been made prior to Christopher's arrest, but I found that hard to believe. It just seemed like too much of a coincidence – especially given that the same officers had been back on the same shift again the following night. Other evidence from the tapes, which I discovered when they were finally disclosed to me years later, was not mentioned at all. All in all, there appeared to be a lot more on the 108 hours of CCTV footage than anyone dared to mention.

In general, the report seemed to address my concerns only to dismiss them. They claimed there was 'no evidence' of an assault by the police – even though Christopher's additional injuries had never been properly investigated – and that there was 'no evidence' of police surveillance of me following Christopher's death. Clearly they had not dug very deep.

Weekends

1963–77

When I was about ten, we started staying over at my father's every weekend. He lived at 32 12th Avenue on the North Hull estate. It was a three-bedroom council house – not one of the cleanest on the estate, but not as bad as Maggie May's across the road. She was known as the cat woman, or the witch, because of all the smelly cats that lived with her. It seemed like she must have had more than a hundred. Thinking about it, we could probably have done with a cat, because my father's house was overrun with mice; there was always plenty of food and crumbs of enticement for them around the kitchen, and many a time they would walk confidently across the linoleum floor in broad daylight. I was scared of them. Keeping a clean house was not one of my father's strengths. But although we might have been the muckiest kids on the estate, with holes in our unwashed clothes and me smelling like a toilet after climbing out of another drenched bed – at Dad's we had our freedom: freedom from the beatings we got in the home, freedom to roam the estate, and freedom to meet the other kids of 12th Avenue.

Our dad wasn't an openly affectionate man to us as children, and refrained from showing his emotions outwardly. I don't ever remember him cuddling us; the only memory I have of touching him was of once crawling onto his knee. That didn't seem to matter to me though; I felt an intuitive connection to my dad, and I could tell he cared deeply about us. The only time he lost his temper with me was when I told him I had a boyfriend. I didn't, in fact, but I had watched the way he reacted, excited, with a big smile on his face when one of my brothers told him he had a girlfriend; I remember my dad laughing and patting him on the back, and I was expecting the same reaction. Instead, I got a slap and was sent upstairs. He also got annoyed with us when he saw we hadn't brushed our teeth. He was very particular about our appearance, and concerned with how we presented ourselves as Black children in a predominantly white society. This was, I believe, due to the many difficulties and pressures he had experienced himself as a Black man at a time of widespread racial prejudice and legalised discrimination in housing and in the workplace. He must have understood that his children would also at some time come across it. To me that is not the behaviour of a man that doesn't care about his children, as made out by some of the social workers over the years, basing their judgement on the untidiness of his home.

One of the social workers, however, did seem to develop a good rapport with my dad. Even after working a long night shift and trying to catch some sleep during the day, my father was quick to welcome him into his home whenever he visited, and they would spend hours talking about all kinds of subjects. I remember my dad explaining that many people from African countries had been brought up to believe that Great Britain is the mother country, holding Britain in very high esteem, truly believing the Queen of England was everyone's Queen, and that they then find that hard to square with the reality of the racial discrimination they suffer when they get here. They even spoke about Nigerian politics together, a subject the social worker said he had studied at university. Over the years he really got to know my dad and his way of expressing himself and began to really like him. He said he found him a very interesting character, and a mutual friendship developed. At last, my father had met a social worker who was able to understand his concerns as to how we would turn out with a lack of cultural identity, as well as our employment options as we grew older.

I loved my dad so much and wanted to be the best daughter he ever had – even though I always felt my half-sister, Patricia, took first place in his heart. I saw his eyes light up whenever she came to the house, and I'd never known him to laugh so much. She was a lot older than us and was, I believe, born to a white mother, perhaps from an earlier marriage or relationship; nothing was explained to us, so I have never known much about it. Social services did nothing to help me understand anything either.

I never wanted to give my dad any trouble; from an early age I intuited that he was a man in considerable mental anguish and suffering. His facial expressions alone revealed more than any words could have said. He didn't speak about the way he felt or how he had been affected by the way my mum deserted us. But I noticed he had become a chain smoker, and there would be mountains of hand-rolled cigarette butts strewn all over the fireplace, and ashtrays piled high; I also remember seeing bottles and bottles of tablets he had to take daily for angina and high blood pressure. I wanted to help ease his stress, so I would clean the house, which seemed to get worse every week. There was an unspoken loneliness that could be seen in my father's eyes, and more than likely a feeling of bewilderment as to how things had turned out. I had become quite expert at reading people's faces and seeing what was *not* being said.

I made some good friends on the North Hull estate, but I was never in a hurry to take them inside our dad's house. Part of me was embarrassed. I had been in my friends' houses, seen their mums cleaning or preparing a nice Sunday dinner, heard the music playing. Ours was nothing like that. Instead I would take my friends out to the back garden, where I could show off the twelve crab apple trees we had, and we could climb on the old concrete air raid shelter to knock off the apples at the top (which were always the sweetest). This was where we had our adventures. I didn't like it when it rained as my friends were not allowed out to play. My brothers and I were allowed out in all sorts of weather, but with no one to play with, rainy days meant a lot of time upstairs in the freezing cold bedrooms while my dad was downstairs, asleep on the couch after a night shift or chatting with his friends.

Our dad's friends were always introduced as uncles and aunties, a common way to address your elders in Nigerian families and a way of showing them respect. My brothers and I didn't speak Yoruba, which could be quite alarming as it often sounded to us as if my dad and his friends were involved in full-scale arguments. I've always thought the Nigerian language sounds somewhat forceful and forthright, and I'm sure it's quite a common experience when hearing unfamiliar languages: it does tend to raise eyebrows and make you wonder what is being said. But more often than not these exchanges would be immediately followed by hearty and vibrant laughing; we soon came to realise that heated and passionate debate is just part of the conversational mode in Nigeria, and not an indication of some major falling out.

We were the only Black family I knew of in North Hull. Yet despite it being a predominantly white community, people on the estate seemed to respect my father: a proud Black man on his own, supporting his children as best he could. He could have been in the pub every night, drinking his cares and wages away, but instead all he seemed to do was work and have the occasional flutter on the horses. His neighbours seemed to like and respect him – except, that is, those that chose to exploit his daughter's vulnerability.

Though I didn't show it, being the only female within a household of males, I was quite vulnerable – and my bubbly, friendly personality was easily exploited. From the age of eleven or twelve I was groomed by one of my 'uncles' who visited the house on a regular basis. Every weekend he would ask my dad if I could go and help him in the house – and, unaware of his motive, my dad agreed. As I write this, the thought of putting on my coat and walking out the door with him holding my hand makes me cringe.

Once inside, he would ask me to undo his trousers and play with his penis. He didn't use physical coercion – it was all done at the level of psychological manipulation, sneaky and sleazy, making it seem like this was something I had instigated myself. He'd tell me to lie on the settee and give me a digestive biscuit, as if this was payment for what he was about to do. I would be staring up at the ceiling, chomping on the biscuit, my body tensing while he fondled me with his hands, then rubbing and forcing his penis in between my thighs until he'd ejaculated all over my legs. I would squeeze my eyes tight and do as I was told, in desperation for it to be over. Once he had finished, he would walk to the kitchen with his trousers still open, get a cloth, wipe himself and then wipe me, which felt horrible. Then he would give me money to go to the shop for him, plus a little extra for some sweets and crisps to keep me quiet. Once I had done the shopping, I was free to go out and play with my friends again, none of them having any idea what had just happened. I was left with a lingering smell. I wasn't sure whether what was happening was wrong or not. And I never told anybody. After all, who would listen? Wouldn't it have just proved what Mrs Goodhand had always said, that I was a tell-tale with an obsessive, vivid imagination, desperately seeking attention? Wouldn't I have got into trouble?

Life with Ben

2002–7

When we first got together, Ben seemed to be sympathetic and caring, at a time when this was exactly what I needed. But it soon became clear that he was not the person I had thought he was, and his behaviour became increasingly disturbing. At first, I just thought he had an illness that needed medication and a kind hand. But now I was not so sure. Whenever I came back from doing something with the press or the campaign, he would start some kind of argument or drama. I just wanted to hide away, but he seemed to crave the fame and attention he believed I was getting, and it would trigger his jealousy. At times he would just sit on the sofa, snarling. It sent shivers down my spine. His health workers visited daily, but he always behaved in a very positive way in front of them, as if he was doing really well, only to revert to the negativity once they had left.

I was confused, and didn't understand what I had got myself into. My home was no longer a place of solace, and when I needed that solace most, he would always introduce some kind of negativity or threat.

Then there was his ape obsession. Once, when he'd come out

of a spell in the psychiatric hospital, I'd gone to his house to try to make it a little more homely. But when I arrived, I got a shock. As he closed the front door behind us, I saw a picture of a gorilla stuck to the back of the door. It would have been the last thing he saw every time he left the house to see me. This was not long after the press had been reporting on the officers making monkey noises on the CCTV footage after Christopher's death.

These 'coincidences' kept happening. Once, when I had been reading through my care records, I told Ben about how Mrs Goodhand would send us to school with coconuts, and about the implicit racism in this that the teacher seemed to have picked up on. The next day he turned up with a packet of coconut mallows.

It was also obvious that he was still very entangled with his ex. With one thing and another I felt I had to get out. So one day I raised it with him – I said I don't think this can go on between me and you. And that was it. It was like he physically transformed: the veins in his neck became massive, and you could see the blood rising up to his face. He let out a full-throated scream, at the top of his voice, right into my face. I turned to jelly. He stormed across the room, kicked a hole in the door and left.

The next day he phoned up, full of tears and apologies. I felt sorry for him and guilty because he had been there for me, and so I let him back into my life. But from then on, any time I tried to confront him about anything, or if he sensed I was drawing away from him, he'd fly into a rage and start lashing out. Once he smashed the mirror above my fireplace, and twice he smashed my television set.

I can see now that my judgement had become seriously skewed. All I had left to believe in were those around me, and the last thing I wanted to do was to judge anyone, especially someone who had suffered so much themselves. My friends kept telling me that he was no good, but once again I had sought comfort in what was familiar to me. Over the years, I had always run to abusive relationships in times of mental stress or emotional pain, and now the pattern, it seemed, had returned.

I didn't seem to be able to keep him away from my house. Sometimes I'd go to a friend's just to get away from him, but I didn't like doing this, because my dog was always a nervous wreck when I got back, gnawing himself and clearly disturbed. It made me wonder what Ben had been doing to him while I was away. Once I got home to find he had pulled my budgie's tail out.

He was becoming more and more aggressive to me as well. He knew I wouldn't call the police, because I was battling them, so I felt like I was completely at his mercy. If I wouldn't let him in, he would just kick the door in.

Another time I tried to end things and asked him to leave. He flew into one of his rages, and the next thing I knew I came round in a heap on the floor.

'Did you hit me?' I asked him.

'No, no,' he said, 'I just slapped you.'

I got out of the house as soon as I could, and a friend of mine took me to hospital. The doctors there said he must have hit me with a lot of force to have knocked me out before I even felt it.

I now think that what was prompting his outbursts was a deep-rooted fear of abandonment. At some point in his childhood, he had been taken away from his mother and put into a secure unit. So every time I tried to leave, it triggered all his childhood fears of loss; he was projecting a lifetime of issues onto me.

I wasn't sleeping at night and through the day I was researching, going through the IPCC report and starting to prepare for the civil case against the officers and the CPS. As I did so, I couldn't help but notice parallels between what they had done and what Ben was doing. Lies and deceit, bullying and intimidation – all those things that were coming at me from the police, were now coming at me from Ben as well. He'd seen my vulnerability and was trying to use it to control me; he hated to see me standing up and speaking out, just like the police did. At the same time, he was projecting all his problems onto me, trying to blame me for his life, just like the police were trying to blame me for what they'd done. I was confronting both a narcissist partner and a narcissistic state.

After Ben knocked me out, I was in a state of permanent anxiety, constantly terrified. Whenever he flew into a rage, I'd be shaking like mad, not knowing his full capabilities. Everything he did seemed calculated to reinforce this perpetual dread, which he used to control me.

A few times I literally ran from him, but he would chase me down the street and grab me by the scruff of my neck or my hair. My fight and flight mechanisms were operating simultaneously as I was battling the system but running from this man who was trying to tear apart what was left of my life. He seemed to be feeding off my energy, and as his confidence built, mine drained away. I felt like a wounded animal on its last legs. My hair loss worsened and I put on weight. I knew I'd got myself into a situation that I had to get out of, but I also knew that that was not going to be easy.

Eventually I plucked up the courage to end things for good. Again, I saw the veins on his neck start to bulge and his face redden. Then, in a voice of pure menace, he said, 'You'd better get your keys and get out.'

My legs felt weak. I opened the door and fled, my little dog running after me, as Ben began screaming at the top of his voice, followed by the sound of shattering glass. It was just like a child's tantrum but with all the power and ferocity of a grown man. It was awful to witness; and felt like something out of *A Nightmare on Elm Street*. I knew then that I was in real danger, so I ran into a neighbour's house and asked her to phone the police, the very people that I had been fighting for the past eight years. It had got to the point where I felt I had no choice.

When they arrived, Ben had gone. I showed them into the house, dreading what we would find. Everything in the living room had been smashed – every lamp, the mirror, all the windows. Then we went into the kitchen, and it was exactly the same, just total devastation. As we went upstairs, it became clear that he had smashed every single window and every piece of electrical equipment in the entire house. The police said they had seen people smash up houses before, but never something so thorough and systematic.

After they'd gone, I noticed the DVD of the CCTV footage of Christopher's death next to the smashed television. When I'd left the house it had been in the DVD player; Ben had obviously carefully removed it before smashing up the DVD player. To me, it showed how calculated the whole thing had been. He knew how important that DVD was to me, and he knew I could never have forgiven him if he had destroyed such crucial evidence. This was not a crime of passion; it was a calculated move to scare me into staying with him, without crossing a line that he knew would have lost me for ever.

Shortly after that, he was locked up. But he was soon out again, his keyworkers telling me how much he wanted to see me. I refused, and I told them there was no way he was coming back to my house. But he would turn up anyway, standing outside my boarded-up window, crying and saying how sorry he was. I wouldn't let him back, and sometimes he would return later and try to kick the door in. Eventually I took him to court and the judge put a restraining order on him. I thought after that I would finally be able to relax, but he took no notice of the order: he kept coming back to the house at night. I learned from a friend that he had been on crack for a while, and suddenly his snarling and aggression made more sense. I had CCTV installed, but I still couldn't sleep at night.

One night, just as I had started to unwind, the now familiar banging started on my door. I jumped out of bed and peeped out of the window to see Ben in the road, shouting.

I could see he was agitated and was not going to take no for an answer. My heart was pounding like mad, and when he came through the gate and started running at my door, I knew I had to phone the police. Just as the door burst off its hinges, the walls flashed blue as a police car pulled up outside. Three plain clothes officers rushed over and took him away.

It was like I had come full circle. The actions of the police – the killing of Christopher, the covering up and lying about what had happened, the contempt with which they had treated me, their refusal to answer questions and then finally their walking away scot-free – had left me in a state of such shattered self-belief and self confidence that I was hopelessly vulnerable and open to narcissistic abuse. And after five years of it, I had had to turn to the very people who had opened me up to that situation to get me out of it.

Still, I didn't feel safe. Ben had not been sent to prison after smashing my house up, so there was no reason to think he would be now. And the restraining order did not seem to have stopped him; as far as I knew, he could still turn up again at any time. I was having sleepless nights, panic attacks and palpitations; my blood pressure was sky high. I knew I couldn't go on like this. So I called Women's Aid and they offered me a place in a refuge. I packed my bags and set off as soon as I was off the phone.

I had my own little room in the refuge, and I didn't tend to come out of it very much, only leaving if I had to travel to another city for the campaign. The rest of the time I used to just sit in my room and do bits of writing. That's when I wrote a lot of what became this book.

I knew I couldn't stay in the refuge for ever, and that I needed to make a new home in another town. But I was scared to go back to my house, even just to pack and move out, in case Ben turned up. So when I heard he had gone back into a psychiatric hospital, six months after I'd moved to the refuge, I took my chance to get away. I returned home and packed what I could, found good homes for my dog and budgie and then, once again, I ran. I had moved out of a mother and baby home when I was just eighteen and it felt very much like life was repeating itself. After twenty years in my house in Bradford, I moved into a one-bed flat in Leeds. Physically it was tiny, but the space it created in my life seemed enormous; it felt like I could finally breathe again. I got myself a little job cleaning pubs and began preparing for the civil case.

Weekends 2

1963–77

It had always been important to my father that we went to church every Sunday, and religious activities played a big role in our lives. As well as church parade and Girl Guides for me (and Cub Scouts for the boys), we attended Sunday school after the service, and then often went on to the vicar's house after that. For some reason, there were three different churches we went to from one week to the next – two Methodists (St Michael's and St Augustine's) and one Pentecostal; I never quite learned the differences between them, nor why we switched between the three.

At the vicarage of the Pentecostal church, the vicar's wife would sit and play piano while they gave us tea and biscuits, a luxury we didn't get at the home. One day the older children told the vicar about the bad things that were happening at number 71. At last, it seemed that someone was taking our suffering seriously – but it didn't have the outcome we wanted. I don't know exactly what the vicar did, but I suspect something must have been said to the Goodhands, because we didn't stay at his church for long after that.

I became well versed in the ten commandments and the New

Testament, which we studied in Sunday School, and as a child I truly believed in the stories. It seemed to me as though many of them were being played out in the home; certainly, the little children were suffering, albeit not in the way the Bible meant. I always hoped that God was watching over us and would cast a miracle to make things better, end our beatings, and strike down Mrs Goodhand and her husband, but the only thing that changed was the churches we went to. It was as though whenever we got too familiar with the vicar, we were moved on.

As I grew older I began to get babysitting jobs around the estate at the weekends. I was good with small children, and it got me out of my father's dirty house. But with one couple I babysat for, the husband started to sexually abuse me as well. He always seemed to find a reason to return home from the pub before his wife; I can't imagine what he told her. I was beginning to get used to this type of treatment and even to see it as normal. I always felt quite insignificant, and believed that if I attempted to say anything no one would take any notice; after all, the Goodhands had not taken any notice when they heard what had happened on the Butlin's trip. I don't think I told anyone about the continual sexual abuse around me, although I now know from my care documents that the social worker was worried that when I was going to visit my father at the weekends I was entering houses of ill repute. So perhaps I mentioned something or acted in some way that made people concerned; regardless, I can't recall any action being taken as a result of it.

Unable to express my feelings about the sexual abuse I was being subjected to every weekend, these feelings came out only in the constant nightmares which caused the wet yellow stains on my sheets.

Over the years, the nightmares would get more and more

vivid. I was frightened to close my eyes at night because I knew that as soon as I went to sleep, I would hear that terrifying bang, the sign the nightmares were about to begin. Witches would start climbing through the windows with sharp red fingernails; the floor under my bed would split apart, and out of it emerged the devil. He would come for me with a red-hot pitchfork, which he shoved in my behind while a gorilla sat on the bed of the girl next to me. Aeroplanes would fly overhead, dropping bombs on us. I would scream, often waking the whole household, but even then the nightmare didn't always stop; in my delirious state I could still see the gorilla running down the garden path. Then I realised I had wet the bed again. And I knew what that meant.

Preparing the Civil Case

2007–8

With the civil case coming up, my solicitor was starting to send me documents and evidence that had been disclosed to her by the police. The original narrative from the police had been about the eleven minutes of CCTV footage showing Christopher's death in the custody suite, but we knew there was 108 hours of CCTV footage from the police station, fourteen hours from nine different cameras, the night Christopher was killed. This had now, finally, all been disclosed to me. I was apprehensive because I knew it was going to be disturbing to watch. We had already learned of the evidence of what sounded like monkey chants and talk of banana boats that were in the footage during the trial, but I did not know what else I was going to find. But now I had a bit of breathing space, I braced myself to start watching it.

This newly disclosed footage started just after midnight, several hours before Christopher arrived. I didn't think there would be much that was relevant before that, but I didn't want to miss anything, so I started right at the beginning of the video; I was dreading coming to the horrific parts after Christopher was brought in.

For the first hour and a half, nothing much seemed to

happen; the custody suite was quiet and empty. Then, just after 1.30 a.m., came what was supposedly an 'April Fool's joke', involving PC Barr calling another police station pretending to be a reporter from the *Hull Daily Mail*, talking about a death in custody. I had been expecting this, because the junior barrister Gareth Patterson had mentioned it in a meeting during the trial. The IPCC had suggested that this conversation had taken place before Christopher was brought in, but listening to it myself, and the way the conversation comes across, it seemed more likely that this was the next day. As well as I could make out, this was PC Barr's end of the conversation:

Hello there, this is Brian Myers from the *Hull Daily Mail*. I understand you had a death in custody earlier ... Oh hang on a minute it's April Fool man ... Who was it? Anyone we know? ... Nobody important ... He was working with us last night, yeah ... Oh good. Just thought I'd get you going ... This is the congratulations officer ... Thanks for your time.

He then made another call a couple of minutes later: 'That's right, he was bubbling, he was bubbling ... Beats me how pissed he was ... He wasn't pissed, was he? ... He was better when he came in then when he went out.'

He went on: 'Death in custody. *Hull Daily Mail*. Hello? Death in custody. Yeah there is a real one ... You're joking ... He's choked on his own vomit.'

How could this possibly have taken place before Christopher's death, when this is exactly what had happened to him?

A couple of minutes later, a drunk white woman was brought into the station, effing and blinding. Once she'd calmed down, she started telling the officers what's happened.

'I've been punched in the sides,' she told them, 'but not by the police.'

'That's reassuring,' one of the officers said.

'See?' said the arresting officer, 'I'm changing my ways after all!'

I shuddered. Was this just a joke? Or did he really have a reputation for beating his prisoners?

It then emerges that the woman has cut her finger.

'It's only a little scratch, nothing serious,' she told them. Nevertheless, both officers insisted on taking a look, to check she is OK. They were attentive to both her injuries and her feelings. The matron arrived and was also greatly concerned about the scratch. She got the woman a plaster and took her off for a proper investigation of the wound. In sum, the police sought to check and attend to her injuries and offer her both emotional and medical support.

Watching this left me gobsmacked; the visible difference between the concern shown for her wellbeing and Christopher's could not have been starker. Before the trial, when I had suggested to the CPS that the officers' contempt was influenced by racism, O'Doherty had written to me claiming that there was no evidence to suggest that a white person would have been treated any differently.[1] Yet here was what seemed to be clear evidence of the same officers, on the same night, treating a Black person and a white person totally differently. For the white woman with a cut finger, they were falling over themselves to give her medical attention; while Christopher, unconscious and struggling for breath, was discarded like a sack of rubbish, despite his clear distress, treated less like a man in need of support and more like a nuisance for messing up their floor with his blood and faeces. I couldn't believe it. The CPS had always told me that, for misconduct charges to stick, 'bad faith' needed to be proved, but they could find no evidence of bad faith. Yet this difference in treatment – potentially showing racism and therefore bad faith – had been buried by the CPS. I wondered what else they had 'overlooked'.

After the woman was led out by the matron, the two officers continued chatting. After a bit of lewd banter, one said to the other: 'I see you're coping with that fatality.'

'Life goes on,' the other replied, 'there is life after Harold, as they say.'

How many fatalities has this station had, I asked myself?

They continued: 'Lying on the floor, breathing in bubbles of vomit out of his nose or something.'

'I'd have just rolled him over.'

'They have his cellmate in here, looking at charging him with a section 18.'

My ears pricked up. Jason Paul had been charged with a GBH section 18. It was seeming more and more like this was footage from *after* Christopher's death, not before. But why would they include such casual discussion of his death and try to pass it off as having occurred before he died? Or if this really did show the hours before his death, who were they talking about – who else had been breathing vomit out of their nose, or should have been rolled over? What other fatality had there been? None of it made any sense.

Later I heard a woman buzzing from her cell to ask for a blanket because she was cold. She was immediately given one; another stark contrast with Christopher, left half naked on the cold stone floor of the custody suite, and a clear example of differential treatment conveniently ignored by the CPS. How much more evidence was needed to show 'bad faith' in their treatment of Christopher?

I stopped the video as the scene showing Christopher's death approached. I had seen enough for one day – and, as so often with the evidence we have been provided, I was left with more questions than answers.

The next day, I started the footage from the point at which Christopher's breathing had stopped. It was horrible to see, but I felt I had to do it, to see what else had been missed – or dismissed.

I continued to question the coughing and sneezing that seemed to happen when Blakey got close to Christopher's body. This could clearly be heard in the original eleven minutes of footage, which made me question whether CS gas had been used on Christopher – especially as a medical expert had said at the inquest that there were signs of irritation. But as I watched Stephen Krebbs, the paramedic, trying to clear Christopher's throat, I was shocked to hear him say what sounded like 'there's gas on his vocal cords to get out'. I had always suspected Christopher had been gassed. It would certainly explain why he was struggling to breathe. Now there was a paramedic telling us there was gas on his vocal cords. But this comment had been overlooked by all three investigating teams – West Yorkshire Police, the CPS and the IPCC – and so Krebbs had never been asked about it.

Moments later I noticed Sergeant Dunn throwing something near Christopher's body; twenty minutes later, Barr seemed to notice something on the floor – perhaps the thing that had been thrown – and kicked it closer to Christopher. God knows what they were doing.

The paramedics tried to get a tube down Christopher's throat before eventually giving up.

Victoria Drennan, the other paramedic, then said, 'I can't believe they took him in', to which Barr replied, 'We can't believe it neither'. Barr and Dunn were now the only two of the five officers involved in Christopher's death still in the room; Blakey and Dawson, the arresting officers, had left. Even when they were there, they were just slouched on the desk, showing no apparent concern over what they'd done.

At one point they were joined by Inspector Ford, a senior officer from Humberside Police who arrived following Christopher's death. Dunn told him, 'we seen them getting him out of the van', before being interrupted by another male saying 'but any – anything that anybody ...' before the recording becomes inaudible. Why was someone in such a hurry to stop Dunn telling Ford about how Christopher had been brought out of the van? And why had Dunn not mentioned anything about Christopher's removal from the van in his statement? Did it not match the arresting officers' accounts? Was Dunn attempting to cover for Dawson and Blakey?

As the paramedics started to clear their things up, Drennan seemed to stand on something on the floor. She bent down and said, 'What on earth's that?' Then she realised: 'It's a tooth!'

'Leave it down there,' Dunn said, 'it could be part of the evidence.'

'It will get picked up by the rubbish and get put in the clinical-waste bin, I bet,' Drennan pointed out.

'It could have someone else's blood on it, if you know what I mean,' Barr commented.

What did he mean by this?

At this point, Dunn started to get quite irate and insistent that the paramedics must leave all their rubbish as evidence. Was this tooth what Dunn had thrown onto the floor twenty minutes earlier? Had Dunn found it somewhere and wanted it to be discovered at the scene? If so, where had he found it – in the van? In the yard? The corridor? Had he planted it in the custody suite to make it look like it had come out during resuscitation? Was this the tooth that was lost after leaving the hospital? If so, what had happened to it? The police only ever had one of Christopher's teeth in their possession, which they claimed was the one from outside the nightclub, which they had miraculously retrieved from a landfill site the following day. But that tooth did not match the one recorded as being missing by the doctor at the hospital. This discrepancy has never been accounted for.

John Dunn, the custody officer, also fails to describe Christopher's removal from the police van in his written notes and statement. Both jump straight from 'being aware of van being reversed into prisoner reception yard' to 'saw on video monitor two officers pulling a male along, up ramp and in through open doorway', with no mention of the moment he was taken out of the van as he had started to tell Inspector Ford.

A little later, at 5.37 a.m., Barr appeared to say to one of his colleagues, 'We're going to have to look innocent.' He then added – and this is crystal clear – 'He got a good hiding before he came in here, didn't he?' I'd always said that Christopher had been murdered, and this sounded to my ears like an officer admitting, on camera, that he had been beaten before arriving at the police station. It was like an electric shock. I had been searching for evidence to confirm my suspicions, but I really didn't expect to find this. This was now the second time I thought Barr had potentially implicated Dawson and Blakey.

Of course, the police would probably claim – had anybody bothered to ask them – that Barr had been referring to the punch from Jason Paul. But that didn't seem to stack up. Why would they be concerned about 'looking innocent' about the fight outside the nightclub?

The concern didn't last, anyhow; a few minutes later, they eased the tension with monkey noises and jokes about banana boats, and all fell about laughing. The CPS claimed that the monkey noises might just have been an unusual laugh and that they were actually referring to banana *boots*. But the comment that followed was not so easily explained away: 'If I do, I hope the hood goes over my chin, pull it all around, tie it up and cut two eyeholes in them.' As far as I am aware, the only people who wear hoods with eyeholes cut in them are the Ku Klux Klan. But once again the CPS had refused to use this evidence in their case against the officers.

After this, Dunn and Barr's conversation turned to whether they should have done anything differently when Christopher was brought in.

'He's laid face down,' said Dunn, 'and you could say we should put him in the recovery position.' Barr then mentioned positional asphyxia; they both knew the dangers of how he had been treated. Later, Dunn said, 'Me and you could've got them to take him to the cells, then we could have got the ball rolling.' But even as they acknowledged their own role in Christopher's death, they were already working out how to stitch up Jason Paul and protect the arresting officers.

'Good thing as well, for the lads transporting him in,' said Barr, 'he's coming in, he's bleeding from an assault ... we've got the assault on camera.'

Then, for the third time now, Barr seemed to hint at the possibility that Christopher had been attacked by Dawson and Blakey: 'I think he's had a good paggering after ... ' – the middle of the sentence was impossible to make out, but then he seemed to finish it with the phrase, 'the white shits'. Who were they talking about? It can't have been Jason Paul, because he was Black. Paggering is Hull slang for a beating. My mind was racing. Barr continued: 'I don't think it's anything to do with him being obnoxious. At the end of the day, he's got any head injuries, then that's going to be the cause of it.' Again, Barr seemed to realise already that the simplest thing to do would be to lay all the blame for Christopher's death on Jason Paul.

Then Barr and Dunn seemed to turn back to the behaviour of Dawson and Blakey.

'I can't believe it,' Barr said.

'They shouldn't have beat him up,' Dunn replied. They? Why had nobody said anything about this before? How could they have missed such important evidence?

Dunn continued: 'Shows you what pearl white is.' What did he mean? That it shows what it's like to be a white police officer with power over a Black man?

Barr replied, 'Oh, it's terrifying.' Then he said something was 'disorientating; what would a good hiding do?'

I rewound the video. It sounded like he was saying, 'CS gas alone is disorientating; what would a good hiding do?'

Barr continued: 'Personally, I've been expecting something, not as serious as this ... throwing a violent fit or something, but not like this. No wonder they couldn't get an airway down him.' Why was it no wonder they couldn't get an airway down him?

A few minutes later, a female voice said what sounded like, 'Sergeant Ralph's just smacked Blakey.'

'If it was me, I would have smacked him,' said Bridget Winkley, the matron.

'Beats what I would have done,' said Barr.

I can't imagine what discussions about Dawson and Blakey

had been going on among the staff behind the scenes. But it definitely seemed like there was a feeling in the air around Dawson and Blakey's actions, as the other staff realised that they now potentially faced the blame for Christopher's death because of what their colleagues had done.

'How often have they been doing it?' asked Winkley.

'I know. They've just spurted it out of a can, haven't they? Spurted it,' said Barr.

'He's come on like the Terminator,' said Winkley, 'and accused the victim as *he's* violent.'

The officers seem to be going from being quite open one minute to then getting defensive when they remember they are being taped. After the doctor verified Christopher's death, DI Brookes – who later charged Jason Paul – arrived on the scene, warning the officers, 'You're putting your neck on the line every time you say that,' to which one of the other officers replied, 'Yeah, you've got to cover your back and say it's a head injury.' Later, an officer could be heard saying, 'We're going to have to be cleverer than that.' Some of these comments were definitely known to the CPS; a memo written by Chris Enzor in 2002, and later disclosed to us, described a message left by the junior CPS barrister Gareth Patterson during the trial of the police officers, noting 'comments about putting the neck on the line, about covering the back and all sorts of things which in Mr Patterson's view are quite crucial.' But this evidence was never used in the prosecution.

It was just shock after shock. Everybody had been trying to tell me that my suspicions about Christopher being beaten were crazy; I'd even begun to wonder myself whether I'd lost my mind. It had been very difficult, psychologically, to deal with what I was thinking and feeling when everybody else seemed to be telling me the opposite. I had kept asking myself, why couldn't I just accept what I was being told? Was it just me, making a big drama out of everything for no reason? But I couldn't help it; something inside me told me not to accept the official story. There were too many inconsistencies, too many unanswered questions, too much of a conflict between what I was being told and what I was reading and seeing.

Coming across evidence that, from my perspective, confirmed my suspicions should have made me feel vindicated, but there seemed to be nowhere to go with this evidence. I'd been everywhere and nobody seemed to want to listen. At least it confirmed to me I wasn't mad. But it didn't feel good. I felt traumatised. It was too late for it to bring about any justice; the officers had already been acquitted.

Once I had seen the footage, the only place I thought I could go was the office of my solicitor, Jane Deighton. I wasn't sure whether she'd seen it all herself and I wanted to show her what I'd found. We put the DVD into her computer and I found the conversations between Dunn and Barr. I was sweating and very agitated; I kept saying, 'Look at this, Jane, look at this! Listen!' But she wasn't as interested as I thought she'd be. I didn't understand what was going on, but something didn't feel right.

It was not long after that that Jane called me and, to my dismay, said that she would not, after all, be able to represent me, due to a 'conflict of interests'. I was stunned. She didn't tell me what this conflict was, but I felt dejected and abandoned. Self-doubt came over me and I started to question my own personality. I already felt confused and uncertain about what was happening and I didn't know what I was going to do next.

Jane told me that I didn't have a case against Humberside

and West Yorkshire Police after all, but I still had a case against the PCA and the CPS. She would continue to represent Christopher's sons in their case against Humberside, but if I wanted to continue the case against the PCA and CPS I would be on my own. I was dejected. Jane had represented me and Christopher's sons, who, when we first initiated the case after the collapse of the trial, had not reached adulthood. I felt used, distraught and confused, unclear about the legal process, and distressed by all the evidence I had been uncovering.

And now I had no representation for the cases against the CPS and the PCA. I knew I would have difficulty getting a new solicitor due to the mountains of documentary evidence we had accumulated. But I still tried. I felt we had a strong case; I knew the case the CPS had presented at the trial could never have been successful. Ruth was unable to take it because she dealt with criminal cases and not civil proceedings. The two of us frantically phoned round the solicitors we had been recommended, but they all seemed to be saying the same thing: that there was no way they could take the case on at such short notice. But I found a law firm that agreed. Shortly after that, out of the blue, a barrister named John Cooper got in touch and offered to take the case on. I was excited, and eagerly accepted his offer. The first test of this new team came quickly. The CPS requested that the second part of our claim, relating to the way they had conducted the case, be struck out, and the County Court judge had agreed to this. Cracks in our team quickly followed.

The barrister and the solicitors didn't seem to be working together, and, not really knowing what I was doing, I ended up dropping the solicitors. It was a naive move, and put me back to square one.

Cooper found another firm of solicitors who agreed to take the PCA case, but advised me to settle out of court because they had accepted liability. But it was the CPS case I was more concerned about, and they weren't prepared to take that on. Still, wanting to focus on the CPS, I took their advice about settling the PCA case out of court. I was awarded £20,000 compensation but I never saw a penny; it went straight to the legal aid board.

Meanwhile, the trial against the CPS was drawing nearer and I still had no legal representation.

I now realised I was going to have to go it alone – to prepare and run the case myself. Luckily, I did have support. My friend Zara, who I had met years previously through her involvement in the Ricky Reel campaign, phoned me daily and kept my spirits up, encouraging me to see this as the next chapter of my life. I also had my barrister friends, Mark and Georgina Firth, from Ian Macdonald's chambers in Manchester. They had supported me financially with my move to Leeds, and also bought me a computer to help me prepare for the case. I still had Ruth, who had supported me for years, as well as Andy and Maggie and the Hull campaigners who had done all they could to highlight the case locally and nationally. I felt so down about everything that if it hadn't been for these people, I could have easily just gone into a corner and allowed it to destroy me. But they accepted me as I was and encouraged me to carry on.

My flat was full of boxes and boxes of witness statements, judgments and documents that I'd collected over the years. I knew most of it off by heart, but now I needed to put it in a form that would enable me to challenge the CPS in court for the way they'd dealt with me and the prosecution into Christopher's death. I didn't have a clue how I was going to do it; I didn't know about law, but I was determined. I spent days and nights researching the thousands of documents, finding things I'd forgotten as well as new shocks. There was a constant stream of new revelations, and it continues even now, twenty-five years after Christopher's death.

Jane Deighton apologised to me years later. It was at a conference organised by the anti-racist Monitoring Group and I had gone along with my friend Zara.

Jane approached us and declared: 'I've come to make my peace. I realise now that you just wanted justice.' I was angry. I can't imagine what she had thought I wanted before. What assumptions did she have about me when she was my solicitor? I think she was giving advice about how to get the best result in the system, but I wasn't interested in that. I was just outraged by what had been done to Christopher and determined that he got justice; nothing else mattered.

After the Goodhands

1974–7

For a while, there were only two girls in the home, but for some reason the other girl, who was white, didn't seem to be subjected to the same physical abuse as me; perhaps because she didn't wet the bed. Nevertheless, my brothers and the other children in the home also went through trauma. Many a time I saw and felt the terrible kick that Mr Goodhand pounded with full force up the backside, either flooring us or sending us hurtling to the other side of the room. My brothers had quieter personalities than me: a bit more withdrawn and less talkative. They bore visible signs of stress, as did many of the children that lived at the home. Christopher and Stephen were both very sensitive and showed their distress by repeatedly banging their heads on their headboards. My oldest brother, Emmanuel, meanwhile, seemed to get picked on a lot. I remember once the house mother caught him with cigarettes in his pocket. She decided to punish him by making him smoke the entire packet – twenty Capstan Full Strength – without blowing out any of the smoke. I pretended to need the toilet, so I could go through the kitchen, where the punishment was taking place, and see what was going on. Emmanuel was huddled in the corner, snot dribbling from his nose to his mouth, choking, coughing, crying. Every time he tried to blow the smoke out instead of swallowing it, she would hit him with a metal pipe from the Hoover. The anger surged through my body; I felt sorry for him but also helpless and guilty. Not long after this, Emmanuel ran away and was not found for days. It was not the first time one of the kids had run away from the home. But on this occasion, once they found him, he wasn't returned to Marlborough Avenue. He must have been moved to another home; I didn't really see him again after that.

It was reported that our behaviour was beginning to deteriorate. The social worker was able to see that the longer we lived in Marlborough Avenue, the more we were showing signs of disturbance. While Mrs Goodhand tried to present this as the result of us being spoiled by our dad on the weekends, the social worker himself put it down to two reasons: firstly, emotional deprivation and secondly, the difficulty of adjusting to two different cultures, one of which presented itself as satisfactory, and the other as unsatisfactory. The fear was that this would lead us to denigrate our Nigerian culture, and thereby devalue ourselves – which we certainly did.

Looking back on my childhood, I can see now how the authorities were so occupied in writing reports about me and my brothers that they didn't notice the abuse we were suffering under their care. In those days children were not regarded as being of much consequence; their feelings could therefore safely be ignored. This made it easier for the social workers to get their responses from the house parents, who knew what words to feed them, allowing them to fill in their forms, tick their boxes, and go back to their offices or homes and ignore or forget about anything too disturbing. And as children, of course, we tended to accept things as they were, knowing that our protests would more likely bring about punishment than help. The lesson for me is that those in authority, all too often, just want an easy life. They might covet the salary, the security and the status but they don't necessarily want the responsibility or the hard work. It was a lesson that would be demonstrated again, in the most horrific way, following Christopher's death.

The same routine carried on for years: new children came and left; new staff and 'aunties' came and left; but everything seemed to change when a young married woman – Auntie Tracy – came to work at the home. She was kind to us, and good fun – she did things outside our normal routine, and even took me horse riding. Her husband was a bit of an action-man type and once took us water skiing with him. Weekends with them were quite pleasant, but she soon saw how we were treated by the Goodhands. At one point I quite freely told her that we only ever got second-hand clothes. I had heard that the house parents were putting the money we were supposed to have for new clothes towards holidays abroad and a lovely bungalow in a picturesque village just outside Hull called Swanland. I think she must have made her own enquiries, because not long after this, we found out that the Goodhands were leaving and we were to get new house parents. Nobody explained to us why it was happening; everything was done behind closed doors. I don't know whether there had been some kind of investigation, but no one had come to speak to us children about what had been going on. We were just confused.

Unfortunately Tracy left as well. A couple then moved in with a young child of their own; but by then the damage had been done. My older brothers had already left, and we had all been emotionally scarred one way or another by what had gone on; none of us had ever had so much as a hug in that home. For me, it comes out as rage – I fight back – but my brothers tend to just withdraw and turn everything back in on themselves. There is no doubt in my mind that this is a big part of the reason Stephen ended up spending his life in a mental institution.

By the time the Goodhands left I was rebelling; sometimes I wouldn't come home at night, or I would turn up with what must have seemed like some less than savoury characters. Once I brought home a man who worked at Hull fairground, years older than me, covered in tattoos, including what were known as 'borstal spots' – blue dots on his face indicating time in a youth detention centre. The new house parents must have had a nightmare, but tried to deal with me sensitively, probably hoping this was a phase I'd grow out of. I even punched the house mother once; she was shouting at me, and I could feel it coming, brewing up inside me – I felt I was going to lash out, and I did. I remember her husband kicking me up the stairs after that – and for once I deserved it. It was not long before the new couple moved out; I think a house full of children as damaged as we were must have been too much for them to bear.

Once my older brothers had left school and the home, I didn't see them much: when Stephen and I went to my dad's at weekends, they were out doing the usual things boys do, living their freedom – or, in Christopher's case, army life. From the children's home, he was used to discipline and life in an institution and I suppose he believed that the army would give him a bit of a career and allow him to travel the world.

At sixteen I got myself a job in one of the local supermarkets, through a local work experience scheme. I was earning £27 a week, from which the care home would deduct £22 for my keep.

I didn't want to live there and for them to still have control of what I was doing just made me more rebellious. I was attracted to anything and anybody that could show me a life that was different from what I had known. But underneath my strong athletic exterior I was still very vulnerable and a magnet for those who wished to exploit me – even if I didn't realise that myself. Eventually I moved into a flat with a friend from school, living on £7 a week and lime marmalade on toast. But for me, this was freedom. I told myself that from now on, I would be the one to steer the course of my life. I had a rebellious spirit, but none of the proper skills I needed to survive in the outside world; this newfound freedom wasn't to last long.

Civil Case Against the CPS

2009–10

In civil cases, it is not enough to prove that an injustice has been done, you have to prove damage has been done to you personally. My case against the CPS was one of racial discrimination: that the CPS had failed to provide a professional service because of my and Christopher's skin colour, culture and ethnic origin, the Macpherson report's definition of racism. My argument was that they had discriminated against me in the conduct of the prosecution of the five officers, failed to take proper regard of my concerns and complaints about a number of evidential matters, and treated me rudely in several other respects.

The IPCC report had applied the test set out in the PCA guidelines and concluded that the police involved in Christopher's death had been guilty of unwitting racism. The officers' assumptions that Christopher was on amphetamines, steroids or alcohol; their readiness to put his problems down to 'bad attitude' rather than head injury; and their use of language like 'coloured' and 'of negroid appearance', said the IPCC, all reflected stereotypical assumptions and attitudes based on Christopher's colour. On the balance of probabilities, they believed that Christopher's race was detrimental to him, and that his treatment would likely have been different had he been white. All that was clear to the IPCC. Yet the CPS had apparently been unable to see any of it, despite Ruth and me constantly pointing it out to them.

In October 2009, a pre-trial review meeting was held at the High Court, presided over by Judge Sedley. These meetings are a chance to discuss some of the details around how the case would proceed, and for the judge to rule on each side's request for documents from the other. I informed the court that I would be representing myself as what is called a 'litigant in person'. And the judge informed me that the case would be thrown out unless I consented to the release of my medical records. In civil cases, each side has the right to demand the disclosure of documents relevant to the case held by the other side. But the judge was much less categorical when it came to my requests for documents from the CPS. Although he said the CPS *might* have to release documents relating to their decision-making in relation to the trial of the officers, ultimately the CPS refused to provide these.

However, one good thing came out of this meeting. I had appealed the court's decision to strike out the parts of my case relating to the conduct of the prosecution, as requested by the CPS. But now, ruling on my appeal, Sedley and the other two judges said that if it could be proved that the CPS discriminated against me in the conduct of the prosecution of the five officers, then this would have an impact on my case. They therefore reversed the earlier decision and reinstated my claim in full. I was relieved. But the whole episode had shown me how desperate the CPS had been to ensure that their handling of the case should not come under scrutiny.

I was still very weak and had by now spent nearly a year and a half sitting night and day looking at the evidence, unsure how to prepare but doing the best I could. This was all new to me; I was not a trained barrister, and once the trial was underway I would not have a team of solicitors behind me passing me points of law and important documents. So instantly I was at a disadvantage. I had to scour through 1,700 pages of documents by myself. Many of them, I soon realised, were duplicates; I began to wonder whether they were trying to drown me in paper, burying the important documents in a mass of useless information in the hope that I wouldn't be able to make head nor tail of any of it. My mind was already damaged from years of psychological trauma, and it was not an easy task. Looking back on it now, I don't really know how I did it. Still I ploughed on, working on the case during the week and spending the weekends cleaning the local pub to pay the bills.

The trial was set for September 2010, and was due to last for twelve days (rather than three days as the CPS had requested). As the date loomed, I was surprised to get a call from Jane Deighton offering to answer any legal questions I had before the trial began. It was good of her, but it was a bit late by then and it really didn't make much difference to my understanding.

The case was heard by Judge Penelope Belcher at Leeds County Court on the 20–23 September, 15–19 and 26 November, and 2–3 December 2010. In her opening remarks, the judge explained that the onus was on me to prove I had been discriminated against, and to do this I would need to give an example of differing treatment of someone else from a different ethnic background.

Next, the CPS QC handed the judge a list she had drawn

up of what she considered to be the principal issues of the case. I was deeply sceptical of the CPS attempting to control the narrative in this way. So I was not surprised that her list had completely omitted all reference to the conduct of the trial against the officers. It was as if the High Court's ruling against their attempt to strike out that part of the claim never happened!

I was first in the dock and would remain there for the first two and a half days of the trial. I was already feeling at my weakest, having been up all night preparing the case for months on end, and now it felt like it was me that was on trial. But the agenda was set; the CPS QC and her team would now spend the next two days attempting to tear apart my claim and undermine my credibility.

One of the complaints I had raised in my statement was that the CPS's O'Doherty had tried to bypass me and deal only with Ruth, despite the fact that Ruth was no longer representing me by that point. Ruth had had to remind him that the CPS had a duty to keep victims informed. Indeed, I was under the impression that this was his sole role in the case, as he himself had suggested to me in a letter from October 2000 about the CPS review of the new evidence from the inquest.

'Do you take the letter from Mr O'Doherty to be racist?'

I was used to this: taking a single incident, painting it as an innocuous mistake, and mocking as paranoid the idea that it could ever be construed as racist.

'I cannot say that any one incident is racist,' I replied, 'but the "collective treatment" of the case and inability or outright refusal to treat the case as a racist case was.'

The CPS had consistently failed to take seriously the idea that racism had played a role in Christopher's treatment, despite the

IPCC's conclusion that it had, on the same evidence. As a result, they had not used any of this evidence in their case against the officers. When their own lawyers found monkey noises and references to banana boats on the CCTV footage, which was subsequently confirmed by their own language specialists, they went out of their way to get a new transcript with a different interpretation. Then, when I asked for an independent review of the discrepancies between the two transcripts, they refused, and none of it was presented to the jury. Furthermore, the officers' use of language such as 'coloured' and 'negroid' was edited out of their statements, so the issue of race was never heard in court.

'Why didn't you raise this issue at the time?' the CPS QC demanded.

'The documents weren't in my possession; I didn't have the documents at the time,' I explained.

'You have them now.'

'I do.'

'Why isn't all of this in your witness statement?'

I was shocked that they were trying to make out this was information that I had sprung on them; in fact, for ten years, they'd been the ones hiding it from me.

'I have no experience of writing a witness statement, I'm representing myself,' I said. 'The words "coloured" and "negroid" were in the officer's statements, which have been in the CPS's possession since 1998.'

One of the most shocking failures, in my view, had been the CPS's refusal to investigate the possibility that Christopher had been assaulted by the police en route to the police station. Christopher appeared to have had a belt on at the club, but no one asked – the CPS included – where this belt was by the time he arrived at the police station. The same went for his extra missing tooth, the additional wounds to his head, lip and neck, and the fact that his trousers were down to his knees – none of this was accounted for. If any of this had happened to a police officer after contact with a member of the public, people would rightly have wanted to know what had happened. At the same time, all the usual procedures were waived with the effect that all forensic evidence that might have revealed whether an assault had occurred was destroyed, by the chief suspects. By any objective standards, this should have been of deep concern to the CPS.

'The physical issues had not been investigated, only the medical issues,' I said in court.

'Physical issues could not have contributed to Christopher's loss of consciousness,' came the reply from the CPS QC; even now, the CPS appeared to deem the possibility of a police assault on a Black man who subsequently died to be an irrelevance unworthy of investigation. My blood started to boil.

'Nobody even questioned how those injuries had been sustained!' I said. 'The issue of assault has never been investigated!'

'They [the injuries] would not cause unconsciousness.'

'Can you provide evidence of that?' I asked, trying hard to remain calm.

The lawyer then read from the account of the meeting of the medical experts in 2001, quoting that 'all agreed that there was no medical basis to prove Christopher's unconsciousness'. I couldn't believe she was trying to use this medical uncertainty to justify the CPS's refusal to investigate what the officers did to Christopher. I noted that one of the experts she was quoting, Professor Crane, explicitly put forward the possibility that Christopher's additional injuries could have been caused by an assault by the police.

'"Possibility" is not enough,' the QC replied.

'The possibility wasn't even explored!'

'You're not accepting anyone else's views, are you, Miss Alder?'

By now, I was fighting back the tears, once again feeling belittled and dismissed. It felt like they were trying to break me.

'I haven't come here to waste time,' I told her, 'I have a point to make!'

Next, the defence read from a document written by O'Doherty stating that I had told him I'd never had any faith in the CPS, and had put the phone down on him.

'Did you tell Mr O'Doherty that you didn't have faith in the CPS?' she asked me.

'Yes, I did say that and I was right to say that,' I told her. 'I wanted to have faith,' I explained, 'but letters were written and nothing was followed up, no answers were provided as to why Christopher's trousers were down to his knees, where Christopher's belt was.'

Part of my contention was that the CPS were reluctant to see the officers go to jail; this was hardly a conspiracy theory – even Lord Butler had concluded that the CPS were reluctant to prosecute the police in his 1999 report. But the CPS QC sought to mock this idea by constantly speaking about the CPS 'plotting', a phrase I had never used. It felt like an attempt to discredit me, as if the case being set to fail was all part of a paranoid imagination.

'These letters "were all a part of a scheme"?' she asked me – again, I felt, wilfully missing the point. The letters were of no real consequence in themselves, they were simply meaningless attempts to pacify me. The CPS may have *replied* to me, but they never *investigated* any of the issues I raised.

'Just because these letters were written doesn't mean anything was followed up,' I said.

'This was a plot?' she asked, sarcastically. I thought, fine, if that's what she wants to call it.

'Yes.'

'Fleming was a part of it?'

'Yes.'

'O'Doherty?'

'Yes.'

'Enzor?'

'Yes. The agenda had already been set; Mr Enzor was brought in at a late stage and it was too late to change the agenda. He had stated that there may have been some grounds for manslaughter. That's not to say that I wasn't affected by his treatment of me.'

The defence QC returned to her documents.

'Hilliard stated that you once called him a racist bigot.'

Nicholas Hilliard was a member of James Curtis's prosecuting team. I had met him briefly with O'Doherty.

'No, I called O'Doherty a racist bigot.'

'Hilliard wrote a letter of committal evidence stating that Ms Alder called him a racist bigot.'

'No, I didn't call Hilliard a racist bigot, I didn't speak to him. But I admit to calling O'Doherty a racist bigot.' As far as I was concerned, that was not simply my opinion, that was established fact; after all, O'Doherty had had a ruling of racial discrimination upheld against him at an employment tribunal.

Then the questions went back to the 'plot'.

'Was Gareth Patterson a part of this "plot"?' Gareth had been one of the junior prosecuting barristers at the trial. I actually liked Gareth; I think he was trying his best, but the hierarchy wouldn't let his findings go anywhere.

'I hadn't spoken much to Patterson, except about the CS gas and the monkey noises.'

'To clarify, O'Doherty, Enzor and Fleming were all a part of this plot?'

It was my belief that they deliberately ignored evidence of racism in order to limit the damage to the police's reputation. 'Macpherson's report had just come out, accusing the police force of being institutionally racist and a police racist death of a Black man would have caused more aggro for the force.'

'They did it because they were racist?'

'Yes, this was another Black death; they didn't want another high-profile case.'

'Racism is despicable, but do you think it's quite questionable as to whether these individuals were being racist?'

'I would be surprised that nobody mentioned race at all, you have five white police officers around him with his trousers down to his knees.'

'This is not enough evidence.'

'There is the comparison of the girl who was in a police cell, cold and given a blanket. Compare that to a Black man, lying on the floor injured, with his trousers down, and not one person covered him up. I asked about the question of race, and the senior members of the CPS immediately rebuffed the idea. But the comparison would have strengthened the case. Statements of the police using racist words to refer to Christopher were never mentioned in the hearing.'

Next, the questioning moved on to the CPS's presentation of conflicting medical evidence, with the QC attempting to justify it out of 'fairness to the defence'. I explained that they had undermined their own case. But I was getting tired; I had now been under a barrage of hostile questioning for nearly an hour and a half. Ruggie pointed this out and the judge scolded him, but he did then offer me a ten-minute break.

After the break, I was back on the stand.

'Was it not the case you wanted a manslaughter charge?' the CPS QC asked me.

The question took me by surprise as I thought that manslaughter charges were supposed to be what the CPS wanted too.

The QC then read out a letter from O'Doherty stating that there might be a real prospect for prosecuting on the grounds of manslaughter.

'This proves that Mr O'Doherty wasn't being dismissive of your request,' the lawyer told me.

I felt we were going round in circles; the CPS had had to be forced, kicking and screaming, to bring the manslaughter charge, and then they had ensured it would fail by conflicting the evidence. I explained that the charges could never have stuck with the approach they took.

'Was this a part of the plot to make sure the prosecution didn't succeed?' There it was again, the word 'plot'. I felt like she was attempting to ridicule me, but I tried to ignore it.

'The fact that the evidence [supporting a case for manslaughter] was put forward alongside contradictory evidence would suggest yes.'

'The voluntary bill was put forward in full knowledge that the case would fail?' she asked, eyebrows raised.

'I'm not a professional,' I told her, 'and I don't class myself as particularly intelligent. But I can see that these people were professionals and have been prosecuting for years.' Of course they knew it would fail, or should have done. The CPS had refused to allow us to see the bill of indictment, precisely because, I believe, they knew we would have challenged the way they were planning to present the evidence.

'Ruth and I asked if we could have the evidence put to the court so we could look over it,' I told the court.

'You repeatedly asked for evidence, witnesses, the voluntary bill, police reports and in each case Mr O'Doherty had said that such evidence was only to be put to the Crown Prosecution – you weren't entitled to that, were you?'

'Yes,' I said, 'but it would have been courteous if they had provided it.'

'Think about the defence, how would they have felt knowing you had all that evidence?'

I was seething. My mind went back to my first meeting with Chris Enzor, when he explained his concern for the 'other five families involved', the families of the policemen, none of whom had lost a loved one, while we were still grieving. Why was I constantly being asked to sympathise with them?

'Think about how *we* must have felt,' I told her, 'when we found out that the conflicting evidence was going to be shared with the defence even before the case started, how must we have felt about that as victims?'

'The bill should have been brought but without the conflicting evidence,' I concluded.

The judge asked me whether I appreciated that, even if this had happened, the defence could then have called experts with conflicting evidence themselves.

'Yes,' I answered, 'then the jury could have made up their minds as to who they believed.'

For me, this was the point. It was not simply that the officers had walked free that was so upsetting; it was the fact that the prosecution had ensured the case was thrown out before the officers had even had to explain themselves. The jury never got to hear both sides and make up their own minds; the police officers escaped not only punishment but any semblance of accountability. Just like at the inquest, they had escaped having to answer a single question about their conduct.

I continued: 'The judge ruled that the case was thrown out because the prosecution produced conflicting evidence. I'm not here to judge the judge, I'm here to judge the Crown Prosecution, their actions and the effect it had on me.'

I was exhausted by the barrage of questions from the QC. My nerves were shattered and anxiety was preventing me from sleeping at night. On top of having to cope with the initial shock of the manner of Christopher's death, I had now had years of additional stress from being rebuffed and dismissed by the very people who were supposedly trying to get to the truth, not to mention the suspicion that I was being spied on by the police. I was exhausted before we had even started. Meanwhile, the CPS were represented by a top QC – who, I suspected, hadn't gone through a fraction of the trauma I had suffered – backed by a team of trained solicitors, all paid for out of the public purse. You couldn't have had a greater inequality of arms.

While it was supposedly the CPS on trial for the way they had handled the case and dealt with me, it felt more like I was being made to defend what I had been through, like it was my own feelings and sanity that were on trial.

'Miss Alder, was it not just the case you would not accept that some questions would ever be answered?' said the CPS QC.

'Yes,' I said. 'As a family member, I believe I had a right to know where Christopher's additional injuries came from, where his belt had gone and his missing tooth.'

'Are you saying the CPS lawyers are racist?' she asked.

Once again, I tried to explain the meaning of institutional racism. Dealing with these people, it was like the Macpherson report had never been written: 'I believe the actions of the CPS collectively and the way they dealt with the prosecution as well as me was institutionally racist.'

By now I was close to a complete breakdown. I wept uncontrollably in the dock; it took every last drop of energy to compose myself and carry on. I had been in the dock for most of the day, with only one ten-minute break. Only after the emotional crisis I was experiencing had peaked did the opposing barrister ask me if I was all right to continue. It was shortly after 4 p.m. I decided to carry on; by then, I just wanted to get it over with.

I continued trying to explain how the Macpherson report described racism as a difference in treatment between members of a different race. I then asked the judge if I could show a section of the custody suite video, which we were told was taken shortly before Christopher's arrival.

I showed them the part of the footage with the white girl being brought in drunk, with the officers and matron fussing over the scratch on her finger. Here, the police were clearly seen to check and attend to her injuries and offer her both emotional and medical support.

I then asked for the court to be shown the video of Christopher – unconscious, bleeding from the mouth, and gasping for his life – being dragged in and dumped face down on the floor. I left the room before it started, having seen this traumatic footage too many times already. Everyone in the court could see with their own eyes the officers, who had shown such concern, care and attention to the white girl, showing total disregard for Christopher's condition, not even bothering to put him in the recovery position. The judge had set out that claims of racial discrimination needed to demonstrate differential treatment for members of different races. In these two videos, taken just two hours apart, and involving the very same officers, that difference could not have been starker.

Yet the CPS, who claimed that they had viewed all of this footage before the trial of the officers, had completely dismissed this clear evidence of racism, which would have demonstrated the bad faith ingredient of gross misconduct which they were supposedly trying to prove. This evidence had played no part in the criminal prosecution – either the CPS had chosen to bury it, or they had never bothered to view the footage in the first place. In fact, it had apparently not been noticed by *any* of the state institutions charged with investigating Christopher's death – not the PCA, nor the CPS, nor Humberside Police, nor West Yorkshire Police, nor the IPCC. Instead it had been left to me to spend months in emotional distress painstakingly going through 108 hours of video footage to find the evidence no one else had been able or willing to find.

When I returned to the courtroom, I asked why the CPS had not found this evidence of racial discrimination. The QC brushed it off by claiming that the difference in treatment was purely due to the white girl being a woman before adding an even more bizarre justification of the different treatment: that the white girl was conscious. As if that meant she required *more* medical attention, and Christopher less! This was the same excuse used by Enzor in the official CPS report into their failed prosecution. It felt like an insult to my intelligence. The defence continued to insist that 'this comparison of treatment would have done nothing for the case'. I asked them why, but they failed to answer. At around 5 p.m., after a gruelling day, the session ended.

Leaving Hull

1977–81

I can't tell a lie and pretend that we remained a close-knit family as we got older. Being in care had done a lot of damage to all of us, and our family was fractured, each going our own separate way.

I left care without much guidance. I had been cocooned in that environment, sheltered from the outside world, but it had not been a protective cocoon. I was left with no great sense of who I was, conditioned to feel like I always had to change myself to my surroundings to please those around me. I was a sitting target. That was when I met Kenny.

It was at the Albermarle youth club. He wore his hair long, dressed in denim jackets and leathers, and he and his brother were part of a motorcycle gang. He was the first person who'd ever paid any attention to me. I was sixteen, still very easily influenced by others, and he was ten years older. We quickly moved in together. I was able to cook nice meals and I kept a clean home. I was far from submissive in my relationships and I hoped the men I chose would see and treat me on equal terms, that they would respect me and I them. It didn't turn out that way.

Not long after we started seeing each other, Kenny would be going out all the time, sleeping with other women, and being very cruel, bullying me and even threatening to kill me.

It was around that time that my dad had a stroke. I went to see him in hospital. He couldn't speak, and would be unable to for the rest of his life. After he came out, he tried living back at home for a while, with Richard looking after him, but Richard was just a young lad; he'd just come out of the children's home and he wanted to live his life a bit. Dad needed constant care. I couldn't take him in because of the domestic violence, and he ended up moving into an old people's home; I remember moving all the stuff out of his house. I went to see him every weekend, as I always had done as a child. It must have been very hard for him; he had been such an independent person. Seeing him in the home felt like a role reversal; it gave me a taste of how my dad must have been feeling when we were in care. When I visited, we'd sit together in a communal area, just as he'd come to see us in the playroom at the children's home. I always felt powerless on those visits to the old people's home, seeing his suffering but unable to help him, wondering if he was being treated properly, and I guess he must have felt the same way coming to see us. That made me think about all the things he couldn't tell us when we were kids. Now he couldn't tell us because of his stroke. But the pain, regret and helplessness was all there – you could see it in his face.

Not long after my dad's stroke I discovered I was pregnant. I'd never felt so strange in my life. I had absolutely no energy. I'd only been with Kenny for about six months. Because of my young age, and my history of being brought up in a children's home, the doctors advised me to have an abortion or to put the child up for adoption. But I didn't want an abortion, and with my experience in care, I didn't want to do that to my daughter either. As for Kenny, I don't remember whether I even told him about the pregnancy at first; he wasn't bothered about me, and he wasn't exactly the type of person I could talk things through with. So, just twelve days before my seventeenth birthday, I gave birth to my daughter Caroline.

A few months later, I found out that Kenny had been messing around with another woman while I was pregnant, and I confronted him. He gave me a vicious beating, but what really scared me was that he then threatened to go to social services to get Caroline taken away from me. At that moment I knew I had to get away, as far away as possible. As soon as he went out the next day, I filled two bin bags with clothes, put my daughter in her buggy and fled to the train station. I saw there was a train going to the very town in Scotland where my friend Maizna had recently moved, as her brother worked in the fishing trade on the trawlers. I jumped on the train, my heart pumping wildly at every stop, sick with fear that Kenny would be there waiting for me. But the hardest part was having to leave my little dog, Shane. He had been my father's dog, and I had grown up with him. Leaving him with Kenny was heartbreaking.

When I arrived in Scotland, I never looked back, and never again thought of Hull as my home. The lack of guidance from my early years had got me into some unpleasant situations, but I realise now I had learned a lot from them. Having seen the light, I definitely wasn't going to go back to an abusive relationship; I didn't consider returning to the ghosts I had left behind for a moment.

It wasn't easy to get accommodation, so at first I stayed in a mother and baby home, a temporary refuge for young women with issues. Then Maizna's brother Hassan and his wife, Rosie, let us stay at theirs for a while – but really I needed to find a proper home for me and my daughter. That was when I met Sheila. Sheila was a close friend of Rosie's and we got on really well; she was around twenty years older than me and had three children of her own, the eldest a little younger than I was. After a while, Sheila invited us to live with her and looked after me while I was waiting to move into my own home. She was the closest thing I'd had to a mum and a female role model since I was two, and she came at the right time, when I was quite isolated. She cooked for me and Caroline and we always had a nice warm bed to sleep in; for the first time in my life I had a little security in a friendly, homely environment.

I started to socialise more, but I was still carrying those feelings of unworthiness that I had picked up in care; I seemed to find it hard to stay away from a certain type of man, and continually ended up in destructive relationships. It's a pattern that I seem to have. In care, they don't teach you anything about who you are or how to make good decisions; you're just brought up to adhere to rules and regulations; it's almost as if they're grooming you for controlling relationships. On top of that, it wasn't easy being one of the few Black people in town at the time; apart from Maizna and her brother, the only others tended to be students at the university. The locals called us 'darkies', and thought nothing of using language like that. It seemed that when people saw a Black person for the first time, they became fearful, and just couldn't get past the fact that this person was Black; this prevented them from ever getting to know us well enough to make the colour irrelevant. So the word darkie stayed. Still, I eventually built up a certain resistance to this treatment; I was as good as anyone, and I wasn't prepared to let other people's ignorant perceptions stop me from doing what I wanted to do.

As far as relationships were concerned, I believed it was possible to have a partnership of equals where each could enjoy the other without resentment or domination; I had seen how Mrs Goodhand henpecked her husband and I certainly didn't want a relationship like that. I tended to pick men I thought I was on a level with, and with whom I could have a laugh and a joke. I was easy-going and didn't cling to men for the sake of it, nor was I looking for someone to provide for me and my daughter. This probably appealed to them at first, but they often came to resent my independence. I think it made them feel like I didn't need them, and this took away some of their male need to protect. They expected their women to cry to them if the smallest of things didn't go right, but I was not brought up like that. I had learned early on not to expect help from anyone; I had learned to survive and I had no option but to be independent. This was my strength, but all too often men viewed it as a threat. So they sought to suppress my personality, my self-expression, even how I dressed, as they didn't want other men looking at me. In the end, they found the only way they could control me was by using their physical strength, which just made me run and escape.

Kenny was like this. One night we were out together when another man asked me out. Seeing what was happening, Kenny immediately came over and punched me full in the face. This was the kind of thing that would happen often, but for a while I found myself attempting to please him, as if the problem was mine; I would avert my gaze to the ground when he was shouting at me, even while I was sat right next to him. Usually, some time after hitting me, he would apologise and cry and say he wouldn't do it again; and sometimes I believed him – but this peaceful intent never seemed to last for very long. The aggression would come out when he was drunk. He liked to get to the pub at 6 p.m. every night; his excuse was that this was the best time to get a pool table. I didn't know he was drinking vodka and special brew all night, and it took me a long time to realise he was, in fact, an alcoholic. The penny dropped one night at the bar, and I finally realised I had to get away from him. Earlier that night a regular at the bar had intervened to stop him pulling me around, so by the time we left, he was already in a bad mood. Outside the pub he attacked me, knocking me to the ground, and started trying to headbutt me. I took off my shoe and used it to fight back, and being a six-inch stiletto, it did him some serious damage. He ended up in hospital with an eye injury and it took him weeks to recover. I stayed long enough to nurse him back to health, but then he was immediately back to his old ways. I ended up back at the mother and baby home. What I didn't realise at the time was that I had been conditioned to think I was not worthy of anything but an abusive relationship. I was continually trying to please, believing that I was the cause of the problems in my relationships. It took me a long time to understand, or even see, what I was doing.

Then, in 1981, my dad died. I didn't find out until after the funeral had already happened. I felt awful; there's still a guilt that I carry to this day. I hadn't seen him since I left Hull; I'd been too scared of running into Kenny to go back. But I felt that at least he wasn't suffering anymore; he was resting. He'd had a hell of a life. Coming over in the 1950s, my mum's struggles with her mental health, all of us going into care – his life was sucked away from him in every way. He must have been knackered with it all, and probably felt like he'd let his kids down. Then he was working all the time, ending up with an illness, going into an old people's home, with nobody there to look after him. It must have been horrendous. I find it hard to understand how some people can have such a lifetime of it and other people's lives can be so simple.

The CPS in the Dock

2010

On the third day, it was finally the turn of the CPS officials to stand in the dock. This was my chance to interrogate them about their failings.

The first thing I raised was why they had put forward the evidence of the anaesthetist at the trial, the one who had claimed that 'negroes' were more likely to die of asphyxia due to their bigger lips and tongues. I asked why the CPS had used this evidence, and failed to challenge its racist description of Black people. The CPS lawyer said he thought it was just the professional opinion of an expert, and still did not seem to understand that such descriptions were offensive. So I asked him to look at one of the court assessors sat next to the judge, who happened to be a Black man. I asked him if he noticed that the assessor had thin lips, unlike mine which were thicker. Does this not show, I asked him, that the anaesthetist's claims, put forward by the CPS in their case, were stereotypical and untrue, and that just like white people and people from all ethnic groups, Black people have features of different sizes?

I went on to question the CPS's failure to make further

enquiries in relation to the additional injuries incurred by Christopher after leaving the hospital. The CPS are, by law, entitled to request further investigations where necessary, but had refused to do so in our case, despite my pleas. I asked them where my brother's missing belt was, but they just said they 'did not know'. I asked whether they had requested further enquiries to be made as to where it could have gone, and was told they had not. I asked where the additional injuries sustained by Christopher en route to the police station had come from, and they told me they 'didn't know'. I asked whether these injuries could have been caused by a potential assault by the officers, and they replied, 'that's possible'. I asked if they had made any further inquiries into this, and they said 'no'. I asked if it was possible that a further assault on Christopher by the officers could have caused the loss of his second tooth. The CPS admitted that it could have done. Their responses confirmed to me that my questions were rational and that answers to them could have been available – it was just that no one from the CPS considered them important enough to investigate.

After establishing to the court that the CPS had not even attempted to investigate a possible assault by the officers, I asked them why they had failed to do so. Their answer was that there would have been no point because any injuries sustained in this assault did not kill Christopher. A chill ran down my spine. How could they possibly know the impact an assault may have had if they had not investigated it? The CPS deemed it irrelevant that Christopher's unconsciousness *was* related to his death, and that an attack on a handcuffed prisoner is a criminal offence in its own right – despite any such attack constituting undeniable evidence of bad faith and therefore supporting the misconduct charge.

If a man received additional injuries while in my care, I asked, following which he lost consciousness and died on the floor (while *still* in my care), would the CPS not be asking if I'd caused the additional injuries he sustained? Would they have deemed a possible assault on him by me irrelevant to a trial concerning my conduct?

It was shocking to hear them admit so openly and brazenly that they did not think it worth their while to investigate Christopher's additional injuries. But I felt vindicated. Finally, they had given answers to the questions I'd been asking them for years, admitting that a police assault could not be ruled out and that these were not unanswerable questions, but were rather questions that they had wilfully chosen to ignore.

Next it was time to call my witnesses. First up was Ruggie. He began by giving a very thorough outline of all the concerns we had raised that had subsequently been ignored by the CPS – about the forensic evidence that was destroyed before it had been tested, including blood samples and Christopher's clothes, and even the tooth supposedly extracted from a landfill site at great expense; about Christopher's missing belt; about the gatekeeper seemingly changing his testimony to make it fit with the officers' accounts; and about the failure of the CPS to question the treatment of Christopher in the hospital by the police. He confirmed that all of these issues had been raised with the CPS. And then he really let rip. He started denouncing the whole legal system as racist, and explaining how it systematically discriminated against someone like him, a Black man, as power was located in the white community. I was cringing at first, because I knew the judge would use it as an excuse to dismiss us, to say that I had been overly influenced by such opinions, and that they had warped my view of what went on. But what he was saying was the truth. I would not have believed it in my younger days, but after twelve years of bitter experience I could no longer really dispute it.

Next to take the stand was Ruth Bundey, my solicitor. She challenged the narrow view of racism that some people seemed to have, explaining that during her many years of experience as an investigator for the then Race Relations Board, she had encountered multiple examples of discrimination that was seldom overt but was nevertheless very much present. In the run up to the trial of the officers in 2002, she had repeatedly asked the CPS to engage counsel with a real experience and understanding of racial issues – but, she said, this clearly did not happen.

In fact, in James Curtis, I don't think the CPS could have chosen someone with less sensitivity to racial issues. She explained how in our meetings with him, the prosecuting QC had spoken about 'Black people banging a drum', about getting a barrister 'from a deprived background' like mine, and referring to his Black friend in Birmingham as evidence of his anti-racist credentials. He was like a hybrid of David Brent and Alf Garnett – he would have been comical if the issues weren't so serious. I can't help but think if the CPS had taken Ruth's opinion into consideration as regards a barrister with experience in race and diversity it might have prevented me and my family from going through this insulting ordeal.

I did raise Curtis's conduct in my questioning, yet having defended his every fool move at the time, it now seemed like the CPS couldn't wait to wash their hands of him, claiming that as an independent QC, they bore no responsibility for his actions.

The problem was that their boss, the director of public

prosecutions, did not agree; at the time of the criminal trial, he had written to me to tell me that 'of course' the responsibility of the CPS extends to the counsel instructed by them. The fact that they now seemed to be doing all they could to distance themselves from him, however, suggested to me that they knew we had a strong case against Curtis. First they had tried to have any reference to the conduct of the trial struck out of my claim, and how, having failed on that front, they sought to pretend he was nothing to do with them. They were running scared. It gave me some hope, but by then I knew better than to think that this meant justice would be served.

Years later, when I was looking through my notes on the trial, it sounded better than I remembered. My head had been all over the place at the time; I'd just come out of the women's refuge after all the domestic violence, and had been living in a tiny flat, preparing for the case by myself, but when I read through my notes, it seemed the questions I'd been asking were good! Like everything else that's happened with this case, it's only when I've sat back and looked at what's happened that I've seen what I've been able to do.

But it wasn't enough to convince the judge. In March 2011, she gave her ruling, concluding that I had failed to prove that the CPS had discriminated against me. I was not surprised; as I told the press at the time: it's the same system, investigating itself again.

Yet reading through the judgment, there were some parts where I felt vindicated – such as when the judge wrote, 'I understand and share Miss Alder's concern of the possibility that racial discrimination played some part in the actions of police officers on the night Christopher Alder died. I also understand and share her concerns as to the standard of the investigation by West Yorkshire Police into the actions of the Humberside officers.' Elsewhere she agreed that Curtis's comment about a 'token Black person banging the drum' was racist, and that it was 'extraordinary' that no one from the CPS had come to talk to me after the case against the police officers collapsed. But I felt insulted when I read lines about the judge's 'concern' that Ruggie's 'views may have impacted' me. It felt like I was seen as not capable of having opinions of my own, that my thoughts and reasoning were simply imposed on me by others. And I thought it strange that Ruggie was being singled out for that; after all, there have been many within the criminal justice system that had for years sought to influence my thoughts, my experience, and the way I felt, and not in a positive way.

Elsewhere in the ruling, the judge said that my presentation of the case showed I was an intelligent woman. For me it simply reflected the fact that I knew the case so well. I had been made to relive Christopher's death for twelve years; I have lived and breathed it and gone to sleep with it in my dreams. Then she commented that I had struggled with the admissibility of some of the evidence and had strayed from time to time into areas going beyond my pleadings. I put that down to the CPS's constant attempts to steer away from the issue at the heart of my claim – their deliberate setting of the case against the police officers to fail. They had tried to have this part of the case struck out and, having been unsuccessful in that, had instead done all they could to move the focus onto other issues.

In the years that followed, I have often found myself reflecting on the things Ruggie said in that court. At the time, I didn't see that they had any relevance to the case – and nor could I agree that most white people were racist, which had not been my experience when dealing with ordinary people in the community I lived in. Of course, some people will always be ignorant of anything outside of their own experience, and many people are misinformed. And I would be lying if I said I had never experienced racism. But by no means did I find every white person racist. I have had good white friends and supporters who have been with me since day one – not to mention a beautiful white grandchild! But Ruggie said he felt his words had been misinterpreted and he had simply been trying to explain the disproportionality in the number of Black people going through the criminal justice system and in prisons in the UK. The years I had spent dealing with people in the police, PCA and CPS have certainly made me question the criminal justice system. So I decided to do some wider research on racism within that system, and came across a landmark report.

In October 2010, the Equality and Human Rights Commission released a report entitled *How Fair is Britain?*, which noted that 'Black prisoners make up 15% of the prison population [in the UK] and this compares with 2.2% of the general population.' In other words, Black people are incarcerated at a rate seven times greater than their share of the population. This is even more disproportionate than the US, where Black people are four times more likely to be incarcerated than the general population. The *Guardian*'s piece on the report wrote that 'experts and politicians said over-representation of Black men was a result of decades of racial prejudice in the criminal justice system and an overly punitive approach to penal affairs.' Other reports have confirmed this conclusion: Black men are 16 per cent more likely to be remanded in custody than whites; and are likely to receive custodial sentences 40 per cent longer than those of white people for the same offences. Reading reports like these always make me think back to Ruggie in the witness stand. Was it really so far-fetched to claim judges were institutionally racist? With statistics like these, is there any other explanation?

Life Before Christopher's Death

1981–98

After my experience with Kenny, I stayed on my own for several years. Over time I began to move into a different circle of friends and tended to socialise more in the town centre. Then one night when I was out with friends, I met a gorgeous young guy at the bar. His name was Josh. We got on really well and spent the evening dancing and joking with his circle of friends. But at some point in the evening we noticed one or two of the women on the next table eyeballing us, giving us disparaging looks; they seemed to be making comments about my race. He went straight up to them and had words. I was surprised. Being Black, you can instinctively recognise covert racism – even if you don't hear it, you can feel it; it's the same feeling you get when you walk into a room and the conversation suddenly goes dead; it makes your hair stand on end and your skin tighten. Other people, however, can often be unaware of it because no one has uttered a derogatory word. Yet Josh seemed to recognise it immediately and had no fear of challenging it. Whatever he said to those women clearly didn't please them at all, and one of them shouted 'just because you can't play football!' as he walked away. He didn't explain the comment and I didn't think anything of it. At the end of the night, we agreed to see each other again and exchanged numbers, and soon we were dating. It was quite a while before he told me he played football for Sunderland. It meant nothing to me, but I eventually discovered that he was a bit of a local celebrity. His favourite pastimes were hunting rabbits and fishing in the River Don. He was a type of person I had never met before, a breath of fresh air, and nothing like the men I had met in the past. I later found out that, unlike most people in town, he actually had some experience of Black people, as his best friend at the football club was Black. I certainly respected his ability to empathise and place himself in my shoes that night.

I liked how he treated me, but I wasn't used to it. I had fallen into another relationship again, and although it was, for once, a good one, I still had a nagging urge to make a bolt for freedom.

Nevertheless, life was looking a lot brighter, and as Caroline got older I started scouting for employment. The first job I got was in Roland Cartier, a shoe shop so exclusive that people were allowed to return shoes for up to a year after purchase. This was certainly not somewhere I could afford to shop, but it gave me a taste for working life: I loved making my own money, and the sense of freedom and independence it brought, as well as the self-confidence that comes from doing a job well. The job bug had truly got me, and after a while I got a job at Dorothy Perkins, which came with the added attraction of a 25 per cent staff discount! It felt like I was able to get any job I applied for, and my confidence was growing fast. I wanted to take every opportunity that was placed in front of me.

Eventually, Josh moved into my house, but he was often away

with his work as a professional footballer. After some months I was pregnant again. It was not good timing; I'd just got a job and was starting to value myself a bit; my life was beginning to turn around. For the first time in my life, I felt like I had been actually *making* decisions rather than just falling into them. But after Nathan was born, I fell into a deep postnatal depression. Everything was a haze, my sleeping routine was non-existent at night, and I was lucky if I managed to snatch a couple of hours in the afternoon while one of my friends collected Caroline from school. I was irritable and agitated, unable to leave the house; I didn't get dressed or wash for days on end, and I had irrational, paranoid thoughts that men were looking at my daughter. It was as if I were living in a completely different world. Even just crossing the road to the shop, my blood pressure would drop so low that with a fizzing on my lips I felt like I wanted to pass out. On top of that, everything was magnified. It was the time of the Gulf War, in 1991, which really got to me. I was getting up every morning to get the newspapers to see what was going on, and I was in a total panic. Since childhood, I'd had recurring nightmares about planes coming over and bombing, and now I was watching it happen for real on TV every night. I would wake up and look out of the window, in total shock that everyone was getting on with their lives as if nothing was going on.

And then Josh moved away to Burnley, where the club had provided him with a house. I didn't follow him there at first; I was feeling nervous about moving away from my friends and everything that was familiar, to a town where I knew nobody. Eventually, I plucked up my courage and, when Nathan was about eighteen months, moved in with Josh in Burnley. But soon after I arrived, my health deteriorated; I got fibroids and had to go to hospital for a hysterectomy. Our relationship wasn't the same after I returned home, and it wasn't long before we split up.

Eventually I picked myself up and got a job with Burton in one of their Evans branches, one of the very few shops that supply modern clothing for the larger lady. I was working up to being a senior sales technician, in charge of what was called 'visually merchandising' the stores, refurbishing them where necessary and ensuring the company kept up with its competitors. I would travel to their stores around the country, using my artistic eye and imagination to help redesign their displays and layout. I was really making an impression with the company: I had a skill, which I enjoyed using, and I was building a positive rapport with customers and staff. I had found some focus in my life, and my spirits were at an all-time high. I felt nobody could touch me or interfere with my goals ahead. I was an independent woman, succeeding in giving my children a good standard of living, as well as supporting them emotionally and providing them with a protective understanding of the world. The last thing I wanted was for them to experience what I'd been through in my childhood, so my determination to do what was right for them was very strong.

I began to see real possibilities and wanted to taste more. I started mulling over job advertisements in the local press until one day I came across a job doing visual merchandising for the Co-op. Most of their department stores around the country had closed, but in the little town of Burnley they were still going. Selling furniture, glass, lighting, tableware and clothing, the long-established store still had an old-fashioned layout. They had ideas for a more 'up-market' refurbishment of their remaining stores and I wanted to be involved. I met up with the area manager and the store manager and sold myself with the belief that this was where my destiny was taking me. They gave me the job, and I thought I would love every minute of it. It seemed like a dream come true: they trusted my ability and experience and were giving me free reign to visually redesign the entire store to catch the public eye. Or so I had been led to believe.

On my first day, the branch manager was away but I was visited by a top manager from head office. His role was to bring the standards up to and beyond those of rival stores like BHS, and his speciality was the lighting department. He wasn't happy with its layout and he told me he wanted the lamp stands rearranged so that all those made of similar materials were together in one place, with the shades coordinated according to colour and size. Though it was not something I had done before, I revelled in the challenge and was quite excited by the new display. But when the branch manager returned the next day – my day off – he was far from happy. This was a manager who was used to taking control of everything that went on in his store and he assumed I'd made these rearrangements without instruction. When I returned I found everything had been restored to its original position. I tried to explain that I'd made the changes according to head office's wishes, but I soon realised that he was not open to change. They say it is dangerous to be right when those in power are wrong and so I didn't last long; I had questioned the manager's system, and I was dismissed just before Christmas. I felt disillusioned, and that Christmas was a subdued one.

For a short while I questioned whether leaving Evans had been the right decision, but I was soon on the job trail again, applying to work at a local shop. I felt confident at my interview and left with a feeling I would get the position; a few days later I received confirmation that I was the new store manager.

I began the job on 3 April 1998. It was two days after Christopher's death, but I didn't know that yet. There was a good atmosphere in the store: I got on well with the staff, my social life was good and all seemed to be going really well. I was visited in the shop regularly by two friends, who would often give up their time to help arrange the mountains of accessory deliveries the store received daily. It only seemed right that I find them a few paid hours and soon enough I was able to do so. These were my close friends, with whom I had spent many a weekend dancing the night away, and it was great to be working with them as well.

I was a working-class single mother, living a very ordinary, pleasurable, life; one that most people would be able to relate to. I was happy: I felt like there were opportunities to be grasped, and had a growing confidence that I could grasp them. But I was also grateful that I had been able to put as much distance as possible from what some might consider to have been a pretty disadvantageous start in life. I was dating regularly, but I did not have a steady boyfriend; my previous experiences had made me cautious. I was content on my own: I was an independent woman in control of my life. I had learned that men tended to resent this and wanted to control me, and I would have no more of that. It felt like I was finally free of the traumas of childhood. I wasn't particularly anti-police or anti-establishment, even after the childhood I'd had; leaving care I believed my involvement with state authorities was all behind me. I had two children who made me very proud, and they were growing up without getting into any great trouble. My daughter was developing a certain rebelliousness, but that tended to manifest in the home rather than outside; like me, my kids were brought up to treat others with respect. Rather than a soft, mumsy type, I was quite a firm, protective mother: having been on my own and experienced many difficult situations myself, I tried to instil in my children a capacity to cope with the worst that life could throw at you – as well as to embrace the best. I only hoped I'd given them enough input to make decisions that would create as few difficulties in their lives as possible. I taught them they were as good as anybody else and that if anyone had issues with their skin colour or the fact that they were mixed race, that was their own problem.

Like most people, all I ever really wanted was the security of a nice home, in a friendly neighbourhood, doing a job that would allow me to fulfil whatever talents I had, with a partner I got on well with. Of course, this was a dream, but one which I was, at the beginning of 1998, on my way to achieving – or so I thought.

Body Swap

2011

By 2011, I'd spent thirteen years fighting for Christopher: collecting evidence, poring over documents, questioning the authorities and demanding answers, bringing court cases, and all while being constantly patronised, looked down on, sneered at and humiliated by the police. I had been treated with so much contempt by the authorities just for asking questions. I had become their target. It had left me exhausted, with no emotional or psychological rest.

All the knock-backs over the years had affected me more than I knew: it was only when I took a short break that I began to realise just how much damage they'd done. I had got to the point where I had no confidence that any truth or justice would come from this horror. I was absolutely shattered, and the hurt was beyond words. I was flagging from years of living on constant adrenaline, and I had become quite ill: I had extremely high blood pressure, and was constantly breaking out in a sweat. I was ready to retreat somewhere else, to pick up the pieces and try to move on with my life.

But it was not to be.

It was the morning of 5 November, a Saturday. I was

preparing myself to go and see my friend Hadiza, who lived in the flat above me in our tenement: I'm an early riser, and I would tend to go round first thing in the morning and have a coffee with her. But that morning, as I was getting ready, I got a phone call. To my surprise, it was my brother Richard. I hadn't heard from him for ages, so it was completely out of the blue and I was really happy to hear from him. But it soon became clear he was not just calling for a chat.

'Janet, Christopher has not been buried,' he said.

I was confused; as far as I was concerned, we had buried Christopher at his funeral in November 2000. I asked him, 'What do you mean?'

He said, 'Christopher's body's been in the mortuary all these years. We buried the body of a woman instead of him.'

I couldn't believe what he was saying, couldn't take it in. He said the police had come over to his place and spoken to him, and they wanted me to phone them.

The last thing I wanted was the police coming to my house. From my past experiences, I had no confidence they would tell me the truth. I told Richard I wouldn't phone them, that they'd have to contact me themselves.

I put the phone down and immediately felt confused and sick. I went upstairs to Hadiza's flat, and though she'd barely opened her eyes, she could see straight away I was in a state. 'What's happened?' she asked. I was distressed and babbling, speaking really fast and trying to get everything out. Her jaw dropped as I repeated what Richard had told me. We were both dumbstruck.

Sure enough, the next morning I got a phone call from a policewoman who introduced herself as Lisa Kramer and told me that she needed to see me in person. I had my own place now, and though it was a tiny little flat, it gave me a bit of solace;

it was all I had. I just didn't feel comfortable with the police coming to my home. I remember what happened the last time they knocked on the door and I had learned not to go back to the same dog that bit me. But she insisted they needed to see me – to make sure I got the 'right information', she said – so I tried to think of somewhere neutral to meet. It was a Sunday, so not many places were open; in the end, I suggested the cafe in Sainsbury's.

Hadiza agreed to come with me, so we went to the cafe and waited apprehensively. My past experiences of these meetings was that they generally amounted to nothing. I had become more and more traumatised over the years having to listen to the people employed to administer justice justify their failure to hold anyone to account. I had become hypervigilant since Christopher's death, and I knew my concerns and feelings were the last things on their minds. They had a job to do, reputations to uphold, and they did this willingly. It was a performance – and they viewed me as a threat, standing in the way of them playing their roles comfortably.

Before long, a policewoman strode over, flanked by two other people. This was DC Lisa Kramer, the appointed liaisons officer from South Yorkshire Police, who had called me the previous day. Alongside her was Trish Dalby, assistant executive from Hull City Council, and DC Richie from South Yorkshire Police's major crimes department. Dalby said that she was there on behalf of Nicola Yates, the chief executive, and that Hull City Council were currently leading the investigation into what had happened. Lisa Kramer explained that her role was to support the family and ensure we got the correct information before anybody else, but it soon became clear that the Home Office, the Ministry of Justice, the Hull MPs, Uncle Tom Cobley and all had got the news before the family had. I asked Kramer why South Yorkshire Police were involved, and she told me that Hull Council had instructed them because they were trained liaisons officers and independent of Humberside Police.

All three of them seemed very unnerved. I understood how they felt; after all, it's difficult to give someone bad news.

Yet I soon got the impression that Kramer was trying her best to spin a narrative that sounded believable. I was already very jumpy, and she seemed to be telling me I must only listen to her, that she was the one who was going to give me the facts, and that I should ignore anything else I heard. But after hearing so many conflicting versions from the police about Christopher's death, and years of seeing nobody held to account, my trust in the police was totally diminished.

Kramer told me that two days earlier, on 4 November 2011 at 1 p.m., a funeral had been due to take place for a seventy-seven-year-old Nigerian lady called Grace Kamara, who had died in 1999 of natural causes. From her death until the day of the funeral, Kramer claimed, it was believed that Grace Kamara remained in the mortuary at the Hull Royal Infirmary. But when E. W. Brown & Son funeral directors had gone to collect the body, they discovered that the body stored under Grace's name was not hers. It was Christopher's. We had buried Grace Kamara on 25 November 2000 in Christopher's grave.

I was sweating and in distress. I felt just like I had when he died, the same kind of disbelief. My automatic response when dealing with the police is not to believe a word they say. I was on the defensive, and naturally I had a lot of questions. I said, wait a minute, we had Christopher's funeral; how could he, a thirty-seven-year-old ex-paratrooper, have been mistaken for an old lady? Kramer just said that they had yet to make enquiries. The way they approached me – the sharply disapproving, authoritarian tone with which they responded to my questions – was as if I were the one in trouble. I told them, 'Don't talk to me like that, I'm not under arrest.' There seemed to be no contrition whatsoever.

She explained that when the undertakers and mortuary staff examined the body, they found a wrist band and a toe tag labelled Christopher Alder. She said they didn't want to inform the family until they were absolutely certain it was Christopher, so they asked the deputy coroner of Hull, Dr McDonald, a pathologist at the Hull Royal Infirmary, to look at the body's distinguishing marks and compare these with the information the mortuary had on Christopher's condition prior to his death. McDonald looked at Christopher's body and noted his two missing teeth, a tattoo of the letter C on his left forearm, a Manchester United tattoo, two piercings in his left ear, a scar on his right forearm, and a scar on his left thumb. The coroner, Geoffrey Saul, was also contacted so they could get hold of Christopher's dental records. Despite his body having been in the mortuary in place of Grace for eleven years, McDonald and Saul were satisfied that it was, beyond all reasonable doubt, Christopher.

Kramer went on to say that Grace's body should have been under the control of the coroner during that time, with the express agreement of her Nigerian relative, Erhumwue Emmanuel. She even gave me his PO box number, phone number and address in Benin City. I felt like they were willingly throwing all this information at me as quickly as possible to try and convince me that they had been doing the right thing, that procedures had been followed and that everything was above board. Kramer then told me that in 2000 the mortuary had been moved to a temporary location, before being moved to the Hull Royal Infirmary in 2001 when the NHS took over responsibility for all Hull mortuaries (I later found out that this was not the case – wrong mortuaries, wrong dates). She told us that Christopher's body had potentially been moved to this temporary mortuary, but that she didn't know where that was. I asked Trish Dalby from the council where it was, but she didn't know either. I thought it was strange that they were so keen to give me all of Emmanuel's personal details, but were unable to provide basic information like the name of the mortuary in which Christopher's body had been held.

The whole experience was very stressful and seemed quite threatening; sweat was pouring out of me, my head was banging, and my blood pressure must have been sky high. I was lucky Hadiza had come along to give me support: she recorded the discussion on her phone while I tried my best to take notes. Because of my lack of trust in what the police told me, I asked them to sign these notes before we left. My mind was overloaded with information and pain. I left the meeting full of anxiety, with no reassurance things were going to be OK, having learned nothing about why Grace's body had been released to my family for burial or how such a thing could have happened. I was in total shock and disbelief. The police had been trying to suggest it had all been an innocent mistake. I was not so sure.

Christine Omoregie

2011

Grace Kamara had no blood relatives in the UK when she died in 1999, so her body was kept in the mortuary. But she did have a friend in Hull called Christine Omoregie who had been trying to arrange visas for Grace's family to come over and attend her burial. For eleven years, they had been refused entry by the Home Office, but Christine would not give up, and had doggedly pursued the issue with the coroner, the council and Hull MP Alan Johnson.

I had found out about Christine through the meeting with Kramer, who had mentioned her name in connection with Grace's funeral. I wanted to meet the other family caught up in this horror story; I realised we were in the same position, experiencing the same shock and probably asking the same questions. One of the journalists I knew from the local paper said he was in touch with Christine, so I asked him to pass her my details; she called me and we arranged to meet up the following day.

The next morning, Hadiza, the journalist Simon Israel and I took the train to Hull and met Christine, a Nigerian herself, at the train station. 'Niggers!' someone shouted at us as we stepped off the train and walked towards Christine – a reminder that

Hull had not changed much since I was a child. Christine was an elderly woman, and as she approached, we could see she had dressed smartly for the occasion, with a brightly coloured dress and a hat she probably wore to church on a Sunday. I could tell she was a god-fearing woman, imbued with the strong religious beliefs with which so many African people are brought up. But she didn't look well, and you could see in her face the stress and strain she had been under. She was as confused as I was, and we both felt there was something sinister about the whole ordeal.

After introductions, Christine quickly began filling us in on what had happened. She told us that, as the funeral approached in early 2011, she had spoken to Nicki Hewitt from the council's bereavement department, requesting to view Grace's body and place a traditional Nigerian ceremonial scarf on her. She explained that it is Nigerian custom for families to see their loved ones dressed in this special scarf after their death, and that photos are taken for those unable to attend the funeral. But Hewitt told her, 'We don't do that in this country.' When Christine persisted, she was told that the body had been thawed so many times that to open the bag again would be a health hazard. She said Grace's body was to go straight from the mortuary to the cemetery and be buried immediately. This was clearly unacceptable to the family, however, who insisted on upholding their tradition, whatever the state of the body.

Christine explained that it was the council who had then organised Grace's funeral: they chose the funeral directors, ordered the coffin and paid for the proceedings; all the family had to do was turn up at the cemetery.[1] This contradicted what Kramer had told me at our meeting two days before, that it was Christine herself who had organised the funeral. Was this an innocent mistake, or were they deliberately trying to hide the council's role in what had happened? After all, Dalby, the council's deputy chief executive, was present at the meeting, yet did nothing to put Kramer right about this. It made me wonder what other misinformation I may have been given.

Shortly before 1 p.m. on 4 November 2011, Grace's family and friends began to arrive at the cemetery as per the council's instructions, with a view to moving on to another venue after the funeral for a commemoration event organised by the family. One p.m. came, but the body had still not arrived. They waited, and waited. Two p.m. came, then three; but still the body wasn't there, and there was no word from the council or the mortuary as to what was going on. It was a cold November afternoon, and it started getting dark; family members were becoming agitated, wondering why it was taking so long for the coffin to arrive. Eventually the group was approached by a man who Christine recognised as one of those who had been looking after Grace's body over the years. He told them they were having trouble locating Grace. The family were angry and disappointed; many of them began crying. They couldn't believe it; they had come all the way from Nigeria to finally bury their relative, after eleven years of being denied entry into the country, only to be told the body could not be found. Cold and frustrated, some of them decided they would go to the hospital mortuary themselves to try to find out where Grace was. Among them was Grace's nephew, who demanded to see the body so he could dress her in the ceremonial scarf and take photographs to send home. Even after all my own experiences, I was shocked that the council would leave them out in the cemetery for hours on end, on the very day of Grace's funeral, before admitting that they didn't have her body.

As Christine spoke to us, she was crying, and she kept saying over and over again, 'We've been lied to all these years.' I felt exactly the same way, and I knew that the lies were not going to stop there.

After leaving the station, we decided to visit the coroner, to see if he could shed any light on what may have happened. Christine had been in close communication with the coroner over the years, attempting to mediate on behalf of the family in Nigeria. The coroner had taken control of Grace's body after her death in 1999 and ordered that she be placed in storage; it wasn't until January 2011 that authority over Grace's body was transferred from the coroner to Hull City Council for the funeral. At our meeting, Kramer had told me that the coroner's authority over Grace's body all this time had been with the agreement of Grace's closest relative, Erhumwue Emmanuel, in Benin City, Nigeria. It was only from Christine that I was to learn that Erhumwue Emmanuel had actually been dead for years, following repeated attempts to get a visa into the UK. I couldn't believe it. Why had the police given me all of Emmanuel's personal details, knowing full well I wouldn't be able to actually contact him because he was dead? And why had Grace's closest relative been denied the right to come and make arrangements for her body? Furthermore, Christine added, Emmanuel had been seeking to repatriate Grace's body to her place of birth. But the council told Christine that, as Grace was now a British citizen, she would have to be buried in Britain, regardless of her family's wishes.

Christine drove us the short distance to the coroner's office, and he agreed to see us there and then. Just as we were sitting down in his office, Christine realised we'd forgotten to put any money into the parking meter – the coroner gave her some cash and she dashed off to buy a ticket. When she came back, she told him he wasn't getting the change, which made me laugh; I sensed a rebellious side to her character and a cheeky sense of humour. But ultimately little came out of the meeting; he told us no more than we had already heard from the police.

After leaving the coroner, we went to the council offices, which were just across the road. We sat waiting for around half an hour when the deputy chief executive, Trish Dalby, approached us and took us to meet the chief executive. As she showed us down the corridor, Dalby started to cry. Hadiza asked her why *she* was crying, saying 'it's the *family* this has happened to'. She took us into a room with a massive conference table: Christine, Hadiza and I sat at one side, with Nicola Yates and Dalby way over on the other.

I felt sorry for Christine. Having been brought up in Africa she, just like my mum and dad, believed Britain to be the mother country, built on respect, truth and justice. She said Nigeria looked up to this country; I didn't feel the same. My toes were curling in my shoes as I saw how insecure she was, how submissive to the authority of the chief and deputy executives of the council. As I watched her speaking as if she was somehow beneath them, it brought back uncomfortable feelings of my own earlier naivety. I couldn't stand it. I interrupted her abruptly and asked the chief executive, 'How can you not know the difference between a thirty-seven-year-old man and a seventy-seven-year-old woman?'

Deflecting my question, the chief executive quickly turned the emphasis on me, telling me I was rude to interrupt Christine. It's true – I was – but I just couldn't bear to see Christine humbling herself, putting them on some kind of pedestal, when really she deserved to be treated with respect and given answers as to why the swapping of the bodies was kept hidden for eleven years, and how they had been swapped in the first place. We both did. But, once again, we left the meeting none the wiser. It was clear that the authorities were going to remain tight-lipped.

As Christine drove us back to the station, she told us about her humiliating visit to E. W. Brown & Son, the funeral directors. I only realised later that this was the very same funeral directors, chosen by the council to bury Grace, that I had used for Christopher's funeral all those years ago. She was already upset when she got there, as – in all her years dealing with the council and the coroner – no one had told her that the body had been moved; she had gone looking for the mortuary that had been demolished years earlier. At E. W. Brown & Son, Christine had again raised the issue of the ceremonial scarf, but they had threatened to call the police if she didn't go away. She believed she had been treated like this because she spoke Nigerian 'Pidgin' English, which she said was perceived by some as aggressive. I knew from my father and his friends that this was just how Nigerian people expressed themselves, with tone and passion in their voices. Christine had even apologised to the funeral directors for sounding that way, even though she recognised that it was they who misunderstood her culture.

It also turned out that on the day I was being told the bad news, officers from Humberside Police had paid a visit to Christine's home. She told me she felt they were trying to intimidate her and her husband, who was not well. They called on her repeatedly over the following weeks, and she told me in a later conversation that one of the officers actually called her a troublemaker during one of these visits. She decided in that moment that she would have no more contact with the police, and refused to answer the door to them from then on. Soon after that, Christine went to stay with her family in London to give herself some space.

I could relate to the way Christine was feeling because I felt the same way. I have also been treated as a troublemaker by the police over the years; I think it was because Christine and I were asking questions, whereas the rest of our families preferred not to. Because we didn't humbly accept what we were told, we were labelled as 'difficult', and this caused us to be blamed and treated unfairly, rather than being seen as victims.

Although we never met up again, I would speak to Christine regularly over the weeks and months that followed. Whenever either of us found out anything more about what had happened to the bodies, we would be on the phone to each other immediately. She was a very determined lady, and I admired her greatly. Having her there meant I never felt alone or isolated: she was just as outraged as I was – and just as determined to get to the bottom of everything.

On the train home, Hadiza and I began to piece together what we now knew. The family had wanted Grace's body repatriated to Nigeria, but the council had prevented this from happening. Then the council and the undertakers had both told the family they were not allowed to see the body, the latter getting very agitated when Christine tried to pursue the issue. And the council had taken it upon themselves to make all the funeral arrangements, using the very same funeral directors who had given us Grace's body in place of Christopher's in 2000, while leading me to believe that Christine had organised it. On top of the family having been denied visas by the Home Office for eleven years, the evidence all seemed to point towards the authorities having something to hide.

Of course, there were alternative explanations. Making life difficult for immigrants was, after all, standard practice in the Home Office, and was soon to become official policy (Theresa

May's infamous 'hostile environment'); the blocking of the visas would easily fall within this remit of petty bureaucratic cruelty. And maybe councils *always* organised and paid for funerals of those whose relatives were out of the country. But after everything that had happened I was deeply suspicious: I don't know if the council *were* trying to hide the fact that they had given us Grace's body in place of Christopher's, but the fact is everything the council had done was going to lead to Christopher being buried in Grace's grave. And, had it not been for Grace's family's insistence on sticking to their traditions, it never would have come to light.

Another Sham Investigation

2012–3

With all the inconsistencies in what we had been told, I decided I would have to go to the mortuary myself to ease my mind that it really was Christopher that had been found. Mentally, I was finding it difficult to accept, especially when they had been supposedly unable to detect they were holding the body of a man and not a woman for eleven years. How could I take it for granted that it was Christopher this time, without finding out for myself? I had presumed it had been his body that was released for the first funeral; I didn't want to make the same mistake again.

I phoned Lisa Kramer and told her I wanted to see Christopher. She advised me not to do so, because his body was 'skeletal'. I asked her how this could be, as he was supposed to have been stored in deep freeze; surely he would not have deteriorated that much? She raised her voice in a passive aggressive tone and said to me, 'He has got a brother called Richard, you know!'

I felt attacked; she seemed to be suggesting I was lucky the police were speaking to me at all, that they could just as easily deal with Richard if I didn't like what I was being told. Over the years, I have often been made to feel that I had no right to say anything, that I was supposed to walk away and ignore the horrors Christopher had been subjected to. It was hard not to feel isolated, like I was being punished for taking the lead when my family was not available, and for doing what I knew was the right thing to do. The police had often implied that I had no right to be concerned about Christopher because I didn't live in Hull, as if there was a hierarchy and I was way down it. I was aware from the 2006 IPCC report that Humberside Police believed I was simply using Christopher's death as a platform to elevate myself, rather than showing real concern that they had treated a member of my family the way they had. I was seen as out to annoy them and tell lies about them in order to make a career for myself. And this from people who had gone to any lengths to hide what had happened to Christopher in order to build and protect their *own* careers. I had given up my career when Christopher died; from that point onwards, my working life had simply fallen apart.

On 6 February 2012, I got a call from Ruth.

'Janet, the police have just told me that Christopher's body is to be released for his funeral on Thursday.'

This was news to me; I didn't even know a new funeral had been arranged. It was another blow. There were still so many unanswered questions about exactly what had happened with Christopher's body over the years, and I was already starting to suspect there had been a cover-up. Was it really feasible that those responsible for his body believed they were holding a seventy-seven-year-old woman all this time? The key evidence was of course the state of Christopher's body. But now they were going to cremate him before any of this had been properly investigated.

Even worse, I still hadn't been to see Christopher's body myself. To be honest, Kramer's gruesome description had unnerved me, as it was presumably intended to do. I knew that viewing him now would leave yet another damaging image in my mind, to add to the ones I already had of him on the floor with his trousers to his knees, gasping for air. What would I see eleven years later? Just the thought of it took my mind to some dark and twisted places. I knew it was very important that I should see him – but I couldn't bring myself to do it. So I asked Ruth to go on my behalf, and she agreed immediately.

Ruth was solid as a rock. She had been there for me all these years, not just as a solicitor but as a friend. She had been with me through the traumatic experience of watching the CCTV of Christopher's death, in the comfort of her home, and now she was going to relieve me of the trauma of seeing him laid out in the mortuary.

Meanwhile, I had to figure out how I had been stripped of my legal responsibility for decisions concerning Christopher's body. With his children both minors at the time of his original funeral, I had stepped in as next of kin and therefore had been legally responsible for his body. As far as I knew, this was still the case. Certainly, all the authorities involved – the council, the police, and the NHS – had assured me that I would be kept fully informed and consulted about any developments. Yet now they wanted to dispose of the body without providing any kind of explanation to me, let alone a consultation. As the executor of Christopher's original funeral, I still felt somehow responsible for the wrong body being buried; now I was being denied the opportunity to put this right. Furthermore, I was suspicious. I could see how this speedy disposal of Christopher's body played into the hands of the police. The authorities were aware that I was concerned about the condition of Christopher's body and whether he had been stored correctly, and to enable these questions to be answered I would have probably asked for an independent expert inquiry. This would have been more than a little awkward for the institutions involved. It seemed very convenient that the responsibility was now being whipped out of my hands before I could make this decision.

The following day, I wrote two emails. The first was to the coroner. I wanted to know why, as the executor, I had not been consulted about the second funeral. The second was to the police – Detective Superintendent Richard Fewkes – asking for an explanation. I asked him what law was being used to take away my right, as legal representative of Christopher's body, for his body to be released to me. I wrote: 'As Christopher's body might contribute evidence in any future proceedings – civil or criminal – I therefore question the wisdom of that evidence being lost, whether he is buried or cremated, before the criminal investigation has been concluded.'

Ruth called me back as soon as she returned from the hospital. It had been agreed that she could attend Hull Royal Infirmary on 8 February, the day before the funeral, to identify Christopher's body, but strictly on the condition that no photographs were taken of him and that what was seen was not put in the public domain. They had placed his body behind glass, covering all but his face with a purple sheet; Ruth could only view him from a distance.

'It's definitely him,' she told me. 'His face was very thin, but it was clearly Christopher.' Thin? Lisa Kramer had told me he was skeletal. If Ruth found him that easy to identify from another room with a sheet over him, how are we expected to believe that all those involved with his body over the years thought they were dealing with an elderly woman? And why had I been told that he was 'skeletal' if that was not true?

Although I put on a brave face to the media, within the safety of my own home I couldn't stop crying. I was a mess. I kept asking myself how no one had been able to see it was Christopher. Christopher's face was well known in Hull: the photograph of him in his stripy polo shirt and peaked cap, gently smiling out at the camera, had been on the local front pages with every demonstration I'd held in the town, and with every court case and revelation that had come out since 1998. But even someone who had been on Mars all that time could at least have seen it was a man. What had been going on?

The day before the funeral, I received a reply from the coroner, confirming that the original burial order still stood. This meant that I still had legal responsibility for Christopher's body – and therefore that the decision to cremate Christopher had been taken unlawfully. But what could I do? Christopher's sons must have agreed to holding the funeral at this time, and I certainly wasn't going to go against their wishes and cancel it. Still, the authorities had managed to bypass me. Only years later did I discover that the front page of the burial order – the page that named me as legal executor – had somehow 'gone missing'.

When the day of the funeral came, I didn't go. To be honest, I felt like I wasn't wanted. Since being dropped by Jane Deighton, I had not had much contact with my family; I felt like they didn't really want anything to do with me. At times like these, divisions emerge within families; people deal with their emotions in different ways – and this is exploited by the authorities. I was already feeling weak and damaged after thirteen years of constant knock-backs in the fight for justice, and on top of this, I was really ill. I felt I was being attacked on all sides. After being accused by the police of using Christopher's death as a platform, I wondered if my family felt the same way.

The first I'd heard about the funeral had been from the police via my lawyer; the only contact I'd had from the family was a text telling me where and when to turn up; I had no idea what had been arranged or what was going to happen – it didn't even say where the funeral would be held. I was just told to turn up at a destination.

I felt unwelcome, and also guilty because the wrong body had been buried at the funeral I had organised. I was also deeply uncomfortable that the funeral was being paid for by the council, the very people responsible for Grace being buried in Christopher's grave eleven years earlier, and who, just months ago, had seemingly attempted to get Christopher buried in place of Grace. It all felt very unsavoury. So I just stayed away. Grace's body was exhumed two weeks later and her family were finally able to give her the funeral they had been trying to arrange for twelve years.

Meanwhile, South Yorkshire Police's inquiry into how the bodies had been swapped was apparently getting nowhere. Shortly after the funeral I received various requests for information from Kramer. She wanted to know, for example, if I had asked for Christopher's body to be dressed in his uniform. I hadn't, and I wasn't even aware that he still *had* his uniform – but I told her I had asked for him to be embalmed. She asked what documentation I had to corroborate this. It appeared it was OK for the police and mortuary staff to make all kinds of claims without documented evidence, but if I told them what I remembered from the original funeral arrangements, I had to provide documentary proof. She even questioned me about the date on which the mortuary released Christopher's body to the funeral directors, and where it was released to. I had no idea when the funeral directors had collected his body from the mortuary; I had simply trusted them to collect him at some point before the funeral and bring him there on the day. I had no access to the records of either the mortuary or the funeral directors, but the police had access to both. So why were they asking me? Once again, it felt like the police were turning the spotlight on me to cover up their own incompetence and culpability.

Ruth was quite perplexed that the police were expecting me to answer these questions. She wrote to Lisa Kramer, 'It would not be for a family to know, whether Janet, Richard or whoever, precisely when a body was transferred from mortuary to funeral parlour – that would be, as we have said before, a matter for public record.' Why were the police treating me as if I somehow had influence over the funeral directors' timetable? It seemed like they were refusing to do the most elementary police work to establish when Grace's body was released and who in the mortuary had released her instead of Christopher, while trying to pin this failure on *me* not being able to magically provide the information for them. I feared I could see the direction that their report was going to go. I could see them trying to create a narrative where their refusal to reveal who in the mortuary had released Grace, and why, would be blamed on me not knowing the date of the transfer. I suspected I was being set up as a scapegoat: they knew someone had to take the blame, and I was their preferred target.

These suspicions were heightened when, following my reluctance to turn my house upside down in order to try to find things like receipts for the funeral flowers, Ruth received the following email from Kramer: 'Can you please confirm that Janet will not assist the investigation and is not willing to provide the originals or copies of any documentation which will assist us in identifying who was involved in the key events surrounding the release of the body in November 2000?' Were the police implying that, because I couldn't provide them with enough documentation, it was my fault that they couldn't identify who released the wrong body? Or was the purpose simply to find out what information I did and didn't have, so they would know what information they could get away with hiding?

Years later, I would discover that I had underestimated the police: they *had*, in fact, obtained the evidence they needed. All along, they had had possession of both the funeral directors' burial order listing the date and precise time (9.02 a.m.) of the body's collection from the mortuary, and the staff rota from the mortuary, which would have revealed who was working at that time. Why did they choose to disregard the evidence they had? Why did they instead try to imply that they couldn't find out who released the body because I couldn't tell them?

On 27 April 2012, Ruth received another email from Kramer: 'Could you please speak to Janet and ask her if she would be willing to assist the investigation by taking the time to be interviewed cognitively in relation to the information she holds regarding the funeral. We are keen to explore and investigate thoroughly every opportunity to establish how this mix-up occurred.' They would explore every avenue, it seemed, apart from using the documents in their possession to identify who was responsible.

I couldn't understand why they wanted to interview me, as I had no idea who in the mortuary had released Grace instead of Christopher. We had already supplied them with all the information we had been able to find about the funeral payments and other information I held.

A week later, another email came through asking whether

I would 'be willing to provide a statement or ... consent to be interviewed cognitively on DVD by interview trained officers.' I read up on what a cognitive interview entailed: it was a method of interviewing eyewitnesses and victims about what they remember from a crime scene. But I was not an eyewitness to which funeral director collected the body from the mortuary, and neither was I a witness to which mortuary worker swapped Christopher's body and released Grace. Again, I couldn't see how them interviewing me could help the inquiry in any way; it was intimidating and felt like another attempt by the police to project responsibility and blame onto me.

By this point, I wasn't at all comfortable with Kramer as the liaisons officer. Some of the things she said during our discussions had really upset me, especially the comment about Christopher being 'skeletal' and her reference to Richard. I didn't feel that South Yorkshire Police saw me as a victim in any way. They must have been aware of the attention I had drawn to Humberside Police and how Humberside Police felt about me, and I found out later that they had profiled the family. I doubt I was seen in a very good light.

I declined the DVD interview and decided instead to make a statement. Ruth wrote to Kramer asking for a list of questions to cover in my statement, but when they arrived, these questions – forty-seven of them – were absolutely ridiculous. They wanted to know what bus I got to the funeral, who I met, where I was staying, who travelled with me, who stayed with me, who I liaised with in the media ... the police even wanted a copy of the leaflet I had put out to invite supporters and friends from Hull. What did this have to do with who in the mortuary released the wrong body and why? It was as if I was a suspect, that I had swapped Christopher and Grace's bodies myself. Or was this simply an attempt to continue surveilling me? I had already provided them with the bank account details of the funds raised for the funeral from the campaign, a receipt for the payment of the flowers and the debit for receipt of payment to the funeral directors, though I couldn't for the life of me see how these could help establish why the mortuary staff gave the funeral directors the wrong body. Again, I couldn't shake the feeling that they were doing their best to taint me instead of focusing on identifying the perpetrators.

My suspicions about what had happened to Christopher and Grace were raised again when I got a call from a reporter I knew. I had instructed the funeral directors, E. W. Brown & Son, to embalm Christopher's body and dress him in a robe. Clearly this did not happen; if it had done, it would have been immediately obvious that they had the wrong body. But the reporter told me that, after the swapping of the bodies had featured on the news, he had received a phone call from one of the funeral directors involved in Christopher's burial. He said that they had been instructed by the mortuary staff, in no uncertain terms, not to open the body bag. It seemed like someone knew they had something to hide.

It took eighteen months for South Yorkshire Police to complete their investigation. By April 2013 they'd written their report, but we weren't allowed to see it until the CPS had decided whether anyone would be prosecuted. I knew from experience that they would try their hardest to avoid any prosecutions,[1] but that didn't make the wait for them to announce it any less agonising. A month passed, then another, and another; I wondered how long it was going to take. Eventually I decided to call Richard Hebbert, the CPS lawyer in charge of the case.

He explained that one of the charges he was looking at used the Vreones test. I'd never heard of this test, so I started reading up on previous cases which had used it. It turned out the Vreones test concerned perverting the course of justice; I couldn't understand how this was relevant to the type of charges being considered in relation to the body swap. I began to feel that perhaps his comment had been directed at me. Was he suggesting that if I was to challenge the CPS, then *I* would be charged with perverting the course of justice? Presumably he knew I had taken the CPS to court in the past. Was he warning me to stop asking questions? It was an uncomfortable thought, but I couldn't see why else he would have brought it up.

Although it unnerved me, the phone call had left me none the wiser. The waiting continued.

Spying

2013–5

I had moved to a quiet corner of Halifax in 2012. I was still trying to process the abhorrent news about Christopher's body and awaiting the results of the police investigation, and the stress was taking a severe physical toll. I had blown up like a balloon from all the cortisol flooding my body, and I desperately needed to reduce my blood pressure and find some calm in my life. Trying to repair some of the emotional damage of the previous years was hard; it felt like there was no let up. Still, I did at least have somewhere I could relax and feel safe. I'd found a cosy three-storey cottage, with a lovely, peaceful garden. The cottage was right on the edge of the countryside, at the bottom of a hill, surrounded by greenery. From my garden I could sit and watch the birds and squirrels, as well as the horses and lambs across the lane. It was a little haven of tranquillity.

This was where my life was at when I got a call from Ruth one morning in July 2013. Ruth and I had built up a deep friendship over the years, so it wasn't unusual for her to phone me just to see how I was. But on this particular call, she had bad news.

'Janet, something's happened.'

'What is it?'

'There's a possibility that you and Leslie were put under covert surveillance by Humberside Police during the inquest.'

I was stunned. How much more were they going to put me and my family through?

Ruth told me that this had come to light through a female Humberside Police officer who was part of the surveillance team that had been authorised to spy on me. Some weeks earlier, it had emerged that the family of Stephen Lawrence had been spied on by the police, and Theresa May, then home secretary, had requested that all police forces around the country see if there was any evidence they had been involved in spying on the Lawrences. The Humberside officer had seen this on the TV news, and became aware that the operation she had been involved in mirrored the concerns about how the Lawrence family had been treated. She reported what she remembered about the operation to her superiors, and from there a referral was made by Humberside Police to the IPCC.[1]

My mind went back to the officer I had seen making notes outside Waterstones that very first day I went to the police station after Christopher's death. Since then, I had always felt edgy about people standing around near me, even after my move to Halifax. I had long suspected that I was being surveilled, and had been suspicious about the clicks and echoes on my calls and missing items of mail. The IPCC had dismissed the suggestion as if I was crazy in 2006. But now my suspicions were confirmed: I *had* been under police surveillance; perhaps I still was. It really did feel like I was seen as an enemy of the state.

So much was swirling through my head. A whole team of police had been established to spy on me during the inquest, and just a few months later, days before Christopher's funeral, his body had been swapped at the mortuary for that of Grace Kamara, ensuring we didn't bury him. I felt completely under attack. It felt like a deep and very personal targeted persecution of me for attempting to hold the police to account: punishment for all the work we had done to help secure the unlawful killing verdict at the inquest. Could the body swap have been part of this vendetta? And if so, what had they been doing with Christopher's body all that time?

I questioned other aspects of what had been happening; I was making connections between the funeral, the spying, the anonymous roses that had been sent to me, even the fling I'd had in the hotel. By this time, the scandal around Mark Kennedy – the undercover policeman whose infiltration of environmental groups had involved sleeping with activists and even fathering children with them – had broken, and it was becoming clear that it was not a one off. Had this bit of seeming respite and comfort actually been a police sting operation aiming to find dirt and discredit me?

It was a terrifying time. I was paranoid about everything, and didn't know who to trust. I felt broken and exhausted, living on adrenaline and cortisol and in a permanent state of fight or flight.

Shortly after the call from Ruth, I got a letter from the IPCC explaining that they would be investigating the allegations. I had very low expectations, and knew that any report they produced would be little more than damage limitation. Still, I spoke to Alan Cary, who would be the lead investigator, on the phone. Straight away, it was clear that he had a different approach from the authoritarian and bullying manner of those I had dealt with in the past. He told me that he had heard and read lots of people making judgements about me, that I was aggressive and all the rest of it, but that no one had really listened to what I had to say, and that is what he wanted to do. I agreed to meet in my house the following week.

Cary was a tall, slim man with a relaxed demeanour. He told me that the police officer who had reported the spying had been told by her superiors to essentially investigate it herself. She was asked to seek out the people who had been part of her surveillance team to see what they remembered about the operation, and then write up her findings. Her own mini investigation was termed Operation Akita, while the spying operation itself was named Operation Yarrow. Cary had seen the Operation Akita report she produced, and it was on the basis of this that the IPCC had believed there were grounds for their own investigation into what appeared to be unlawful surveillance. I asked if I would be allowed to read the report myself but, although it was about me, he said I would not be allowed to because the officers had not been interviewed under caution.

I later discovered that an Akita is a breed of Japanese dog, powerfully aggressive to strangers, but deeply loyal, especially to their own family. Was that how I was viewed by the police? Or perhaps it was how they viewed themselves; a reminder to those involved in the investigation of their own institutional loyalties – and the need to close ranks.

Cary was good to his word, and willing to listen. I told him of all my concerns and suspicions over the years, and he asked me to write everything up in a statement, which I agreed to do. I believed he was sincere, and that he would try to find the truth to the best of his ability. Yet I still doubted the IPCC: they had supposedly investigated my concerns about surveillance back in 2006 and found no evidence. And yet now we knew an entire team had been assigned to follow me. That is an awful lot to miss, and it didn't inspire confidence in their investigatory capabilities. I did believe that Cary would go as far as he was allowed to go in his pursuit of the truth. I just wondered how far that would be.

Finally, in October 2013, after six months of supposed deliberation, the CPS announced their decision about the body swap: no one was to be prosecuted.

The BBC headline read 'Christopher Alder Hull mortuary mix-up: no prosecution', and their report carried a quote from South Yorkshire Police: 'After careful consideration of all the circumstances and the evidence available, the Crown Prosecution Service has concluded that there is no realistic prospect of a conviction for either misconduct in a public office or the prevention of the lawful burial of a body.'[2] DS Fewkes, who led the investigation, said: 'While the investigation will not lead to a criminal prosecution, I am now in a position to explain to the families of Christopher Alder and Grace Kamara the likely circumstances that may have led to these very tragic events.'[3] The article then quoted me saying, 'We are devastated. Nobody has answered any of my questions before, I can't expect anyone to do so now.'[4] The investigation had not revealed when the body was released, nor who released the body, and had apparently found no evidence to show that it had been done intentionally.

Although this was the result I had expected, I was still sickened; how could they confuse a fit thirty-seven-year-old ex-paratrooper for a seventy-seven-year-old woman? I just couldn't see how the two could be mistaken. And it seemed incredible that it just happened to involve two Black people – in Hull, which had an ethnic minority population of 2.6 per cent. That it had been an accident simply wasn't believable.

The Operation Almond report, when I finally received it, was heavily redacted; it was like trying to piece together a jigsaw puzzle. There were so many anomalies. It didn't do anything to answer who released Grace's body from the mortuary for Christopher's funeral; in fact, it seemed to me like its purpose was to make reading it as confusing and traumatic as possible, rather than to provide any clarification.

For example, the report stated that Christopher's breastbone was under his body and that his head was not attached to his body, but an anthropologist who had viewed pictures of Christopher's body reported that it was fully intact, and in reasonably good condition. It made me question whether the photos she had been shown were even of Christopher at all. Rather than providing any real answers, the report just added to my feelings of desperation and despair.

I also wondered why they had given the report the name they had: Operation Almond. Almond was the name of the psychopath who had knocked me unconscious and smashed my house apart. He was well known to Humberside Police, who were effectively in charge of the operation; before smashing my house, he had twenty-nine previous convictions.[5] I couldn't help thinking that naming their operation after my tormentor was just another psychological attack.[6]

I had fully expected the report to be a whitewash; I knew I would hear more horrible details about what had happened to Christopher, but that in the end, they would exonerate themselves. It was standard procedure. But nothing could have prepared me for the shock that was to come.

Since 2011, I had been in a state of total confusion as to what had gone on with Grace and Christopher's bodies. I couldn't see how the swap had been a mistake, but nor could I comprehend why it would have been done on purpose. And either way, I couldn't see how it could have gone unnoticed all these years, as Christopher's body was clearly recognisable and labelled with his name; the bodies had both been moved between mortuaries on several occasions, and the mortuary's own procedures required each body to be identified with every move.

But what I discovered on page twenty-three of that report, tucked away at the end of a section listing the mortuary's processes and procedures, shocked me to the core. For it turned out that it was *not* only mortuary staff who had had access to Christopher's body. In fact, police officers had been visiting the mortuary, repeatedly, to view his body. And they had been asking for him specifically – by name. Humberside Police, it emerged, had been using Christopher's body for some kind of 'police training'. Far from being hidden away where no one could have realised their 'mistake', Christopher's body was being regularly 'used' by the officers who stood by while Christopher died.

The report stated that '59 officers have stated that they were shown the body of either Christopher Alder or Grace Kamara or of a frozen body'. Now the only frozen body during this period – other than Grace's between 1999 and 2000 – was Christopher's, so any frozen body they viewed would almost certainly have been his. And several of the officers said they viewed Grace Kamara *after* 2000 – after, that is, we had buried her in Christopher's grave. So they must have been viewing Christopher as well; I can only surmise that referring to him as 'Grace' – when all the evidence shows he was clearly recognisable as a man – must have been some kind of sick in-joke among the police.

On top of everything that had happened already, this was an unbelievable shock. I kept asking myself – why would the police use Christopher's body for training? Supposedly it was for 'sudden-death training', for the police to desensitise themselves by getting used to seeing dead bodies. But why would they choose two Black bodies in a predominantly white town? And besides, these bodies had been dead for some time – in fact, they were the only two in long-term storage – so why would you use them for sudden-death training? It didn't make any sense.

In fact, nothing in the report made any sense. It didn't reveal anything useful. All it told us was that the police had come into the mortuary to do training, and that there'd been ten missed opportunities (such as times when the body had supposedly been moved) when mortuary staff could have realised they had the wrong body. It gave all the details about when people started working and didn't work, when they started at the mortuary and about the joining of the public mortuary to the hospital mortuary – bureaucratic details, basically. And then it told us that Christopher was found with his head not attached and that they didn't know if the body was a man or a woman when they found him. It was like a maze. It wasn't presented with any intention of providing understanding of what had happened. It just posed more and more questions.

Rosie Brighouse, my lawyer at the time, who had taken our case to the ECHR, wrote to the police to ask them for a meeting. They wanted to come along with the CPS, to have a joint meeting with them, but I refused. I thought they'd have built up a story between them, and all sat together and supported each other in what they were saying, so I just said no. I told them I wanted to see the police first, and then speak to the CPS afterwards.

So in early November, Andy, Ruth, Rosie and I met with South Yorkshire Police in Ruth's office. I hated meeting the police: to me, it was like walking into an ants' nest, knowing I would be bitten viciously, but I still felt compelled to do it. My anxiety levels were through the roof. I had been in this situation many times over the years, but it didn't make it any easier – and in some ways, it made it worse, as I knew what to expect: my questions would be treated with contempt and left unanswered, while I would be made to feel as if I was being difficult, like I was the problem. Yet even knowing all this, I couldn't help hoping that things would be different this time.

When the day of the meeting came, I was deeply apprehensive. I had not slept properly for weeks; in fact, when I think about it, I have not slept properly since Christopher's death. I've spent years surviving on nervous energy mixed with adrenaline. My blood pressure was up, my heart beating like I don't know what; I was on edge. I was also on high alert, as I always am around the police.

They came in and we sat down. The investigating officer, DS Fewkes, was unable to attend because he was having surgery. At first I thought it was an emergency: perhaps he'd been in an accident, or been attacked while doing his job or something. In fact it was a pre-arranged minor appointment: it seemed he'd arranged to have our meeting at a time he knew he couldn't attend. It felt like an insult, as if we weren't important – either that or he didn't have the guts to see me face to face. In his place, he sent Detective Andy Stephanak, Deputy Detective Phil Etheridge, and Kramer. Stood together, the two men looked quite comedic: Stephanak was built like a bodybuilder, muscles bulging out of his shirt, sharply contrasting Etheridge's skinny frame; I thought to myself that they looked like the Hulk and Where's Wally. It had become part of my survival mechanism over the years to look for the light side in these meetings, an attempt to take away some of the anxiety and to lessen the disappointment when nothing came out of them.

I could tell from their body language they weren't comfortable. Stephanak seemed to have it all scripted in advance, and he didn't want to be interrupted. I was trying to ask questions, but he kept saying, 'we'll come to that in a minute, just let me finish'.

One thing that was clear is that the standard procedures had not been followed the day Grace's body was released in place of Christopher's. Stephanak told us, 'What should have happened on the day of the release is as follows. You have two bodies in the freezer, you would do two things: fill in the document and check the wristband. We know nothing was written on the outside of the bags, therefore there was no excuse not to check the wristband. At that point they didn't check and should have.'

Andy asked for clarification: 'So the body was not checked and the form was not filled in?'

'Correct,' said Stephanak.

Andy asked: 'Can we identify the person? If we find their identity, can we prosecute them?'

Stephanak replied: 'If we could identify them, we would try for misconduct in a public office.'

But Etheridge was not so sure: 'Although not necessarily, as it could be a genuine mistake. We are somewhere between the two at the moment.'[7]

The problem, they claimed, was that they had no way of knowing who had released the body: 'We have tens of thousands of documents for this case,' Stephanak said, but 'the upshot is it's not possible to identify the dates for the mortuary and who released the body. Without that we can't narrow down who did it.' After a year and a half of investigation, and half a million pounds of public money, this is what they had come up with.

But there were serious holes in their story. For a start, they told us that they didn't know if Grace's body had been collected from the mortuary on the Saturday morning and taken straight to the funeral meeting place, or collected earlier in the week and stored at the undertakers. But it had been confirmed by the mortuary staff and funeral directors that the mortuary was closed on a Saturday and bodies were not released, except in the unique circumstances of Muslim or Jewish funerals. Being neither Muslim nor Jewish, then, the body was obviously not released on the Saturday. It appears the only people who preferred this Saturday scenario, dismissing what they had been told by the mortuary and funeral directors, were South Yorkshire Police.

I asked whether they knew who worked on particular days. Yes, Stephanak told me, they knew who worked all week, they had the staff rota; but because the body had not officially been released, there was no paperwork to show which day it was collected. I asked him who was working on 22 November, the day the funeral directors called the cemetery to request the coffin: I thought they must have had the body in order to be able to know what size coffin was needed. But he didn't tell me.

Thinking back to what the reporter had told me about his call from the funeral directors, I also asked why the funeral directors didn't open the bag.

'The only reason there could be is that he was frozen. This is clearly not a reason. It's just a possible excuse. They ALL say they would have checked the wristband,' Stephanak replied.[8] I asked, 'Is it possible they had been told not to open the bag?' But another question was asked at the same time by someone else, and the conversation moved on.

Then there was the elephant in the room – racism. They tried to close this conversation down straight away.

'I have raised race because people are treated differently,' I said. 'No one else has gone through this. The Macpherson report: one culture is treated differently to another. We are treated differently because we are Black.'

'There is no evidence of this,' was Stephanak's curt reply. There was also no evidence that they had ever investigated it; if they had, this would surely have been the time to mention it.

Andy elaborated on exactly how racism works: 'Racism may consist of unspoken assumptions. People acted in a way to suggest that the fate of Christopher Alder and his body is of no significance. We ask: did the police inquiry throw up questions of prejudicial assumptions, callous indifference?'

At this point, Phil Etheridge chimed in with an amazing twist of logic which reminded me of the old line, 'some of my best friends are Black': 'There were other Black bodies that would have been buried during this period,' he said, as if that put an end to the matter. By this logic, anyone who does not abuse *every single Black body* that crosses their path, cannot be considered racist under any circumstances.

'Did you ask about attitudes?' Andy queried again.

'Yes, we looked at the treatment of other bodies,' Etheridge replied – a reply, I thought, that was more of a 'no' than a 'yes'. I'd had enough.

'You have looked at this from the assumption that it's an accident,' I told them.

'No we haven't,' Etheridge replied.

The minutes then record that I 'became agitated and the mood became heated' and that my lawyer suggested a break.

After the break, Rosie asked about the use of Christopher's body for police training. Her questions were simple: 'What, how and why?'

'There were two reasons for people to come and see bodies,' Stephanak told us. 'One, to identify a loved one and two, police training. For police, this was an opportunity to see bodies in a controlled environment. We then enquired with the training department. 849 or 851 police trained in the period 1999 to 2011 from Humberside Police only [and] we ended up with forty to fifty who gave information "worth considering" ... they give a number of accounts: either being told about Grace Kamara, others told about Christopher Alder. Others just see the body bag. After the burial, police are shown a body, we don't know whose. It's a possibility that they were shown Christopher Alder described as Grace Kamara.'

'Why?' I asked. 'If the police need to see a body, why are they showing a frozen one?'

'Exactly,' answered Stephanak, 'that is why what the officers are saying doesn't make sense ... There are different opportunities to show people in a bad state. The freezers were on the upstairs floor. To show Christopher Alder's body they would have had to go upstairs and unzip six bags.' He later added, 'On a practical level ... there was no reason to show a frozen body over a fridge body.' They were clearly going to a lot of effort to specifically view Christopher's body – despite its irrelevance to their training requirements.

'How did you become aware of this practice?' Rosie asked.

'A female officer came forward having heard the story of the body swap,' Stephanak replied. 'She had remembered Grace Kamara as she thought it was a pretty name.'

I left the meeting, as so often, feeling frustrated and confused, with no real answers and yet more questions. The investigation didn't seem to have given any consideration to the possibility of someone purposely releasing the wrong body and then covering it up, hoping to later bury him out of the way at the funeral of Grace Kamara in 2011. It was as if a decision had been made in advance to conclude that it was all just an unfortunate accident: Grace's body being buried in place of Christopher was no more than a mistake, while not knowing who the mortuary worker was meant there were no suspects. This supposed 'criminal investigation' seemed to have been founded on the assumption that there was no victim, no suspects and therefore no crime. With that as its starting point, no wonder its outcome was so depressingly predictable.

It felt as though there were only two people standing in the way of this convenient narrative being accepted: Christine, who the police saw as a 'troublemaker', and me, who they deemed an 'agitator'.[9] Certainly the police investigators had seemed more interested in asking me irrelevant questions about funeral flowers than establishing who had released the wrong body and broken the law by keeping it all off the books.

But what disturbed me even more was that although every single one of the people that had dealt with Christopher and Grace's bodies or had any dealings with the case will have buried, or will bury, their own loved ones – and will probably have cried buckets at the loss of their family members and felt the pain and disillusionment that comes with a family member's death – they seemed to have no empathy or ability to understand how we felt. It was as if they believed that, because Christine and I asked questions and didn't fit the social norm, we lacked the mental capacity to feel the same pain. I've never felt like I've been treated as a victim, but always as a nuisance; those in authority have always attributed my questioning not to the pain and anguish of having had a loved one killed without any accountability, but to some kind of pathological desire to infuriate them. This investigation just seemed like more of the same: an obstacle to justice rather than a means to it, with me cast in the role, not of traumatised relative seeking answers, but annoying troublemaker intent on causing problems for no reason.

The police didn't know or care what my state of mind was at the time; these people never thought for one minute about how I was feeling. Throughout all of these traumatic revelations, none of them showed any concern for my mental welfare. They saw me as a threat to be neutralised, and with each new piece of evidence of their inhumanity, they went on the attack. To defend themselves, they didn't care how callous they were being.

It was like I was in a dark hole looking for a glimmer of hope anywhere. And yet all this stress was being brought to me. It was not as if I'd done anything wrong; I was just continuously dealing with the after-effects of their actions against me. The state kept coming into my life, as they had done in childhood, and all the trauma I thought I'd left behind was regurgitated.

I decided to appeal the CPS decision not to prosecute anyone over the body swap, and also to request that the IPCC investigate the police's apparent use of Christopher's body for training exercises. I felt like I had to push their processes as far as they would go, although by now I knew not to expect any justice.

In March 2014, the CPS announced that they had reviewed their decision not to press charges in relation to the swapping of Christopher's body and had upheld that decision. It was not a surprise but was nevertheless a knock-back. Another followed in July, when we were informed by the IPCC that they would not investigate the revelations that the police had been using Christopher's body for training purposes. Instead, Humberside Police were left to investigate it themselves – the same force that the allegations were about, the same force that was at that very moment being investigated for illegally spying on me, the same force that the inquest had found had unlawfully killed Christopher in the first place. It was clear how that would go. It felt like these people could get away with anything.

When the report finally came through, I thought it was a pretty unsophisticated whitewash. Most of the twenty-page document had simply been cut and pasted from the South Yorkshire Police's Operation Almond report. Like that report, it contained dozens of gruesome accounts of officers viewing a Black body in various stages of decomposition, often referred to as 'Grace Kamara' (even though she was by then buried in Christopher's grave), but concluding that all of them were mistaken and that 'no officer had viewed Christopher's body and recognised it as being him.' Once again, it was all assumed to have been an innocent misunderstanding. Nevertheless, there was some revealing information contained within it. In a meeting between the investigating officer and the senior coroner, the latter 'firstly expressed concern as to what basis the coroner had to allow the police officers to view a body within the mortuary and confirmed that he would not have allowed this. He indicated that the only time any other person such as a police officer would be able to view a body within the mortuary would be where they were present with a legitimate reason to be present for a post-mortem.' This suggested that the police viewings of bodies, which no one denies took place regularly, were either unauthorised, or were authorised on an improper basis.

My state of mind at this time came out in an interview I did with the *Yorkshire Post* in December 2014. I told reporter Simon Bristow that my belief in humanity had been crushed and begged for anyone who knew anything about what had gone on in the mortuary to come forward if they had a prick of conscience.

Throughout this period, I regularly asked Alan Cary of the IPCC about the statement he had asked for, and to request the Operation Akita report (to no avail). The IPCC completed their report into Humberside's spying operation against me in January 2015, but I was not allowed to see it until the CPS had decided whether or not to bring charges. Shortly after this, Cary and some of his IPCC colleagues agreed to meet up with Andy and me to give us an update. Once again, they had brought in a Black woman, Cindy Butt, as part of the investigation. I told her straight that she was being used by a racist organisation to hide their racism and shield them from criticism; she responded by saying something about working within constraints. You could say that again.

Nevertheless, they told us they had evidence against a couple of police officers for a misconduct charge. It got my hopes up that something might come out of it, but the wait for the CPS to make their decision was agonising. At the same time, my head was swimming with images and questions about what was being done to Christopher's body all that time, while wondering exactly how far the police surveillance operation against me had gone – and whether it was still underway.

Finally, in late November 2015, we received a letter from Piers Arnold of the CPS, ten months after they'd received the IPCC report into Humberside Police's surveillance of me. The letter informed us that a total of eighteen of the officers involved in Operation Yarrow had been identified as potential suspects. The IPCC had concluded there was no case to answer against fourteen of the officers, but four senior officers had been reported to the CPS 'for the consideration of the offence of misconduct in a public office'.[10]

The letter explained that two surveillance 'authorities' – documents authorising covert surveillance – had been granted under Operation Yarrow. The first one was dated 26 June 2000, a week before the start of the inquest, and authorised surveillance of protesters outside the court in order 'to gather evidence and identify suspects involved in offences that may be committed outside the Court'. The second authorised much more intrusive surveillance beginning at 5 p.m. on 28 July 2000, when the first authority expired, and was in effect until 31 August 2000. This second authority mandated the use of 'mobile, foot and technical surveillance' in 'all areas covered by the Humberside Police boundaries'. This was effectively open season to follow any of us anywhere at any time. And they did. The letter went on: 'There is evidence that Operation Yarrow involved surveillance of you and Mr Thomas. The overall picture [that] emerges is that part of the surveillance team followed a group including you to your hotel, and that another part of the team followed another group to a car park. Mr Thomas may have been in one of those groups, and there was surveillance targeted deliberately at him.'[11] All the years of gaslighting, by the police, by the IPCC, trying to make me think I was mad for suspecting I was being followed, was suddenly laid bare.

In his interview, the commander of the surveillance team had mentioned 'someone connected to his family. Something around his solicitor,' while the deputy operation commander had stated that 'somebody went for a drink with a solicitor. One remit was to try and overhear the conversation.' Such conduct, the CPS explained, would clearly be an offence.[12] The acting superintendent, explained the letter, had 'extended the geographical authority for surveillance, on the day in question, without it being requested, and without any obvious justification for doing so.' He had attempted to justify this extension by referencing some supposed 'previous disorder' at the demonstration outside the police station on the anniversary of Christopher's death, but Arnold said he was 'not persuaded' that this disorder ever took place.[13] On top of all that, 'there is reason to think that the mobile and technical surveillance, specifically allowed for in the Assistant Superintendent's extended authorisation' actually started before it had come into force.

In summary, Arnold wrote that 'following the family of an alleged victim of police negligence/ brutality and their legal representative ... would involve a high level of intrusion and would require good reasons. No such reasons are discernible from the evidence.'[14] Instead, he wrote, 'The evidence indicates that [the surveillance] was not properly authorised.'[15]

But there was a problem. The most incriminating evidence had come from the original Operation Akita report, conducted by the police officer who had blown the whistle on the surveillance in the first place. But these statements had not been made under oath, and could not, therefore, be used in court in a prosecution. When the IPCC came to question the officers under caution, 'with limited exceptions', all the officers refused to answer any questions – just as they had at the inquest and in the previous IPCC investigation – instead handing over a prepared statement, omitting key information contained in their original comments.[16] References to the targeting of Leslie and my family had all been scrubbed from the new testimonies provided by the commander and deputy commander.[17] 'Any prosecution would necessarily rely heavily on the evidence of police officers involved in the surveillance,' Arnold wrote, 'yet the response of almost all those questioned by the IPCC was to decline to answer questions, which in itself strongly suggests that they would be reluctant to provide evidence.'[18] The police wall of silence had prevailed. Consequently, he wrote, 'I have decided that on the existing evidence provided to me by the IPCC no prosecution should take place against any individuals for an offence of misconduct in a public office.'[19] They had got away with it. Again.

I wasn't surprised. Ruth said that we'd ask for a review of the decision-making, although I held out no hopes for that either, as it would be based on the same limited evidence as the original decision. I had hoped to testify at the major public inquiry into police spying that was taking place in London,[20] as this would have forced them to disclose all the evidence. But I wasn't allowed to because access was limited to the Metropolitan Police. I have never been allowed to read the original Operation Akita report into Humberside's spying operation against me.

By now my personal life had again descended into chaos: my health was rapidly deteriorating and I was constantly on the verge of physical and emotional collapse. But I was still trying to make sense of the mass of contradictory information and reports I was wading through, and to stand up to the obfuscation and lies. Shortly after the letter from the CPS, I was sent a copy of the IPCC report on the surveillance operation against me; but like all the other investigations, it left me with more questions than answers.

It was a lot to take in, on top of everything I was still learning about the body swap. Even the IPCC concluded that the spying operation had improper and likely racist motives.[21] But despite the damning revelations it contained, I could see the report was still an exercise in damage limitation. It had already come out in the press that I had been followed around Hull, when the policewoman had first raised the matter. That couldn't be denied. So instead, they tried to make out that it only happened on one occasion – between 3.20 p.m. and 5.17 p.m. on 28 July. But I know this cannot have been the case, for the simple reason that they described me being followed into my hotel, and having a meal in the restaurant and a drink at the bar – and I never did this on a Friday. I only stayed at the hotel from Monday to Thursday night – on Fridays, I only stopped there to pick up my bags from reception before going straight back home for the weekend. They had taken all the various descriptions of me being followed and tried to make out they all happened during that one brief two-hour period. I believe that not only were we surveilled during the whole period of the inquest, but before and after this as well. I still remembered the policeman following me on the very first day I set foot in the police station in Hull in 1998.

They did refer briefly, however, to my complaint about the police filming us inside the foyer of the court during the trial of the officers in 2002. The report referred to 'intelligence and information provided by Humberside Police'[22] to Cleveland Police, who supposedly used this information to justify following us. I wondered what was in this intelligence; if it was based on prior surveillance, which seemed highly likely, it would have been crucial evidence for the extent of the operation undertaken by Humberside. Yet the IPCC appeared never to have requested this intelligence, or even asked about its contents. It was as if they were determined not to find anything that might undermine the police's account. And, of course, they claimed not to have been able to find out who authorised the surveillance.

*

The IPCC report made me aware that there were nearly eighty people involved in the two spying operations, including officers urgently taken off another surveillance job to take part. I have been shown no justification for this. I'm left feeling that Humberside Police were coming after me because they had the power to do so and a bottomless public purse to do it with. I was ultimately on my own, highlighting and drawing public attention to Christopher's death, and seen as causing trouble for officers and their organisation.

It sickens me that the police chose to target me at such a vulnerable time in my life, following me wherever I went in Hull. It cuts deep to know their targeting was deliberate. They were not bothered about justice; I was stripped of all rights – even to the point of them listening in to my private conversations with my legal team. Leslie was the only African-Caribbean barrister working within the inquest court, and because he was a Black barrister he too was treated with total contempt. The hostility Humberside Police showed for me meant my barrister too became a target of their racist operation.

I can't find words strong enough to describe the fear I felt, and at times still feel, to find out the police turned their investigative powers on me and Leslie. Rather than looking at the behaviour of their own officers, Humberside Police were focused obsessively on what felt like a vendetta against me for daring to speak out. I had become their prey, a canvas on which to project all their negative feelings and actions.

When I dare to think back to this traumatic time, I realise it was extremely intimidating. Every time I entered the court, I was surrounded by the uniformed police officers that had been deployed both outside and in the foyer while the inquest was being conducted, and their visible presence already made me feel edgy and uneasy. They were well aware that no public order offences had been committed by me or anyone else there, but if that was genuinely their fear, their attendance was more than sufficient to handle the four to six of us who attended the court on its busiest days, so why did they need covert surveillance to follow me wherever I went? I have my suspicions.

I believe the real purpose of this surveillance was to see if they could find something with which to discredit me, especially after it became clear the inquest was not going their way. It was painful enough for me having to sit and listen to emotive, heart-wrenching comments and slurs being made by the six barristers representing the police officers, attempting to assassinate Christopher's character while he was not there to defend himself. Yet still they felt they wanted revenge on my attempts to hold them to account.

The number of officers involved in the spying operation – an incredible eighty officers in total – showed there was a collective targeting of me as an individual by Humberside Police, and a united show of support for police colleagues under scrutiny. The resources, man-hours and money spent on trailing me must have been authorised right from the top. Yet, as ever, no one has been held accountable. Neither Tony Stead, who signed the unlawful surveillance order, nor Michael Dixon, who deployed the surveillance team, have been reprimanded in any way, whether by criminal sanction or internal disciplinary.

The Horror Never Stops

2016–23

In 2016, I took out a civil case against the institutions involved in the swapping of Christopher and Grace's bodies: Hull City Council and Hull and East Yorkshire Hospitals NHS Trust. In the process of preparing this case, South Yorkshire Police disclosed to us more than 8,000 documents from their investigation, and it has taken me years to go through them all. Among them were some of the most astounding and shocking revelations of the whole case. But the single most important document in ascertaining who was responsible – and the most obvious starting point for any investigation – was not included. This was the funeral directors' document clearly outlining the date and time when Grace's body was collected from the mortuary in place of Christopher's.

South Yorkshire Police had told me, both in person when we met, and in their official 163-page Operation Almond investigation report to the CPS, that they had been unable to find out when Grace's body was released from the mortuary. They said that with this information they would have been able to find out which member of the mortuary staff was responsible for releasing the wrong body, as they had the staff rotas from that week, and knew exactly who was working when. Despite their best efforts, they told us, they had simply been unable to glean this information. The mortuary records were missing, and they weren't sure, they said, whether Grace had been collected on the day of Christopher's funeral on Saturday 25 November 2000, or earlier in the week. In fact, they knew perfectly well that the body would have been collected in advance of the funeral, not on the day, to remain at the funeral directors' chapel of rest. But more than this, I obtained, by means of a simple phone call to the funeral directors, the documentation surrounding Christopher's body, known as the 'Dignity' burial form. This form clearly states the date and time they collected the body they believed to be Christopher from the mortuary. Under the heading 'First Call' is printed: 'Tuesday, 21st November, 2000, 9.02am'. 'First call' is a phrase used by undertakers to refer to their collection of human remains.[1] By matching this date with records of who was working when, the police would have been able to pinpoint which member of the mortuary staff was responsible for releasing the wrong body.

I found it hard to believe that South Yorkshire Police, who spent £500,000 of public money in their investigation, including a return trip to Australia to interview a former mortuary worker, did not think to phone the funeral directors and ask for their documentation. In fact, we know they had the burial form in their possession all along, as well as the funeral directors' own ledger which included the same information. The CPS confirmed in their meeting with us that 'the police have looked at the funeral directors' records', and, besides, they had explicitly asked the mortuary staff about the burial document. They even knew which member of the mortuary staff wrote Grace Kamara's name on Christopher Alder's body bag.

Also recorded on the funeral directors' burial order is that Christopher was to be buried in a robe. In fact, we paid £2,200 for him to be embalmed and robed before burial. Had this been done, the funeral directors would have seen clearly that the body in their possession was not Christopher, but Grace Kamara. No answers have been given by the police as to why the body bag was not opened to carry out this request. The CPS, in their meeting with us, confirmed that 'there was no reason not to open the bag'. None of this appears to have been investigated by South Yorkshire Police.

The police officers' testimonies collected by South Yorkshire Police confirmed that mortuary staff and police trainers were well aware that it was Christopher's body in the mortuary all those years. One Humberside police officer had been into the mortuary six months after Christopher's supposed burial. A mortuary worker opened a drawer and told him they had Christopher Alder but could not release him for legal reasons. That was in April 2001, the exact time we were holding our annual commemoration of Christopher's death outside Humberside police station.

Another officer remembers being told during training exercises that Christopher's body was still being held in the mortuary long after he was supposed to have been buried. Dozens of other officers testified that they had been shown a body that was either frozen, in long-term storage, or described as Grace Kamara, at a time when Christopher (labelled as Grace Kamara) was the only body that was frozen or held in long-term storage at the mortuary. Year in, year out, for more than ten years after his death, police officers – according to their own testimonies – were being shown a body which can only have been Christopher's.

Yet, despite all of this, in their eventual decision not to bring charges in relation to the body swap and subsequent cover-up, the CPS appear to have concluded that the true identity of Christopher's body was unknown until 2011.

That the true identity of Christopher's body was known as early as 2000 and all the way up to 2011 was confirmed by multiple other exhibits in the possession of the investigating officers but hidden from their report to the CPS. One is a mortuary admission form in Christopher Alder's name, dated 2005. Another is the minutes from a meeting held in 2011, in which Mike Wright, chief executive of the local NHS Trust, explains that 'at no point *since 2007* has the contents of the body bag labelled as GK [Grace Kamara] been opened'. The clear implication that the bag had been opened in 2007 was apparently never investigated by South Yorkshire Police, who never even bothered to interview Wright about his comment. Instead, they concluded that 'there is no evidence to support the possibility that this [body swap] was discovered before the 4th November 2011'.

For me, it was incredible that South Yorkshire Police were even running the investigation in the first place. South Yorkshire and Humberside are effectively two branches of the same force, with a shared head of HR, a shared data centre, joint support lines, shared training programmes, a shared recruitment website, a string of collaboration agreements and several jointly run investigations under their belts. Humberside chief constable Tim Hollis publicly recognised that it would be inappropriate for Humberside to be involved, and council boss Nicola Yates noted that Humberside were 'conflicted' as Christopher had died in their custody. Both stated an 'independent' investigation would be required. Yet a *less* independent organisation than South Yorkshire would be hard to conceive.

But it was worse than this. As I read through the 'Gold Command' minutes of the meetings between bosses of the council, mortuary and police from November 2011, it emerged that it wasn't even South Yorkshire in charge of the operation at all. It was being directed by Humberside Police all along, even as they were under investigation by the IPCC for illegally spying on me. Minutes from the meeting held on 7 November 2011 note that the South Yorkshire team 'will be working under the direction of SD'. SD was Stuart Donald, the deputy chief constable of Humberside Police, the very force responsible for Christopher's death. Meetings of the 'Almond Gold Command' groups were composed *entirely* of officers from Humberside, with only occasional appearances from South Yorkshire Police officers such as Richard Fewkes, who was supposedly 'leading' the investigation. Documents relating to the investigation are even labelled 'Operation Almond – Humberside Enquiry'. Humberside were also paying a substantial amount of the costs of the investigation, and Humberside officers were used in the investigation; the Operation Almond meeting to arrange the exhumation of Grace Kamara from Christopher's grave, for example, involved four officers from South Yorkshire and four from Humberside. Operation Almond was effectively a Humberside Police investigation using South Yorkshire officers to do some of the legwork.

Humberside Police were responsible for the unlawful killing of my brother and their actions were motivated by racism (as officially concluded by the IPCC report of 2006). They had destroyed key evidence during the investigation, including blood samples and clothing and possibly a CS gas canister, presumably to hide their culpability. They had smeared Christopher in the press and had illegally spied on me during his inquest. There was thus clear evidence of hostility towards Christopher and his family, and thus a possible motive for desecrating his corpse. And yet they were directing the very operation that would supposedly reveal the truth about all of this. It was like the West Yorkshire investigation all over again – Humberside calling the shots in an investigation into activities they themselves were involved in.

In the 'Gold Command' minutes it was stated that South Yorkshire Police were 'trying to prevent this being a criminal investigation'. Even though in the end it *did* technically become a criminal investigation, they ignored or buried the most important leads and never asked key questions of the prime suspects. Questions that should have been put to the suspects – for example, who released the body from the mortuary – were instead put to me, as if I would know!

It was only by reading through the documents night after night that I realised that South Yorkshire Police had left all the most significant information out of the report. If I had relied only on their report, I would never have known what had really gone on.

For years, my head was in turmoil with all of this, and I was pinning all my hopes on bringing it out in court. But once again, I was let down.

Despite all that we had found out, in his preparation of the case, the lawyer who took on the civil case didn't even allege that anyone was aware of the body swap before 2011. His case was simply that the mortuary was at fault for handing over the wrong body in 2000, which was of course undeniable. The council, who were responsible for the mortuary at the time, admitted it and that was that. The case never came to court, none of the evidence we had saw the light of day, and no one was held to account for what was being done to Christopher's body during the thirteen years he was in the mortuary. I felt let down again, especially as this lawyer had told me I needed to 'put what had happened in the past out of my mind' and whose advice seemed to uncritically accept the police psychiatrist's biased claim that I was 'paranoid'.

I then made enquiries about pursuing a civil case against South Yorkshire Police for misfeasance in a public office. I found a new solicitors' firm and, right up until a week before the deadline for filing the claim, they seemed great. The police had tried everything they could to delay the release of the documents (which I already had, but, due to a court order, was not allowed to show my new solicitors!) but the solicitors stood firm and finally gained access. I sent them several emails highlighting key parts of the evidence I was concerned about; after wading through 8,000 documents, I did not want them to miss anything. When they saw the evidence, they told me that the prospects of winning warranted the case moving forward. Furthermore, the police's defence case seemed very weak. In response to our questioning of South Yorkshire Police's omission of some of the crucial evidence, the Police Legal Services department sent us a letter stating that just because the evidence is not in the report, does not mean they have not seen it. To my mind, this was an admission that they had wilfully left some of the most important details out of their report to the CPS.

So I was in total shock when, a week before the deadline to file the particulars, I was told by the barrister I didn't have a case. I took the knock-back personally and began to feel judged, especially when the barrister stated bluntly, 'I am not going to represent you'.

The barrister gave two sets of reasons for reaching this conclusion – one, that proving I had incurred a psychiatric injury as a direct and wilful result of the South Yorkshire investigation – which we would apparently need to prove to show misfeasance – was a non-starter. And two, that the evidence was not strong enough. This made no sense to me, and I searched through the documents she had drafted; she had not used the evidence I thought was strongest. I ran around frantically that week trying to find another barrister to take it on, but with only a week to go, it was too late. No claim was filed and the case fell.

I was outraged. It felt like all my efforts – twenty-five years of my life, with all the toll on my emotional and psychological wellbeing and my family life – had been for nothing. The police had won again. And they let me know it by coming for me.

My solicitor informed me that the police were now demanding that we pay *their* legal costs. I couldn't believe that all that money, donated by ordinary people – we'd raised £16,000 through a crowd justice fund – could end up in the hands of the very institutions that had killed my brother, spied on me, and messed around with Christopher's corpse for thirteen years.

In our initial case, my lawyer had written that '[even] the unredacted Operation Almond report was not, in fact, a representative summary of the evidence. Rather, significant details were omitted or glossed over.' Yet I have been left unable to speak about these significant details due to a court order that was placed on me before the documents were released. I have been advised I could be sent to prison for two years if I do so.

The Struggle Continues

2020–4

More than twenty-five years on, there has still been no justice. None of those responsible for Christopher's unlawful killing, nor any of the police officers or mortuary staff involved in using his dead body for training and then covering it up, nor any of the eighty police officers involved in illegally surveilling us, have ever had to answer questions about any of it in court. Instead, the institutions involved have conducted whitewash investigations of each other, with Police Federation lawyers shielding their members every step of the way. Those charged with upholding accountability have instead upheld impunity, whether under Labour or Conservative governments.

It is very common for families to be split by deaths in custody – some want to fight, others want to move on. I wanted to move on too, but I knew I couldn't until we had found out the truth, and had some kind of accountability and justice.

The police exploit these divisions, attempting to intimidate members of the family to make them scared to challenge their power. I believe this is what they were doing with their malicious arrest of Richard a few months after Christopher's death, when they bundled him into a van and told him they were taking him 'to where your brother died'. They even tried to use my brother Stephen's psychiatric illness, as well as the Black presence in the campaign more generally, to try to present the family and the Black community as a threat. They project everything onto us to deflect blame from themselves. When they found out about the body swap, the authorities immediately focused on the Black community in Hull, scared there would be an eruption, and seemed more concerned about that than about finding the culprits. Our campaign involved people of all ethnicities, but somehow the police just focused on the Black community, just as they did during the inquest, singling out Black supporters for surveillance. From the start, the police never missed an opportunity to attack me in the various inquiries, saying I used Christopher's death as a 'platform' for my supposed political ambitions, that I was an 'agitator', and so on. I never got a right to reply to any of that. They knew that my family would read all this, and these things have an effect. I have now lost all contact with my family, and can't help thinking they harbour some sort of resentment towards me, holding me responsible for what's happened in some way.

Legally speaking, much has gone backwards since Christopher's death, making it even harder for families to get justice. The one high point in Christopher's case was the unlawful killing verdict at the inquest in 2000 – but since then new rules have made it more difficult for such verdicts even to be considered.

Up until 2013, coroners were obliged to give inquest juries the option of an unlawful killing verdict wherever sufficient evidence had been presented to reach that conclusion. Unlawful killing was significant as it was the only verdict that was equivalent to a criminal offence (that of manslaughter). But in 2013, new coronial rules said that this option should only be given if the coroner has concluded that such a verdict would be 'safe'. In effect, coroners were being ordered to judge the evidence themselves, rather than leaving it to the jury to do so. It is no coincidence, then, that though there were a string of other unlawful killing verdicts following deaths in custody after Christopher's case, there were none at all between 2013 and 2020. Juries are simply not being allowed to even consider it as an option.

Another change in the law in 2020 supposedly 'redressed' this issue to an extent, by lowering the standard of proof required to reach an 'unlawful killing' verdict. Previously, as in Christopher's case, a jury was required to be sure to the criminal standard of proof – that is, 'beyond reasonable doubt' – in order to reach a verdict of unlawful killing. In 2020, this was lowered to the civil standard – the balance of probabilities – i.e. more likely than not. While this made it easier for juries to return unlawful killing verdicts – and for coroners to allow them to be considered – it also reduced the *significance* of such verdicts. In Christopher's case, the fact that a jury had already concluded, *beyond reasonable doubt*, that he had been unlawfully killed, made it much harder for the CPS to refuse to prosecute the officers for manslaughter (although they certainly tried). The 2020 ruling, however, has handed the CPS an invaluable weapon to resist demands for prosecution. In the past, an unlawful killing verdict was the exact 'equivalent' of manslaughter – requiring the same level of certainty and the same evidence; today, it no longer carries the same weight, and the CPS will be much more able to dismiss unlawful killing verdicts, arguing that, because the standard of proof was lower in the coroner's court, the verdict does not have any bearing on whether a prosecution for manslaughter is likely to succeed. The last link between inquest verdicts and criminal charges has been broken, making prosecutions of police officers much less likely in the future. Up until 2021, despite thousands of deaths in custody since 1969, only one police officer had successfully been prosecuted for murder or manslaughter over any of these deaths.[1] Christopher's case was one of those that came the closest, and I believe it rattled the state, who wanted to ensure we never came this close again. But the events of summer 2020 changed the equation.

When I saw the video of George Floyd, in which a police officer kneeled on his neck for almost nine minutes while his life drained away, it triggered everything I'd experienced watching Christopher's death on camera. I'm sure the Floyd family felt that same combination of disbelief, shock and powerlessness when they watched that video. And I am sure they felt, as we did, the devastating frustration when none of the other officers attempted to step in, even those who can clearly see the distress he was in. Just as in Christopher's case, one of the officers seemed to be concerned about his position, suggesting they 'roll him on his side'. But it didn't happen; the murderer Derek Chauvin simply continued to choke the life out of him while his colleagues stood around watching.

Then came the gaslighting. Just as they did with Christopher, state prosecutors tried to blame George Floyd's death on some supposed 'underlying health conditions' in order to deflect attention away from the officers and justify their initial refusal to prosecute. Only after the Minneapolis police precinct was burned to the ground was Floyd's killer charged with second degree murder. All my years of dealing with state authorities have taught me that, in the end, it is only pressure from the people that forces institutions to move. Without that, impunity is the rule, no matter how much evidence is produced, or how many reports are written.

The murder of George Floyd had an incendiary impact. The video of his death could not fail to produce gut-swelling anger in anyone who viewed it, and people took to the streets in their millions across the planet. Even small towns that had no tradition of protest saw hundreds gather in solidarity. In Hull, a Black Lives Matter group sprang into action, and a new generation of activists took up Christopher's case and breathed new life into the campaign. One of them was Jordan Matfin:

> Christopher Alder was one of those names I'd always heard of, but never quite knew the ins and outs. I just knew he had died in a police station a long time ago, when I was six. Then, after George Floyd's death and the worldwide Black Lives Matter protests, I started doing a lot of research and properly read about the case and I just couldn't believe it: the way they've got away with it and never done anything about it. The government's just swept it under the rug and forgotten about it, they don't care. It's disgusting really.
>
> Then I read about all the stalking of Janet by the police, and I thought – Hull needs to get angry about this. It's just not spoken about enough. I read about the police officers getting early retirement and the payoffs and stuff – they got between 44 and 66 grand each – but Janet, obviously she had been campaigning for twenty-two years and never got anything out of it. So I set up a crowdfund – I just got it going and it reached £1,000 within two days. I know it's not about the money but Janet needed funds, to write the book, and for court cases, and people wanted to help with all that.

Soon after, there was a Black Lives Matter protest in Hull. It was organised last-minute, but I emailed Janet to ask if she could come and speak and she turned up on the day which was awesome.

The response was brilliant. So many people have wanted to get involved since then: people have been doing Change petitions; we've got another protest coming up this Saturday, and we're going to start doing 'street conversations', with signs inviting people to come and talk about the case. Since we've started raising awareness, people have started taking so much initiative. A girl called Joanna has started a raffle to raise money for the campaign, which is doing really well – loads of local businesses have donated prizes like food vouchers, tattoo vouchers, trainer vouchers, all sorts.

It's woken a lot of people up and his name's finally being spoken about by pretty much everybody now.

Speaking to Janet, I think before all this, she was feeling – not lost exactly, but feeling like she wasn't being listened to. And seeing that the youth has taken such a big initiative with these things, I think it's lifted her spirits up. I hope she can take a breather now, after twenty-two years non-stop. We're doing as much as we can for her – I guess we've relit the spark in a way, so we just need people to keep lighting the fire, just keep it going.

I read the other day that more has been done to attack systemic racism in the two weeks since George Floyd's death than in the past two years. It affects us all and it's going to keep affecting us all, and now we've got to go beyond the protest and keep doing what we can to keep it going.

JORDAN MATFIN, Hull, 2020

The movement clearly rattled the British state. When the next high-profile prosecution for a police killing came along, concerning the tasering and kicking to death of former footballer Dalian Atkinson, they made sure to get a conviction. The last thing they wanted was a repeat of Minneapolis. In 2021, Atkinson's killer, PC Benjamin Monk, was found guilty of manslaughter and handed an eight-year sentence. I noted the CPS this time used the correct criteria for manslaughter – that Monk's actions contributed to his death – rather than the nonsensical criteria they insisted applied in Christopher's case – that he would definitely have survived had the officers acted differently. I have no doubt that the CPS only took the case seriously because they feared a repeat of the 2020 uprisings.

In 2022, my younger brother Stephen died. He had been a long term resident in psychiatric care, and supposedly died of natural causes – although his postmortem report said he had potentially toxic levels of medication in his system. I was shocked to find out he had a Do Not Resuscitate order placed on him on 14 February, just weeks before his death, seemingly without his family's consent. The reason given on the form was that he had schizophrenia and hypertension. It was an even bigger shock to learn that he had died on 1 April, just like Christopher. And both in state custody. Was it just coincidence? Is it my previous trauma making me feel like history is repeating itself?

In June 2023, I was watching Channel 4 one evening when a report came up about deportations of African and Caribbean people with psychiatric illnesses. According to recently declassified documents, around four hundred people had been deported from the UK between the 1950s and 1970s under a scheme that 'was supposed to be voluntary but that may not have involved a proper consent process'. Watching this, a chill ran down my spine. I had always thought that my mum had wanted to return to Nigeria, and that my dad had eventually allowed her to do so. Now a different explanation emerged. Had my mother in fact been deported against her will? Is that how we came to spend our childhoods in care, Stephen from the age of just four months, my dad hounded to pay for the privilege?

I went online to see what else I could find out. Apparently, the National Assistance Board, the forerunner of today's Department for Work and Pensions, had made an agreement with the Colonial Office in 1949 that they would pay for the repatriation of 'coloured British colonials who through ill health, or inability to adapt themselves to conditions in this country, were unable to support themselves' adding that the 'institutions concerned regard mental disorder and in some cases chronic illness as grounds for repatriation of Commonwealth citizens regardless of whether adequate treatment and care are available'.[2]

I got in touch with the journalist who wrote the article to see if she could find out if my mum had been one of those deported. She said she would check the data and get back to me. A few days later she confirmed that someone had been deported from Hull. I knew pretty much all the Black families in the city in the sixties; you could count them on the fingers of one hand. It had to have been my mum.

I immediately dug out the care records I had received from social services a few years earlier to look at them again in the light of this new revelation. Suddenly it made more sense. One of the social service memos said, 'When we started discussing the children and the possibilities of Mrs Alder going home, she walked out of the house in disgust.' Later it was recorded, 'Whether she agrees or not, I do not know.' This did not sound like consent.

My dad was supposed to pay the travel fare and had apparently been saving up. But one of the memos notes that he had spent the money he'd saved on a car. It sounded like he too was having doubts.

These discussions began before Stephen was born. When this pregnancy was mentioned in the social service records, it is recorded that it 'will spoil the plan'. It sounded like the deportation had been planned for some time but was delayed until after Stephen was born.

Thinking of my mum being deported in such a vulnerable state left me feeling disgusted and sickened. What she needed was help; instead it looks like she was forcibly separated from her children and young baby, compelled to leave them in an uncaring 'care' system, never to see them again. It seems the abuse dished out to my family by the British state had begun almost from the moment my parents arrived.

As for Christopher, the campaign for justice continues.

Acknowledgements

With many thanks for your continued support:

Everyone in the United Families and Friends Campaign

Ruth Bundey

Ken Fero and Migrant Media

Ruggie Johnson and his family and the Monitoring Group

Andy and Maggie and the Justice for Christopher Alder campaign in Hull

Eunice and Rachel

Georgina and Mark of Ian MacDonald's chambers in Manchester

Peter Herbert and Maria Bamieh

David Baker

Simon Bristow and James Campbell

Black Lives Matter

Netpol in Manchester

Calendar News and *Look North*

All the unions who have supported the campaign, especially the RMT, FBU, Unison, Unite and Aslef

All the students and lecturers who have invited me to speak at their universities

And everyone else who has supported the campaign over the years. Your support has been a lifeline for me.

My friends who have stood by me, especially Zara Pradyer who has been on the end of the phone for daily chats from the beginning.

Notes

Introduction

1. Christopher's case was still to be heard in the European Court of Human Rights, but this was being led by the campaign group Liberty and I was more or less leaving them to it.
2. 1,870 people died in police custody or following contact with British police between 1990 and 2023, an average of fifty-seven per year. https://www.inquest.org.uk/deaths-in-police-custody.

The Custody Suite

1. It is worth noting the existing procedures at the time. The police officers' duty of care, section 9, treatment of detained persons, notes that 'the custody officer must immediately call the police surgeon or, in urgent cases – for example where a person does not show signs of sensibility or awareness – must send the person to hospital'. Furthermore, the report into the death in police custody of Ibrahim Sey noted that 'current guidance ... places great emphasis upon moving a violent detainee from the prone position as soon as possible'. Christopher's death occurred within hours of this report's publication.

Christopher

1. Alexandra Topping, Steven Morris and Richard Norton-Taylor, 'Two servicemen die on training exercise in Brecon Beacons', *Guardian*, 14 July 2013, https://www.theguardian.com/uk-news/2013/jul/14/two-servicemen-die-training-brecon-beacons.
2. Robert Kershaw, *Sky Men* (London: Hodder and Stoughton, 2010), p.292.
3. Ibid., p.2.
4. Toby Harnden, *Bandit Country* (London: Hodder and Stoughton, 2000), p.12.
5. Ibid., p.11.
6. Peter Morton, *Emergency Tour: 3 Para in Northern Ireland* (William Kimber, 1989), p.37.

7. Chris Byrne, ex-Royal Marine, quoted in Aly Renwick, 'Racism in the British Army', Veterans for Peace UK, January 2019, https://vfpuk.org/2019/03/01/racism-in-the-british-army/.
8. Harnden, p.11.
9. Kershaw, p.287.

The Nightclub

1. Independent Police Complaints Commission (IPCC), 'Review into the events leading up to and following the death of Christopher Alder: Vol I' (IPCC), 27 March 2006, p.61. https://assets.publishing.service.gov.uk/media/5a7c1c72ed915d1c30daaa18/0971_i.pdf.
2. Ibid., p.80.

Making Enquiries

1. *Hull Daily Mail*, 2 April 1998.
2. 'Death probe: Man charged', *Hull Daily Mail*, 3 April 1998.
3. *Hull Daily Mail*, 3 April 1998.

Campaigning

1. The case in 1969 concerned the death of David Oluwale, a Nigerian man who had come to Britain in the 1930s. He had hidden himself on a ship destined for Hull where, upon docking, he was arrested and placed in Armley prison. When released he tried to start a new life in Leeds, got married and had two children. In 1953 he was charged with disorderly conduct following a police raid on a nightclub and spent another twenty-eight days in prison. During this time he began to show signs of disturbance; some believe this was due to a head injury inflicted by a police truncheon during his arrest, but it may have been due to the several years he had earlier spent in mental hospital receiving electric shock treatment and medication. Friends reported he was a shadow of the man they knew and had lost all confidence in himself to the extent where he was no longer able to hold down a job. Several times he reported being harassed by Leeds Police. After spending another couple of years in hospital he became homeless. It was at this point that he was hounded and beaten by several police officers, leading to his death. They called him names like 'darkie' and two officers made him bow to them on his knees and kicked him in the groin. They drove him to the outskirts of Leeds and he was later found drowned in the river; an eyewitness recalled him being chased along the banks of the Aire by police officers. Whether they threw him in, or he fell during the chase is not clear, but a subsequent inquiry found the police responsible for his death. During the police officers' trial, the judge described David Oluwale as a dangerous, dirty, filthy, violent man, in stark contrast to how the people that knew him described him. The manslaughter charges against the officers were dropped on directions of the judge but both officers were found guilty of assault and sentenced to three years and twenty-seven months respectively. This was the first, and to this day only, time any British police officer had been found guilty of any crime relating to the death of a Black man in police custody.

2. The way I looked at it, Christopher should have been alive. The post mortem had not found a natural cause for his death so he must have died because someone had done something to him, or had failed to treat him as they should have done. The injuries caused by Jason Paul did not kill him. Having no experience of these matters, I naively expected that it would be someone's job to look into everything that happened to Christopher once he left the nightclub, and work out if anyone had done anything that they should not have done, or not done something they ought to have done. Those who had carried out their duties properly would then be able to move on, knowing that Christopher's death was not on their conscience. And anyone whose conduct was questionable would be investigated thoroughly to decide whether their conduct was criminal. If all possibilities were not investigated and ruled in or out, how would we ever know for certain what had happened, and learn lessons to ensure that similar incidents were avoided in future? Experience has since shown me how wrong I was. Not only did I come to realise that it was not someone else's job to pursue all possible lines of inquiry, but I soon felt as though it was down to me to point out all the possibilities and try to force others to investigate them. No one seemed interested in recognising that it was possible that something untoward had happened to Christopher between leaving the hospital and arriving at the police station. Neither did they seem interested in doing anything to rule the possibility out. When all other possibilities had been ruled out, and with no other sensible explanation having been offered by anyone, I was left with the conclusion that Christopher died because of something the police did or did not do. In my simple view, if he was left to die by people who should have been looking after him (and that's looking at things in the best possible light), they killed him.
3. Brian had been stopped by the police while on his way home from a nightclub in 1995. Officers said he was armed and that they had acted in self-defence when they struck a blow to Brian's upper arm which then slid up his arm to his neck. But eyewitnesses said he was unarmed and that an officer had struck him directly on the head with a downward blow from his baton. He was then detained in Kennington Road police station for several hours before being transferred to hospital where he died five days later from a fractured skull and internal bleeding.
4. The CPS also seem to have ignored the CCTV footage of Christopher's death, showing the police officers standing around Christopher for eleven minutes while he lay, face down and unconscious, audibly choking to death on his own blood.

Disclosed Documents

1. IPCC, p.172.
2. The note in Stephens's notebook read '10:15: Resume I/C Dawson and Blakey to HRI examination HRI by Dr Grout Negative.' The one in Dawson's: '9.35: Attend HRI for medical examination by Dr Knox.'

The Inquest

1. The Hull Afro Caribbean Society were being kept updated by PC Beatrice Ogunleye-Smith, who was, I believe, being used to reassure the African-Caribbean community in Hull.
2. Where witnesses were called by a particular lawyer, it was standard practice that that lawyer would be last to conduct their questioning; but for 'neutral witnesses', who had not been called by a specific lawyer, it was up to the coroner to rule on the order of questioning following representations from the various parties.
3. The coroner's summing up of Christopher's death at the start of the inquest, for example, noted that 'although not all the witnesses to what transpired agree exactly with each other as to what happened, the preponderance of evidence from the written statements suggest that Christopher Alder connected with blows to Jason Paul before Jason Paul struck one blow to Christopher Alder's face'. Most witnesses do indeed describe Christopher hitting Jason first, but several do not. Richard Hilyard, for example, testified that Jason 'as the fight was getting split up, walked over there. As he got close enough to Chris Alder he just took one step back and swung in with a really big punch'. Ian Lynch also says he did not see Christopher hit Jason before Jason hit Christopher.
4. IPCC, p.99.
5. 'Excited delirium' is a controversial and contested medical diagnosis often put forward to explain away the death of young Black men while being restrained by police officers.
6. The other being the police station matron Bridget Winkley (IPCC, p.140).
7. IPCC, p.123.
8. 'Had Mr Alder been unconscious during the whole or most of the journey, it seems likely, given that the van had to turn corners en route, that he would not have been able to remain in his seat' (IPCC, p.118).
9. IPCC, pp.121–2. He actually told West Yorkshire Police, 'I'm not sure how many were in the vehicle [the van] – obviously there was at least one.' West Yorkshire Police do not seem to have asked for clarification on this.
10. Inquest transcript, p.636. Years later, in his interview with the IPCC, Crichton is more unequivocal that there was only one officer in the car, stating that he 'does not recall seeing another officer in the police car at all', that 'any passenger would have had to get out of the car and walk directly in my line of vision to get to the caged area' and that 'if there were two, I would have seen them, to the best of my recollection there was only one'. The IPCC report notes that 'Mr Crichton was actually watching the car when it pulled up' and that Crichton confirmed that he knew Blakey and would have recognised him (IPCC, p.122).
11. The IPCC report does not mention Crichton's answer to this important question, and concludes that this is probably what happened, despite all three officers having claimed that they parked before getting out, and despite Crichton ruling out this scenario as well.
12. IPCC, p.115.
13. IPCC, p.132.
14. The IPCC report curiously makes no comment as to the wisdom or

otherwise of placing Christopher in the back of the van on his own in this state (IPCC, pp.337–41); however, in later questioning, Kane suggests it would not be uncommon for this to occur (Inquest transcript, p.928).
15. IPCC, p.334.
16. Blakey had told West Yorkshire Police that he was sat upright (IPCC, p.132), although the police had told Leak that he had been 'slumped in the back of a van with his head supported in the corner' (Inquest transcript, p.940).
17. The team comprised Superintendent John Holt as senior investigating officer, with Keith Tolan and Paul Morris assisting him. These three were, says the IPCC, 'almost the only officers' who ever worked on the investigation, with only one other officer (Inspector Grubb) identified as playing any role in it at all (IPCC, p.153). This stood in stark contrast to the dozens involved in Humberside's investigation into Jason Paul, on which no expense was spared. While Humberside, for example, took 193 statements in the early stages of their inquiry, West Yorkshire took only twenty-seven during the same period, thirteen of which were simple negative statements, containing no information about what happened, from other attendees at the hospital or police station. Indeed, they took no statements at all for the first month of the inquiry (IPCC, p.367).
18. The US CDC lists one of the possible symptoms of exposure to tear gas, of which CS gas is one type, as 'respiratory failure possibly resulting in death'. https://emergency.cdc.gov/agent/riotcontrol/factsheet.asp.
19. As specified in official police guidance: see npcc.police.uk/SysSiteAssets/media/downloads/publications/publications-log/2018/guidance-on-the-use-of-force-data---march-2018.pdf.
20. IPCC, p.185.
21. In 2006 the IPCC said that for an experienced SIO, John Holt seemed to have no concept of the purpose of forensic scientific analysis and the destruction of samples; the principles of openness and independence were evidently not considerations that occurred to him.
22. Gallagher later told the IPCC that he was 'flabbergasted' to find out that the samples and fingerprints had never been tested, adding that 'I don't honestly know why it [sic] hasn't been examined, I would have thought it was of paramount importance' (IPCC, p.163).
23. When interviewed by the IPCC six years later, the matron didn't mention anything about me supposedly intimidating her. She said that the interview was her first opportunity to tell anyone about what she saw that night, other than when she gave her statement. She said no one had ever asked her to give an account of the night of Christopher's death, as she was ill at the inquest and the subsequent trial ended before she had been called to give her account (IPCC, p.348).
24. Para 20 neutral citation number 2001 EWHC Admin 352 in the High Court 3700/2000.

The Funeral

1. William Wilberforce led the parliamentary campaign against the transatlantic slave trade from the late eighteenth century onwards. However,

some believe he has received undue credit for its abolition in 1807, which was more a reflection of the British ruling class's strategic fears following the Haitian revolution. This was the first successful rebellion by enslaved people in recorded history, and British elites worried that continuing the trade would provoke further rebellions that might threaten the whole colonial enterprise; besides which, by that time, two-thirds of kidnapped Africans were being sold on to French and Spanish plantations, directly enriching Britain's rivals and enemies. These strategic calculations were likely far more influential on British policy than Wilberforce ever was. Ironically, Wilberforce had voted in Parliament to send British troops to Haiti to crush the revolution, the largest ever naval mission to leave British shores, resulting in 49,000 British deaths. Had this expedition been successful, it is likely Wilberforce's pleadings would have continued to fall on the same deaf ears they had done for the previous twenty years.

Mr O'Doherty

1. They claimed the coroner should not have left a verdict of unlawful killing as an option to the jury as the breaches of duty alleged against the officers could not have amounted to gross negligence manslaughter.
2. I later learned that this was due to the previous year's Butler report, which had recommended that senior lawyers should be responsible for bringing prosecution cases following unlawful killing verdicts at inquests. I had been given a copy of the report by the Douglas family, but at the time I didn't appreciate its significance. It was only much later, during the years of reflection as I attempted to heal and make sense of Christopher's death, that I read the report. In it, Judge Butler stipulated the importance of having a senior lawyer review the evidence, as well as any new evidence brought out at inquest, when considering whether or not to press charges.

The inquiry's remit had been to look at 'Crown Prosecution Service Decision Making in Relation to Deaths in Custody and Related Matters'. The report concluded that in sixteen cases, restraint by officers had been the direct cause of death, of which four were classed as 'positional asphyxia'. The majority of deaths were ruled to have occurred due to natural causes, many involving drug or alcohol abuse, and the authors called on the Home Office and Department of Health to pilot facilities with medical care to replace police cells.

The report came out just over a year after Christopher's death, in August 1999, and criticised the Crown Prosecution Service for failing to take action over a number of previous high-profile deaths in police custody. He made several recommendations aiming to improve accountability, and expressed 'unease' over the current system. In his report, Butler said that 'there can be few prosecuting decisions more important than whether to charge a person with having unlawfully caused the death of another. To fail to charge could mean a serious crime – and any unlawful killing is a serious crime – goes unpunished, leading to loss of confidence in the rule of law and administration of justice.' One of the recommendations he made was that lawyers from the CPS could consult with others and may also require further investigation into unresolved issues to be carried out. In

Christopher's case, further investigation clearly was necessary, in particular into Christopher's additional injuries and the destruction of so much forensic evidence. Yet the CPS had never requested that this be carried out.
3. In their descriptions of just a few uneventful minutes outside the hospital, the officers seem to have made no less than five false statements: i) that Christopher was trying to get back into the hospital; ii) that they called for a police van before arresting Christopher; iii) that Christopher was making personal threats against them; iv) that he poked PC Dawson in the shoulder; and v) that Dawson had drawn his gas canister.
4. The IPCC report comments on Christopher's removal from the hospital: 'the police were not requested or instructed by anyone to remove him, and therefore had no authority to force him from the building,' concluding that 'manhandling him in that way, without actually arresting him, was probably unlawful' (IPCC, p.332).
5. Para 31 neutral citation number 2001 EWHC Admin 352 in the High Court 3700/2000.
6. Para 44 neutral citation number 2001 EWHC Admin 352 in the High Court 3700/2000.
7. Although the CPS's own website today states the following with regard to gross negligence manslaughter: 'The breach of duty must cause the death. It does not have to be the only cause nor even the principal cause of death but it must have more than minimally, negligibly or trivially caused the death ... It is unnecessary for the breach of duty to have been the sole or even the main cause of death, provided it contributed significantly to the victim's death.' https://www.cps.gov.uk/legal-guidance/gross-negligence-manslaughter.

Battling the CPS

1. A voluntary bill of indictment is a legal process whereby charges are brought that had previously been dismissed – because, for example, new evidence has come to light. See https://www.cps.gov.uk/legal-guidance/drafting-indictment.
2. He stuck to this line in correspondence with Ruth. On 21 January 2002, Ruth wrote again to ask O'Doherty for a copy of the voluntary bill for information purposes. As the CPS had now made their decision, she also asked when the date of the trial would be and to know if the officers had made any representations, so that any views we had could be taken into account. She was doing no more than requesting information as per section four, paragraph five of the Butler report.

On 29 January 2002, O'Doherty replied to Ruth arguing that it was a confidential matter between the Crown, the judge and the defendants, and therefore he was not prepared to release a copy to her. Ruth wrote back explaining her concern that this refusal to allow us to see the contents of the indictment did not facilitate my involvement in the investigational process to the extent necessary to safeguard my legitimate interests.

On 21 February 2002, O'Doherty's reply noted that he had taken into account all of my concerns but that his obligation was to act in a manner that was fair to everyone, which would naturally include the police officers as defendants as well as the family of the victim. But, he added, this did not mean he would simply agree to my demands. I found this comment strange as it was Ruth who requested the application of the voluntary bill so she could explain the process to me. He added, however, that he would ask the judge to provide us with a copy of the voluntary bill after the hearing. In the event, this never happened.

3. It sank further when O'Doherty started demanding Ruth hand over all her correspondence with Crane and Adgey. What exactly they thought they would find I don't know; Ruth had simply sent the medical evidence to the doctors and asked them to give their professional opinions. But it seemed very one-sided – after all, the CPS had not even taken proper minutes of their 'conferences' of medical experts, an issue prompting a letter of concern from Maria Boumieh from the National Black Crown Prosecution Association. It made me wonder whether the CPS might have been doing what they seemed to be accusing us of, and steering their experts towards certain conclusions, especially given Dr Cary's unexplained 'change of heart' following one such meeting.

4. Peter Herbert QC, from the Society of Black Lawyers, who represented Neeta Amin in an employment tribunal against O'Doherty, explained that O'Doherty had victimised her due to her complaints of racial discrimination. I began to think that my suspicions were correct: that the CPS were incapable of taking up my concerns due to my race and ethnicity. O'Doherty had done nothing to reassure me that things would progress in a positive manner. I felt he was engaged in some kind of battle with me and the last thing he saw me as was a victim.

At Maria's suggestion, on 25 March 2002, I wrote to both the attorney general and the director of public prosecutions (the head of the CPS) to tell them how shocked I was that O'Doherty had been instructed to deal with such a sensitive case, having already been reprimanded for victimisation connected to issues of racial discrimination. I told them I felt that such tendencies could well explain why O'Doherty was treating me as he was, and that I would not be engaging with the CPS any further.

5. When Ruth made inquiries as to why the venue had been moved so far from Hull, the CPS admitted that there were other venues available that would have been easier to access, but blamed the decision on the circuit judge. He had apparently made a comment that the case could not be heard at the sort of venue being suggested by the prosecution for 'reasons known to those present'. I certainly didn't know what those reasons were and no one had ever thought it necessary to explain them to us, so I asked the CPS what he meant. I was shocked when they told me that they thought the judge was referring to the fact that there had been race riots in the recent past in Bradford. I couldn't understand why the CPS didn't protect the family's interests and contest the judge's ruling; after all, as far as the CPS were concerned, this case had nothing whatsoever to do with race.

Before the Trial

1. Namely, his additional injuries, the mud on his thighs, his unconsciousness, his missing belt and trousers round his ankles, the officers' visit to the hospital the following day, the destruction of Christopher's clothes and

dry cleaning of the officers' uniforms without testing, the destruction of blood samples without testing, the removal of blood from the van before the forensic examiner arrived, the blood on the corridor seemingly from the officers' clothes, and the destruction of the CS gas canister.

The Trial of the Officers

1. One of those who attended to watch the case made a formal complaint to the court manager about being videoed in this way, and Ruth also wrote asking what was going on. The court manager said he had just started working there and had not been aware of this situation but that he would look into it. After investigating the matter with Cleveland Police, he wrote back to Ruth to assure her that the footage had been destroyed.
2. IPCC, p.333.
3. Later in the year, at the Annual General Meeting of the CPS, Maria challenged O'Doherty from the CPS about the way the evidence had been presented. He claimed it was common practice – to which Maria replied that it most certainly was not. Her letter to the CPS on the issue noted: 'I was so concerned about what I was being told as the reason for this unusual course that I felt that it may have been my own lack of experience in such high profile cases. I felt this so much that I began to doubt my own beliefs. I therefore consulted with more senior colleagues in the CPS and I even spoke to Courtenay Griffiths QC who has defended many murder cases at the Old Bailey. All agreed that this was so unusual that they had not seen it before and that the way I would have dealt with the expert evidence [only bringing forward the witnesses that supported your own case] was correct'.
4. IPCC, p.255.
5. The 'Sheppard test' refers to the definition of 'wilful neglect' as it applies to the 1933 Children's Act as established by the 1981 House of Lords ruling on the case of Regina v Sheppard (1981).

The Trial Takes Its Toll

1. I later discovered that Justice Jackson's ruling against the police appeal of the unlawful killing inquest verdict at the Divisional Court in April 2001 had actually been *removed* from the voluntary bill of indictment following discussions with James Curtis QC (see IPCC, p.250). This ruling was arguably the most important single piece of evidence the CPS could have placed before the Jury, as it contained detailed legal arguments, already upheld in court, that there was enough evidence to support, to the criminal standard, a case for gross neglect manslaughter (and therefore that the Coroner had been correct to leave unlawful killing to the Jury as an option to consider). In his ruling, Jackson accepts that *none* of the experts can be sure that Christopher would have survived had he received appropriate medical treatment. This is for the simple reason that the cause of Christopher's sudden lapse into unconsciousness had not been established, and if it were due to some kind of catastrophic biological event (for which there is no medical evidence, but still could not be 100% ruled out), he might have died anyway. Nonetheless, Jackson, argues, this is not necessary to prove

causation. The correct test is whether the officers' actions or omissions more than minimally contributed to his death. And here, he argued, there was enough evidence to reach a secure verdict to the criminal standard of proof. Indeed, he noted that even the officers' own lawyers accepted this definition of causation. His conclusion was that 'I am quite satisfied that there was sufficient medical evidence to support a finding of causation on the basis which the Coroner put to the Jury,' that is unlawful killing – the equivalent of gross neglect manslaughter, requiring the same criminal standard of proof. He noted that 'the evidence of Professor Crane alone would enable the Jury to find causation to the criminal standard,' but that in fact the views of doctors Carey, Clark and Porter also supported that conclusion.

This judgment, therefore, was the most important case law available for demonstrating a) the correct legal understanding of 'causation' for this case and b) that the medical evidence was sufficient to allow such a finding, to the criminal standard of proof.
2. R (Dawson) v HM Coroner; neutral citation number 2001 EWHC Admin 352, p.10.

Christine and Herbert

1. The *Empire Windrush* was a ship which in 1948 brought workers over to Britain from the Caribbean, then still part of the British Empire. Although it was not the first, it received significant publicity – as well as some hostility – and came to symbolise the post-war Caribbean migration; those who came during that period are still known today as part of the 'Windrush generation'. It is worth noting, however, that many did not think of themselves as 'migrants' – after all, they were British citizens, moving to the 'mother country', often seeking refuge from the destitution visited upon their homelands by British colonialism.
2. E.g. Elizabeth J. Corwin, Ruth Kohen, Monica Jarrett and Brian Stafford, 'The heritability of postpartum depression', *Biological Research For Nursing*, 12(1) (2010), 73–83, https://www.ncbi.nlm.nih.gov/pmc/articles/PMC3342683/.

Going into Care

1. Smith & Nephew is a medical technology manufacturing company, which was a major employer in Hull at the time.

Injustice

1. The family successfully challenged this the following year, when a judicial review by the High Court ruled there had been 'insufficient inquiry' and ordered a fresh inquest. The second inquest returned a verdict of unlawful killing, leading to the officers' suspension in 2004. However, this led to an 'effective police strike' when over a quarter of the Met's four hundred firearms officers handed in their firearms licences in protest at their colleagues' suspensions. The officers were reinstated and the High Court overruled the jury's unlawful killing verdict.
2. Four other officers – Superintendent Christopher Burton, acting Detective

Chief Inspector Kevin French, Detective Inspector Christopher Paul Stiggs and PC Robert Shoesmith – were all charged with misfeasance in a public office – i.e. neglect of duty or abuse – in relation to the shooting. The officers had been bailed to appear at Bow Street Magistrates' Court in London. Four senior Sussex officers – Chief Constable Paul Whitehouse, Deputy Chief Constable Mark Jordan, Assistant Chief Constable Maria Wallis and Assistant Chief Constable Nigel Yeo – had also been under investigation by Hampshire Police in connection with the operation and its aftermath, but did not face any charges. Whitehouse and Jordan had both been suspended.

The only other officer to be charged with murder was PC Patrick Hodgson, who was acquitted at the Old Bailey of murder and manslaughter in connection with the shooting of a car thief in 1995.

Police Disciplinary

1. In 2012, Sean Price was himself sacked for gross misconduct, making him the first police chief to be dismissed in thirty-five years, after being found to have directed a member of his staff to lie to investigators. IPCC commissioner Nicholas Long said Price had 'attempted to intimidate and bully staff under his leadership and mislead an independent investigation' and described his conduct as 'shameful'. He had been due to face a separate misconduct hearing into eighteen other matters, but this was dropped after he was sacked on full pension. Price had been arrested the previous year on suspicion of misconduct, fraud and corruption, but the CPS refused to prosecute. The investigation was part of Operation Sacristy, a wider investigation into corruption in Cleveland Police. See https://www.bbc.co.uk/news/uk-19840069.

The CPS

1. CPS, p.19.
2. CPS, p.29.
3. CPS, p.19.

Life in the House

1. When I went home to see my dad at the weekend, it would enrage him: he would make me sit on the floor as he raked the comb through my hair, the pain coursing through my tender scalp, not used to being attended to.

Death on Camera

1. The comedian Tommy Cooper's death had been broadcast during a live performance in 1984.
2. Press Association, 'Watchdog to review police custody death', *Guardian*, 14 April 2004, https://www.theguardian.com/politics/2004/apr/14/immigrationpolicy.ukcrime.
3. The role of the Black and Ethnic Minority Members Committee is (in their own words):

- To offer help, support and to encourage networking by our members.
- To assist Fire and Rescue Services in ensuring that their BME recruitment, retention and progression strategies recognise the diversity in the communities they serve, and actively seek to reflect the very best of those communities.
- To advise and assist the FBU [Fire Brigades Union] in educating its members in order to recognise, appreciate and respect cultural differences thus eradicating the effects of racial/cultural prejudice in the workplace and the community.
- To take full advantage of learning opportunities and to offer career guidance and influence in the creation and maintenance of supportive working environments.

4. In the CPS report into the conduct of the trial, Enzor suggests that the CPS did not view the tapes until late February 2002 (p.20).

School

1. This character is almost always shown from waist or torso down. According to Wikipedia, out of about 160 episodes, only two or three show her head, and her face is shown just once, very briefly. See https://en.wikipedia.org/wiki/Tom_and_Jerry.

Holidays

1. This is clearly something that has stuck with me: when I raised my children, they always got something to do, something to wear and something to eat.

The IPCC Report

1. 'It is now clear that [Christopher] was not faking his unconsciousness in the van or custody suite, and the view put forward by the two arresting officers was not only wrong but positively misleading ... PC Blakey claimed in his interview with West Yorkshire Police that Mr Alder was breathing 'evenly' while lying on the floor. It is evident from the soundtrack to the CCTV that this was not the case and that Mr Alder's breathing was uneven and laboured. PC Blakey was, therefore, either deluding himself or being deliberately untruthful about this ... The difference to the plight of the man on the floor and the cynical dismissal of his obvious distress, is simply disgraceful ... My assessment of PC Dawson and PC Blakey taken together is that they ... were less than fully frank in their explanation of the events and their reactions, in order to justify their positions.' (IPCC, pp.341–5).
2. IPCC, p.342.
3. IPCC, p.312.
4. 'It appears to me that there are a number of aspects of the behaviour of the officers that suggest that unwitting racism ... may have influenced the way in which Mr Alder was treated ... I conclude that the treatment of Mr Alder did indeed reflect the definitions of "unwitting" racism described by Lord Macpherson ... I do believe the fact he was black stacked the odds more heavily against him ... the grim conclusion I have reached is ... that

Mr Alder ... did not matter enough for [the officers] to do all they could to save him.' (IPCC, p.28).
5. IPCC, p.261.

Preparing the Civil Case

1. In the Stephen Lawrence inquiry, Sir William Macpherson had defined racism as consisting of conduct, words or practices which advantage or disadvantage people because of their colour of skin, culture or ethnic origin, which can be just as damaging in its subtle form as it is when overt. Institutional racism, he said, consisted of an organisation's collective failure to provide an appropriate and professional service to people because of their colour, culture or ethnic origin. He said it can be seen and detected in processes, attitudes and behaviour which amount to discrimination through unwitting prejudice, ignorance, thoughtlessness and racist stereotyping which disadvantage minority ethnic people.

Christine Omoregie

1. Christine later passed on to me a letter to the *Hull Daily Mail*, confirming that the funeral had been arranged by the council.

Another Sham Investigation

1. This is not just my view. The government's own Butler report (1999) was severely critical of the CPS's failure to prosecute police officers over deaths in custody and concluded the system was 'fundamentally unsound'. Five years later, Parliament's joint committee on human rights issued a report on deaths in custody which warned that the current system cannot 'be considered to be compatible with the obligation on the State under Article 2 [of the European Convention of Human Rights] to conduct an effective investigation' into a death in state custody, adding that 'the effect of repeated failures to prosecute is to signal tolerance of conduct, whether negligent or deliberate, which causes deaths in custody'. The attorney general's review of the CPS's role in deaths in custody the same year similarly highlighted several shortcomings. (Joint Committee on Human Rights, 'Government Response to the Third Report from the Committee: Deaths in Custody: Eleventh Report of Session 2004–05', 10 March 2005, https://publications.parliament.uk/pa/jt200405/jtselect/jtrights/69/69.pdf; Nick Hopkins, 'CPS at fault over custody deaths', *Guardian*, 12 August 1999, https://www.theguardian.com/uk/1999/aug/12/nickhopkins1; Joint Committee on Human Rights, *Third Report*, https://publications.parliament.uk/pa/jt200405/jtselect/jtrights/15/1513.htm.)

Spying

1. This chronology differs from that presented in the IPCC report into the surveillance, which suggests that the Operation Akita interviews began in June, while Theresa May did not order forces to look for evidence of surveillance involving the Lawrences until 3 July (IPCC 2, p.11).

2. 'Christopher Alder Hull mortuary mix-up: No prosecution', BBC, 3 October 2013, https://www.bbc.co.uk/news/uk-england-humber-24383324.
3. Ibid.
4. Ibid.
5. 'Father "offered crack at daughter's birthday"', *Lancashire Telegraph*, 16 August 2007, https://www.lancashiretelegraph.co.uk/news/1622947.father-offered-crack-daughters-birthday/.
6. We later put in a complaint about their choice of name. They simply said they named their investigations 'after nuts'.
7. What Etheridge was getting at is that to prove misconduct you must also prove malicious intent. This makes it notoriously hard to prove, and functions essentially as a get-out-of-jail-free card for anyone accused of it; if you can make out that, rather than being malicious, you are simply lazy or a cretin, you can break any rule you like.
8. Emphasis in original minutes of the meeting.
9. A policeman who had visited Christine's house had called her a troublemaker, and police officer Paul Cheeseman had called me an agitator in comments to the IPCC.
10. Letter from CPS, 26 November 2015, p.4.
11. Letter from CPS, p.3.
12. 'The offence of misconduct in a public office would be ... clearly made out if the surveillance that was authorised was intended to eavesdrop on the contact of [the] family with their legal representative in violation of legal professional privilege' (Ibid., p.5).
13. Ibid., p.7.
14. Ibid., p.8.
15. Ibid., p.7.
16. 'With the exception of the former deputy chief constable and former chief superintendent, they all provided a preprepared statement at the outset of the interview and subsequently refused to answer the majority of questions put to them.' (IPCC 2, p.5.) 'There are some inconsistencies between the two sets of accounts [given to Operation Akita and to the IPCC], and for the most part the accounts given to the officer in the initial investigation are slightly fuller than those subsequently given to the IPCC.' (Letter from CPS, p.3.) 'Many of the officers provided more information to the officer who was tasked with conducting the initial investigation, when they were not under immediate suspicion, than they did to the IPCC. However, the accounts that they gave to the officer conducting the initial investigation were not made under caution, were not produced in the form of witness statements, and would be unlikely to be admitted in evidence at trial' (Letter from CPS, p.5).
17. Letter from CPS, pp.5–6.
18. Ibid., p.5.
19. Ibid., p.1.
20. 'Stephen Lawrence case: Theresa May orders inquiry into police spies', *Guardian*, 6 March 2014, https://www.theguardian.com/uk-news/2014/mar/06/stephen-lawrence-theresa-may-inquiry-police.
21. 'It is not considered likely that the decisions made by Humberside Police on 28 July 2000 were based on poor judgement or incompetence as the

actions appear to have been deliberate and considered. From the information obtained during this investigation there is evidence to support the conclusion that discrimination and bias is likely to have been a factor when Humberside Police decided to conduct the surveillance operation on 28 July 2000.' (IPCC 2, pp.68–9).
22. IPCC 2, p.72.

The Horror Never Stops

1. According to Wikipedia, the 'first call' is the initial 'pickup of the remains of a recently deceased person [to] 'transport that person to the funeral home for preparation'. See https://en.wikipedia.org/wiki/First_call_vehicle.

The Struggle Continues

1. Alwyn Sawyer of Merseyside Police was convicted of manslaughter in 1986 after beating to death a handcuffed sixty-seven-year-old man in his cell. Maya Wolfe-Robinson, 'The death of Henry Foley: A 1985 case of police manslaughter', *Guardian*, 23 June 2021, https://www.theguardian.com/uk-news/2021/jun/23/the-death-of-henry-foley-a-1985-case-of-police-manslaughter.
2. Amelia Gentleman, 'Windrush generation: Hundreds "sent back to Caribbean from UK hospitals"', *Guardian*, 21 June 2023, https://www.theguardian.com/uk-news/2023/jun/21/windrush-generation-hundreds-sent-back-to-caribbean-from-uk-hospitals.

Bringing a book from manuscript to what you are reading is a team effort.

Dialogue Books would like to thank everyone who helped to publish *Defiance* in the UK.

Editorial
Hannah Chukwu
Adriano Noble
Eleanor Gaffney

Contracts
Anniina Vuori
Imogen Plouviez
Amy Patrick
Jemima Coley

Sales
Caitriona Row
Dominic Smith
Frances Doyle
Ginny Mašinović
Rachael Jones
Georgina Cutler
Toluwalope Ayo-Ajala

Design
Ben Prior

Production
Narges Nojoumi

Publicity
Tom Neilson

Marketing
Mia Oakley

Operations
Kellie Barnfield
Millie Gibson
Sameera Patel
Sanjeev Braich

Finance
Andrew Smith
Ellie Barry

Audio
Dominic Gribben

Copy-Editor and Structural Editor
David Bamford

Proofreader
Antonia Hodgson